T0158851

Should I "Go Walkabout" Again

(A MOTORHOME ADVENTURE)

Diary 2—Part 1 of "The Big Lap"

JOHN TIMMS

AuthorHouse™ UK
1663 Liberty Drive
Bloomington, IN 47403 USA
www.authorhouse.co.uk
Phone: 0800.197.4150

Published by AuthorHouse 11/09/2018

ISBN: 978-1-7283-8067-4 (sc)
ISBN: 978-1-7283-8081-0 (e)

authorHOUSE®

INTRODUCTION

This is not a travel documentary although you will get a lot of information about Australia and a great deal of detail about a few places. This book is more about being confused, the things that went wrong, the things or places that surprised us and those that disappointed us. It also touches on living with your partner twenty-four seven, along with two dogs and what joy those two dogs gave us when we arrived at, for example, a deserted beach. Sometimes when things went wrong I cried and so did my friends but their tears were those of laughter as I continued to send them out our weekly diary via email. It's about the accidents that happened to our vehicles to us and the dogs, unusual physical ailments and boredom which is not what you see on the television when you listen to travel shows. Here in Australia the interviewers always seem to find happy travellers who are sitting on the edge of beautiful beaches with close friends, sipping wine as they watch the sun sink over the horizon and they are all such happy campers. I haven't yet met these people and if I ever try to sit near the beach at sunset, in a warm climate, my only companions are mosquitoes and sandflies! I could spray myself all over with some sort of near lethal mosquito repellent of course but I hate the smell and can't get away from myself quickly enough. So, this is what happened to us (me my husband and the dogs).

It took this second and a third extended tour to get around the rest of Australia. Am I glad I did it? Yes but there is a lot more behind that answer as you will find out because there were times when I nearly ran away – to catch the nearest plane back home!

This second Diary commences with a short journey to the Sunshine Coast in February 2005, but the big road trip really started in April 2007 when we had itchy feet for "The Big Lap" around Australia anticlockwise. Starting from Gold Coast to Central Queensland, Northern Territory, Western Australia, South Australia, Victoria and New South Wales back home to Currumbin.

This took over ten months, so this diary was taken only to Bremer Bay in the south of Western Australia, to keep the diary to a modest size. Diary three will cover part two of "The Lap" and later a further marathon down the coast to Melbourne and on to explore Tasmania, to complete the Continent.

Should I Tour Australia?

By
Lisa(Elizabeth) Timms

DEDICATED TO MY DEAR WIFE
WHO SHARED THESE MEMORIES WITH ME
BUT WHO DIED SUDDENLY
ON 5th November 2015.

Chapter 1

February 1st 2005

I had just scrubbed the kitchen sink unit down when I noticed the plugholes glaring at me. I had forgotten to clean them. I apologised sincerely and got the cleanser back out. Afterwards I stared at them in admiration and they twinkled back in delight and it was then that I knew that I had to get back on the road.

We had returned from our first big trip (Gold Coast/Melbourne/Cooktown/Gold Coast) in November to face so many problems that we are now no longer on speaking terms with our rental agents. Little problems like being unable to open the front door because the timber floor had swollen so much which was apparently caused by rain! I tried to explain that it quite often rained and asked whether there was a more plausible explanation such as the tenants allowing the pool to overflow thereby flooding the lounge and hallway but no-one apparently had a sensible explanation. So we put in an insurance claim. Then I noticed that there was a small damp patch on the ceiling over our bed and added that to our claim at the assessor's suggestion. That was obviously from the damaged roof claim from the previous storm we experienced before we had set off for our travels the year before.

All our furniture and belongings had to be unpacked from the granny-flat and it was as painful as moving house. I had just finished unpacking the books and ornaments and had erected the Christmas tree and adorned it with trinkets and presents when a storm hit. For some reason our patio drain did not work and our living areas were flooded and so was the hall floor! (We found out later that the road drains were blocked and water was backing up). We rescued our electrical items and most of our furniture as the water entered the lounge. The lounge was now practically empty. A new insurance claim was lodged. Huge drying machines arrived and we spent three horrible days with the house being dehumidified. As the machines also dehumidify humans, we had to keep out of the rooms. Luckily we could use the outside patio upstairs to move from bedroom to study and into John's den to watch TV

As it was so close to Christmas we put everything back in that we needed for Christmas and then the doctor told me two days before Christmas that I had a fungus on my lungs from the carpet and we needed to move out immediately. And so it went on. The furniture was moved back out to get the carpets cleaned, then again when the carpet had to be cleaned again. Then I had two different assessors and two different flooring companies trying to compete for the work to the timber flooring that flows from the hallway into the kitchen (which was now also damaged). We suffered frustration upon frustration and far too many phone calls. The painters turned up to repaint the bedroom ceiling but all the plaster fell off onto our bed and it ended up having to be replastered. We had to get both of our bathroom showers re-grouted because of mould growth. We had to get our lounge suites cleaned and our motor home seats and carpets cleaned and they were all done on different days. As fast as we cleaned, we had more dust flying around the house be it ceiling plaster, fungus or floor shavings. John and I became quite ratty, I had trouble sleeping and Helen (my daughter) found five large plastic balls choking the patio drainage pipe which had obviously added to the flooding problem (we have three drains).

I think that the satisfaction over cleaning the sink holes was because it seemed to be the only job that had been completed. We decided to get away for a few days and we left with promises that our timber floor would be repaired whilst we are away.

EUMUNDI

We left the dogs behind with Helen. I was like a mother leaving her toddlers. I had a long list of possible problems and remedies ready for Helen. Would she please put Callie's cream on her face three times a day and hose them down if it is too hot and not to worry about tick treatment because I had done it that morning. There were phone numbers for local vets and emergency vets and Colin (one of my sons) promised to come over to help out with walking them.

Our journey here was not without its problems as John drove too fast for me. He was in front and I was following in the Ute. Since our last trip I am quite happy to travel at a maximum speed of 100ks in a 110k zone but he starts at 110k and speeds up to play chase with the semi-trailer truck drivers. When we stopped on the north side of Brisbane for a coffee I found that my legs were like jelly and we proceeded to have a 'quiet' argument in the cafe. Suddenly a semi-trailer driver piped up 'Are you discussing the laws in Queensland?' and proceeded to tell John the road rules. I made my escape and took my coffee outside. When John came out to find me I apologised and told him that I had no idea that the truck driver was listening in to our conversation. John didn't seem to mind at all and said that the driver had said the same as I had said. We then set off at a more leisurely pace and although John twice went to overtake trucks, he changed his mind and slowed down again which was just as well as I was going to let him go on ahead of me but he doesn't like losing sight of my car in his rear view mirror.

As we approached Eumundi I felt pleased that we had chosen to come back here. The scenery enfolded me with its soft green hills. Many shrubs and trees are in blossom - purple, pink, red, yellow and white and with the recent rains the grass is lush and green.

I found the jobs that I had to do to set up on arrival were easy and seemed to take less time than I had thought. John had a bit more difficulty recalling everything that he had to do outside, probably because it was a pretty hot day and he was dripping with perspiration. Once we'd had a dip in the pool we felt hungry and had an early dinner of salad and cold meat. I had a blissful night's sleep. I had forgotten what it is like to go to bed and actually go to sleep straight away. The night before we'd left I had had to resort to one of my rarely used morphine tablets and had been occupying the spare bedroom for about five nights out of seven because it was often 3am or after before I could get tired enough to overcome the pain all over my body. I awoke at 7am bright, fresh and relaxed.

I sat outside and had a coffee and then went for a walk to take some photographs. I haven't missed the dogs at all! I then returned for breakfast and sat outside on John's lounge chair and finished off a section of last weekend's newspaper. We had only brought one chair with us as we had both thought it a waste of time to bring both of our new chairs as I hadn't sat in mine since we'd opened them on Christmas Day! I don't sit outside and relax! I never did on our nine month trip. I thoroughly enjoyed it! I cannot help wondering if it is because I do not have to worry about the dogs. This is why we had bought our bus – to get away from home and relax.

Usually when I go outside at home I notice hair balls scudding across the patio and end up either brushing Jack or getting the broom out or both. Then, off course, we have to go through our greeting rituals with the dogs even though I was outside only two minutes before. Then I wonder if they are too hot or I notice that one or all of my plants need watering or perhaps a swimming towel has fallen off the pool fence and is covered in dog hairs. Or perhaps I see clouds building up (this is the wet season) and remember that I have a heap of washing on the line that should be dry or some red back spider webs under the roof eaves or a new wasps nest being built and so it goes on and I never seem to actually sit down for long.

Have you ever watched a wasp trying to find its nest? They find the most amazing places such as in our exterior air conditioner vent or tiny cracks in brickwork but they seem to forget where they put them. I spent a frustrated half hour last week watching a wasp go back and forth over one of our walls. I wanted to find out where the nest was so that I could get rid of it but by the time the wasp found the nest I was so tired and so full of admiration for it's perseverance that I didn't have the heart to get rid of it. Come to think of it, I've now forgotten where it is.

VIEW FROM MT TINBEERWAH

This morning we were supposed to go into Eumundi and look at the Real Estate windows as we are wondering whether or not to move to this area. I don't think we'll make it as we're too relaxed. Isn't this what it's all about? I cannot believe that John is so relaxed though. We must return to places that we've visited before in future so that I can relive this experience. He obviously feels in no mad rush to go and explore. Rather different to our previous trip. I saw people relaxing as we are now doing but I'd not yet experienced it! I do miss Greg and Sue though who were here with us on that last trip and it's not quite the same without them.

WAITING TO GO OUT

It's now the end of our first week and we have looked at the outside of homes in Eumundi, Cooroy, Pomona, and Boreen Point and have checked out Tewantin. All of these areas are so lovely and so different. We noticed a turn off to Lake MacDonald near Cooroy and one morning went sightseeing around that area. We also spent an afternoon at **Boreen Point** watching the wind surfers on **Lake Cootharaba** but have decided against living there. I have totally fallen in love with **P**omona, which is a village. I like Cooroy but that is a town and I have wanted to live in a village again for so long now. We went there yesterday again. As I walked across to the greengrocers shop I wandered what a Father Christmas was doing at the cafe but it turned out to be an old lady who must be 120 years old with a hand knitted red hat on her head and a red woollen cardigan. She was very nimble despite her widow's hump and wanted to chat and she smiled so much that you forgot the walnut appearance of her face. She told me that she had only lived there for one and a half years and then added 'Give or take a few days'. She also told me that her daughter comes to check on her and that she gets taken out by some organisation for the day and they pick her up from home. She purchased two small bananas from the shop and returned to her seat at the cafe and I've never seen anyone consume bananas at such speed. After she had left, a man at the next table asked me if I'd been talking to her and I asked how old she was. 'I don't know' he replied looking rather surprised 'but if she doesn't stop picking through the rubbish bins she won't live much longer'. Bins or no bins, I rather liked her and she has my admiration for having reached such an ancient age and being so spritely, friendly and smiley. You've got to have the 'village character' haven't you and she's obviously it. They make the world a much more interesting place.

So the guy asks me to join him and his other friend and they proceed to tell me about their lives. I'm not used to this anymore. People at my local shopping centre rarely get chatting to complete strangers. I do, but eight out of ten times people look at me rather oddly and turn away. Like when I tried to help a mother who was trying to negotiate her way out of the check-out with three kids, a push chair and a trolley full of shopping recently. I only said 'Can I help you because my kids can manage themselves now they've reached thirty but I do remember how hard it was?' and she looked at me as though I was nuts. If had I had been her I'd have said 'Yes, you take the three kids and push chair and follow me' and I'd have shot off with my trolley to my car. Then I'd have suggested that I strap my children in whilst this other peculiar woman store all my groceries in the boot! I can still recall with annoyance the bus driver who told me scornfully 'Madam, you need Pickford's removals, not a bus with that lot'. Surely three kids, a push chair plus shopping and an exhausted mother is not that unusual? Perhaps it is in Australia where most women seem to have cars.

John has gone to another coastal area today and has taken the camera. I didn't want to go in case I love it because I know that there are a lot of sand flies and mosquitoes there and I would hate that but might get caught up in the dream of owning a seafront block of land. It's also just that bit too far away from my kids.

Carmen and Arthur are joining us here tomorrow, just for the weekend. It will be the first time that we'll have been parked alongside another American motor home. They knocked on our door before our last trip and asked if they could see inside our van and whilst we were away they bought one too. When we returned home they called around to visit us and as we couldn't stop talking they suggested that they try and join us at some point when we next went away. It may be the last time any of us enjoy this park as we have just found out that it has been sold, as has the land beside the park and the land behind. No doubt it will be subdivided for houses but the Eumundi town folk may take action against such planning permission because they do not want their village to change, so I've been told. They like it just as it is and have enough people here on Wednesdays and Saturdays when they hold their famous markets. It will be interesting to find out what happens. I adore this land but I doubt we'd be able to afford to buy land and build even if they do chop it up as it will be very expensive. We headed back home, stopping at The Gold Coast.

Chapter 2

SURFERS PARADISE – 'PRETTY WOMAN'

Actually, that's not true as I'm no Julia Roberts to look at but I had put my make-up on for the first time for a year in honour of John's Birthday. My treat to him was a visit to a new attraction called the Space Walker 'The Ultimate Space Odyssey' as I knew that this was right up his 'orbit'.

First stop though was a visit to the new Q1 building which was supposed to be the tallest building or apartment block in the world but whatever 'tallest' it is supposed to be, it won't be for long as I don't doubt Dubai or some other country will soon beat the record before the last unit is sold. It's not finished yet but we were zoomed up far too many floors for my liking to see the display units. My ears were immediately affected and I kept trying to yawn so that I could hear again. By the time we'd been through the third apartment I was beginning to feel queasy but have no idea whether it was because of my ears or from the odours from all the new furnishings and floor coverings. Each apartment had mirrored walls everywhere and both John and I walked into the mirrors when we saw a door reflection. Then I panicked as I couldn't find my way back down!

When John rejoined me outside, we drove down to the beach to park the car and walked along the front to Cavill Avenue in the heart of **Surfers Paradise**. It was very windy and the lifeguards were being kept busy watching the tourists who were ignoring the warning flags and were happily racing down the beach and into the sea for a swim. As we strolled down Cavill Avenue we were given a leaflet inviting us to dine at a restaurant in Raptis Plaza. We eventually found the Space Odyssey attraction in Elkhorn Avenue near the junction of Orchid Avenue. By this time John wanted a coffee and we were warmly welcomed at an Italian cafe/restaurant right next door to the entrance. As well as comfortable internal seating and street tables, there were two outdoor sofas by a coffee table and we happily settled in for a rather longer stay than anticipated because we found the owner so interesting to talk to. Although he still has a heavy continental accent, he had moved to the Gold Coast about three years ago having lived in Melbourne for over thirty years. To him, Melbourne is home and he misses it deeply and he still has property and businesses down there. However, his wife does not wish to return because having suffered from very bad asthma for so many years, she has felt completely cured of it since moving to Queensland. As I said to him, the fact that she will probably live a much longer and healthier life is enough reason for her to never wish to return there. However, it also surprised me because I thought that the Brisbane region was one of the worst areas for this illness. Perhaps they did not live by the sea before. Anyway, we went on to discuss the attitude of the shop assistants in Surfers Paradise and he was telling us that he has been going to the same shop, every day, for three years to get his paper and they still don't recognise him! Pomona seems even more inviting!

John left us chatting whilst he entered the Earth Station to be dematerialized via the Earth Station's Teleporter to be beamed to Star Station Zeta! I, on the other hand, decided to conduct some research.

As you walk along Cavill Avenue and around into Elkhorn you will see a plethora of shops selling cheap clothing, cafes, real estate agencies trying to get you interested in their new high rise apartments, bars, night clubs, cafes and restaurants. Then there are endless gift shops selling a lot of cheap and mostly imported memorabilia such as koala bear key rings and boomerangs usually made in Taiwan or China. Amongst this lot are the duty free shops, entrances to the high-rise buildings and car parks or the odd shop that you don't expect such as the Condom Shop. However, the streets are tree-lined with wide walkways and offer considerable seating for the exhausted shoppers and it's really rather pretty. There are plenty of arcades to explore and it is not hard to lose your bearings as you wander in one end and exit to find yourself in a different street.

However, from where I was enjoying my very good coffee I could see some of the shops that are found in Rodeo Drive. I was dressed in old jeans, my old trainers, an obviously cheapish jumper and my hair had been blown all over the place whilst walking along the sea front. In a nutshell, I looked as if I didn't have a couple of bob to rub together, as the old saying goes and when I approached the door to Cartier I immediately showed my ignorance as I did not realise that you have to ring the bell to gain admittance and nearly walked into their glass front door not realising that it wouldn't move as I pushed it. There was only one customer inside and he left as I was admitted. I was warmly welcomed however and I responded by saying the blatantly obvious. 'I have never been into a Cartier store in my life and decided that it was time that I did.'

I also wanted to find out what kind of welcome I would receive. They must have all seen Pretty Woman because I was treated with the utmost respect but the staff went further than that and were truly friendly. They told me about the evenings they have when a new watch or whatever is introduced and how the red carpet is laid out and all manner of wealthy people are invited and some well-known celebrities as well. The assistant's enthusiasm was genuine but as this information did not seem to impress me that much she offered me, what she described as, a coffee table book to take home with me which she took from a cupboard and proffered with a warm smile. I glanced through and thanked her sincerely because it has some extraordinary photographs in it. However, having looked through it whilst enjoying another cup of coffee later in the afternoon, I now have no idea what to do with it. I have long ago given up having a choice selection of suitable reading material upon my coffee table just in case a visitor turns up whom I feel I should impress. Unfortunately, I have to admit it, I was once like that! Of course, that old Lisa would not have walked into Cartier in the first place dressed as I was now and certainly would not have admitted to never having been in their store before.

Hermes was unfortunately undergoing renovations so I couldn't go in there. I received another smiling welcome in Gucci and was left alone when I said that I just wanted to browse. It was like walking into a field of freshly flowering spring bulbs when I walked into Escada and their welcome was as equally fresh and beautiful. The assistant seemed so genuinely excited by their new range that had only arrived the day before and the theme was mainly pink and green. I was a little surprised because I thought they were last year's colours but it mattered not because I came out smiling and feeling that spring has sprung instead of autumn settling in, which is the case in this part of the world.

George Jenson was empty except for the staff as was Salvadore Ferguson and I didn't go in either of their shops as the assistants appeared to be hanging around with nothing to do and the thought of three pairs of eyes following my every move out of sheer boredom was just too overwhelming. However, I admired their wares through the windows. I went around the corner into Orchid Avenue and found the Louis Vuitton store by the tiny plaza on the right. The staff were busy yet relaxed and friendly and I felt very comfortable wondering around there admiring their stock. By this time I had kind of latched onto looking at handbags as they seemed to be in every store except Cartiers and I was getting kind of hooked on the different designs. I, therefore, did not go into Charles Jourdan (Paris) as they stock mainly shoes. At Loewe Madrid I received such a warm welcome that I actually responded 'What a wonderful smiling greeting!' The assistant told me that some people stay for up to an hour looking at stock (it wasn't a large shop) and leave without purchasing anything but that didn't matter as they might well be back next month to buy something. "Via La Moda" mainly sold handbags and by this time I had started to feel like this area is the handbag capital of Australia.

I now understand, for the first time in my life, what 'retail therapy' really means. I'm sure the term must have been coined by those who have the money to visit stores like these and it has nothing to do with going out to just buy a new skirt from K Mart or whatever to try and cheer yourself up. I didn't buy a thing and I felt wonderful. In fact, the only item I came away with was the book given to me by the assistant at Cartier and I had received so many genuine smiles that I was smiling myself as I returned to talk to the proprietor of the coffee bar. I sat back down on the sofa and as he brought me my coffee I told him that I had been doing some research and he was visiting the wrong shops! I also showed him the book. We then discussed the option of him and his wife perhaps living in Melbourne for six months of the year when it's warm there and spending the other months at the Gold Coast thereby meeting her health needs and his emotional needs. At that moment John turned up and his head was in another dimension altogether (black holes, the stellar vortex wormhole, hyperspace and a journey to the edge of the universe).

We were meant to be visiting another attraction called Infinity where you dance with giant spheres in a world of glow tubes, feel the light in the laser zone and cross the bottomless Light Canyon but I decided that perhaps we'd wait a couple of weeks and go on my Birthday instead as it is an attraction that I want to visit and I felt that both in one day would be too much. (Big mistake as we never did get back there! I recall a notice on one of my employer's desk which read 'Do it Now')

We wandered back to Cavill Avenue as dusk was falling and the nightlife commencing. We went into Raptis Plaza and I marvelled at the statue of David again before settling down comfortably in a rather quaint and small restaurant called Naomi's Shoe Cafe. We received yet another warm and personal welcome and relaxed, listening to gentle music whilst waiting for our Veal Scallopine and steak dinners. The total bill was only $20.80 and as our Australian dollar is only worth about 40 pence sterling at that time you will realise why we were impressed. The meal was basic, accompanied by salad and chips but the ambience and friendliness outshone the reception we have received in some of finest restaurants we have visited in Brisbane and the Gold Coast and far surpassed the service at the Versace hotel when we stayed there. The food was a lot better than what we ate at Versace too. In fact that was so bad there that John returned his dinner and left his hot breakfast.

As we walked back along the beachfront to our car we stopped to watch some men flying kites on the beach. There was just enough light from the promenade lighting but no moonlight as the sky was thick with dark clouds. The kites whirred and whizzed as they flew at amazing speeds overhead. We had enjoyed a wonderful afternoon in Surfers Paradise.

August 2005

We'd just got the house back to normal when the south-east coast of Queensland and the northern New South Wales received somewhat too much rainfall within 24 hours. The Gold Coast was flooded and some emergency service workers needed rescuing and then they in turn got into trouble and needed rescuing so perhaps that epitomises the sad state of affairs along the coastline. It was truly awful and there were landslides at the top of our hill, one being at the top of our road. Some homes were left without back gardens and the foundations of these homes so precarious that all levels of government became involved. There has been a lot of pontificating but very little action so far and that was about eleven weeks ago. The State Government put their hands in their pockets for a geotechnical survey, the insurance companies ran away and the local Council has stepped in to help now and will argue later as to who pays for the cost!

Well we too got flooded, Helen ended up in hospital a couple of days later and we have done some major renovations! Luckily our Insurance Company has come up trumps again but we have also spent a lot of money and we have, of course, put more drains in! So we'll have been stuck at home for about a year by the time we are free to go and now we can't wait to get back onto the road.

In the meantime Helen has bought herself a year-old car with only a few thousand kilometres on the clock and I've bought myself a bike. John adjusted the seat height to the lowest it will go and I can just about reach the ground (my short, fat, hairy leg problem) and he raised the handlebars so that I can sit a little more upright but must have done something wrong cause I only rode about 800m and had to walk with my legs apart when I got off. That saddle! My legs were like jelly. I fiddled about with the gears whilst I tried to circumnavigate the roundabout outside out house whilst at the same time listening to John screaming 'Look behind you - cars - get to the side of the road!' He was on top of the motor home out the front and I think his legs were like jelly too just from watching me.

As I wobbled along the road a couple of guys said hello and as I returned some young guys in a car slowed down to get a better look at me - they must have had a fright when they saw my wrinkles! John reckons I was handling the bike better when I got back but I pushed the bike along our flat driveway as I was worn out! The thing is, is that the helmet (which I did not want to wear) is quite spunky and what with all the straps it sorts of lifts my double chin up so I look younger!! I'm thinking of wearing it on the beach and in restaurants. I might have to when I go to the shops because I can fit the clasp together but I cannot undo it without help!

Now I've recovered (3 hours later) I've decided to read the manual. These gears are called derailleur gears - where on earth did that come from - well from France I presume but it's not in my French vocabulary. I now find that the left hand ones control the front wheels and the right the back wheels. Isn't that amazing! Of course, even kids know these things. I peddled backwards to put the brakes on until I realised I was supposed to use the levers at the front (I haven't got to those instructions yet). It didn't matter though because I was in the middle of the road when I tried the brakes out and had plenty of room.

These instructions tell me that if I want to select a lower gear 'shift to a bigger rear cog and a small chain wheel'. What on earth does that mean? Which way do I turn it? Why do things have to be so complicated? It also tells me that I cannot change gears when pedaling backwards!! Is this a common practice? I'm having enough trouble going forwards! I have to stop to change gears now as I'm so confused! Are there driving lessons for bikes nowadays? I have to admit that I miss a rear vision mirror as I can't turn my neck very much. On top of all this, before every ride I am supposed to check the tyre pressure, check brake operation, check wheels for loose spokes, make sure nothing is loose and after every ride, wipe down with a damp cloth! Oh yeah - I can see me doing that. This bike was the cheapest I could find on special at Big W (Woolworths for UK friends).

So am I excited at getting a bike, having wanted one since we were allowed to ride one at that caravan park when we were travelling before (making this the second time I have tried to ride a bike in 30 years)? No. John thinks I'm excited but I'm not. What I really wanted was one of the old fashioned ones that we used to ride when I was at school and I kept insisting that any bike I bought had to have a basket at the front. I haven't got my basket. I would have bought almost any bike with a basket. I want one of those old bikes where, when you peddled backwards it activated the brakes. So, if anyone out there has an old bike with a basket at the front and a big, comfy old saddle, I'm here to ask 'Do you want to swap it for a brand new bike?'

Chapter 3

ON THE ROAD AGAIN - 20TH MAY 2006 (Part 1 of "The Big Lap")

THE ROUTE TAKEN IN THIS DIARY MARKED IN GREEN

The last time I wrote anything it was around April of 2005 and we've finally started on our journey around Australia again. In fact this is our second night on the road. Delays, delays, "Murphy's Law" again,?

Previously we had found a house in Pomona and put our house on the market, the seller took her house off the market and we couldn't find anything else we wanted. We subsequently took our house off too! Then the gas fridge broke down and there was only one person prepared to take on an American fridge and as he had never repaired one before he offered to 'learn' on ours. He did learn – a lot – and it took four months. We sent to America for parts ourselves. As it was taking so long I decided to get a medical check up done on something that was 'niggling' me which resulted in me being admitted to hospital a week later for surgery. Complications arose out of that, such as having my gall bladder taken out and then finding I had two duodenal ulcers as well and having a cat gut stitch left inside which caused an abscess – it's all so boring but it's done now and the other surgery I had has relieved a lot of problems with my back.

Then I had to have three biopsies on my forehead for skin cancer and then that area frozen. I'm full of tablets, have had far too many antibiotics and am very run down from packing up and cleaning the house. Both John and I ended up very stressed from lack of time as the house got rented within hours of it going on the internet and we weren't really ready! We put it on the rental list on Friday afternoon and whilst we were eating our dinner the rental lady phoned us to ask us if we would accept her recommended tenants who were presently in Sydney. It all happened too quickly in the end which is ironic. John had been so frustrated waiting for the fridge and then for me to get repaired and the night before we slept in the van only to find there was a gas leak and that the water spout is leaking so badly in the kitchen, we can only use the bathroom sink. He also has a rear brake light not working. To think he had all that time waiting to go and getting frustrated!

We now have duel fuel as he had an LPG gas tank installed. John is driving beautifully now and waits before speaking via the 2-way phone so that I don't miss the first half of every sentence but has now picked up a new habit of pressing an arrow when he picks the phone up which sets it to the wrong channel which means he can't get it to work and he thinks it is my phone at fault! We also managed to leave together, at the same time and on the same route this time. If you read the first trip we did together you will remember the fiasco on our very first day.

We will arrive tomorrow at Gracemere (Rockhampton) where we will catch up at long last with Sue and Greg again. They accomplished their trip around the Northern Territory and Western Australia last year, which we were supposed to be doing with them and left home some time ago to start this year's travels. So although we are several hundred kilometres north of Brisbane, we have changed our plans to visit with them before heading to Longreach, Mt Isa and on to Alice Springs, Uluru (Ayers Rock), back to Alice Springs and then up to Darwin. From there we head to Broome and then right around Western Australia, past Perth, across the desert and eventually Adelaide and then towards home. We have to complete this trip in 50 weeks and are spending the first two with Sue and Greg just winding down and relaxing.

Our first two nights were spent 'off road'. Our neighbour tonight is a lovely lady driving a big old bus on her own but as she had a career as a truck driver she is very happy. She has just finished a course of chemotherapy and accompanied by her little dog named Gidget, is heading right around Australia with no time limits. She has told us lots of stories of other people's lives and as before, we find the permanent travellers so much more interesting to talk to than those that just go on holidays to escape the winters and who usually stay in the caravan parks. Anyway, this lady is going to go and stay with a male friend in the Kimberley region and fly around in his helicopter shooting buffalo which is their kind of fun apparently.

John Timms

GRACEMERE-QUEENSLAND.

When we arrived, Sue was hugging me as we were trying to sign in! A fish and chip dinner and a good bottle of white wine helped us unwind but everything Sue was talking about where we should go to in the Northern Territory and Western Australia was a blur of names and I was beyond comprehending a word she was saying despite her animated descriptions.

Sheer exhaustion is a weird feeling. You are not exactly ill but you feel very odd. I was incapable of reading a paper, holding a conversation, watching television or even cleaning my teeth yet I found it hard to get to sleep the first night. The next day I was a zombie. Today I am gradually coming back to an awareness of what is around me yet still feel kind of detached and Sue is still telling us names of places we should or shouldn't go to. I keep imploring her not to and to wait, as I am not really here yet in my head although she can see my physical form! I did manage to get us onto a mobile phone plan this afternoon and we are eating sensibly and well and my mouth ulcers and face sores and sore ear, which all arose from infections picked up in hospital, are all healing up. Greg and John repaired the kitchen sink connection yesterday but the T.V aerial doesn't work now. I think John has repaired his brake light – must remember to ask him.

We had to go into town yesterday as there are two dog chains and a stake laying around at our last overnight stop! We bought some more and John got his reading glasses repaired. I bought Callie a new rubber ball which she has got bored with pretty quickly as she is not allowed off her chain in this park so I can't throw it for her. Seemed like a good idea at the time. So we have continued to do the mundane chores that we would do at home.

It is cool and wet and miserable outside which doesn't help although the locals are almost dancing with delight to see the rain and the T.V news announcers are so excited that it is headline news! I hand washed some clothes today that won't be able to go into a machine and felt a great sense of achievement despite the fact that I have had to hang it on a rack in our shower compartment as it is too wet to put outside. I thought it might 'ground' me to do this small task! We are actually on the road at last. How come I cannot seem to 'know' it?

I'm way behind on this diary and will attempt to recall what has happened. We stayed for two weeks at Gracemere but the local chemist was overrun with people seeking help for gastroenteritis and I was one of them. Tablets gave me two days respite and then it was back so I took two more and so it went on and I became convinced it was the water that was causing the problem. It spoilt our time there but we did get back to one of our favourite beaches one day where Callie delighted us with her exuberance and her energy until she ran into Jack and knocked the poor old man flying! It used to be the other way around. He was so sore that we had to give him a doggy painkiller that night!

The park owners held a splendid free 'pancake night' with maple syrup, strawberry syrup and oodles of ice cream around two camp fires with free tea and coffee and biscuits included. Sue taught me how to make some of my own greeting cards and I bought all sorts of craft materials and some painting equipment and I completed my first two cards and am looking forward to having the time to get more done.

John visited **Mt Morgan** which has the largest open-cut gold mine in the southern hemisphere and took lots of photos for me to look at. The town itself is not that exciting though so you need to be interested in gold mining. You can travel back via a different route and there are some lovely views.

On the day we left we did not get away until midday and had two coffee/dog stops before reaching **Emerald** around 4pm. We stopped at the information centre and there was a dump point so John decided to empty the black water tank and noticed that there was something stuck up the grey water tank outlet. I eventually released it with a stick and we had to use a lot of water to clear out the tank and by the time we departed it was getting rather too late for driving. Driving at dusk is not recommended because you are more likely to see kangaroos or wallabies on the road. Driving in the dark is definitely not recommended. John said I drove like the fury and he had difficulty keeping me in sight.

We arrived at **Sapphire** in the dark and I was in front and had had enough so pulled in at a petrol station which served food. We were looking for an off-road site mentioned in one of our books but all that remains of it is a piece of land as the Council has removed the toilets and water tank. I smelt the aroma of fish and chips and exclaimed to the lady behind the counter 'Dinner. Can we have some?' She told us that we could also stay there because there was a van park behind and why didn't we go and get settled in whilst she cooked us our dinner. How nice to have a Mum again.

In the morning we drove further into the gem fields to **Rubyvale** and it is absolutely fascinating and a lovely little hamlet. I can well understand how people get hooked on fossicking for the gems because there is a startling array of different colours in the stones and they are worth vastly different amounts! John could not take his eyes off a yellow/amber coloured sapphire worth $95,000. Luckily it was not for sale! The stories are endless, the people there fascinating and you could write a book about their lives and their tales and the stones they have found. One road had been named Desperado Street which I found amusing.

I will write about the journey to remind myself at a later date, just in case I get it into my head that it was a great trip! From Gracemere Caravan Park onwards it was endlessly boring. The land is parched and although it was a bright sunny day with enough breezes not to need the air conditioner on in the car, I had to turn it on at times because I thought I would fall asleep. John and I both called each other on the two-way phones to check on each other. The trees became sparser and what vegetation there was could at best be described as bushes and dry grass. Dead Kangaroos and Wallabies lined the roads. If there was a hill it became more interesting and if we saw a vehicle of any description going either way it was exciting! When we crossed the railway line and it was on our left instead of to our right it required further discussion as a point of interest! We could see a couple of hilly areas to our left which must have been part of the Blackdown

Tableland National Park which apparently has gorges and waterfalls and were sad that we could not visit Carnarvon Gorge but as it is also National Park land we cannot go with the dogs, so they will be a trips for the future.

For those who want more information on the National Parks there are many books available and in each State or Territory you will find leaflets at any Tourist Information Centre.

There were two areas only where the road climbed and dropped and winded back and forth. **Blackwater** was really ugly and seeing a huge slag heap it reminded me of Mum telling me that when she was in Sheffield for a while, she would put the sheets out sparkling white and bring them back in grey. When I saw some dried grass with pink heads I realised that I had felt starved of colour. When we passed through one small town and I saw a stunning red bougainvillea I was overjoyed.

For the rest of the trip the road was straight and endless and as you looked ahead it seemed that you were approaching water and I realised I had seen my first mirage. John told me that from his height it looks like the sea. And so it continued, on and on and on.

We passed through odd sounding places like **Alpha** and **Jericho**. I started doing exercises whilst driving, arching my shoulders back and forth and up and down, turning my neck (there wasn't a car in sight!) and clenching my buttocks to strengthen my 'core' as my Pilates teacher terms it. Then I'd adjust the seat so that I changed the position of my spine. I realised that I could not have done this trip without having had that operation because before when we travelled I would get out of the Ute and be doubled over with pain and would stagger around trying to get straight. Now I am jumping out of the car with no pain having driven much further.

BARCALDINE IS A PRETTY, SERENE TOWN

Because of our diversion out to Rubyvale we again left late and arrived at **Barcaldine** late afternoon. I had been warned not to call it Barcald-Ine as I was doing but to remember 'bar-called-in' or the locals would be offended! It was so good to arrive in a pretty town. The locals are friendly, the town is spotless and there are enough attractions to keep the tourist happy. I was still ill and after a four hour wait at the local hospital without seeing a doctor I decided we should return to our van and change all our water as the local artesian water is so pure. It took a while to empty the tank, wash out our water bottles, clean our water filter and refill but this morning I woke up and felt well and I was able to eat last night! There was one doctor trying to cover the hospital and the local doctor's surgery and they had two emergency arrivals yesterday afternoon. Apparently they find it hard to keep doctors and I'm not surprised! You could only work at that pace for so long and you'd burn out.

We saw a program only the night before about rural New South Wales and the problems they are having in some towns where there are no doctors and women having to travel for hours in cars whilst in labour to try and reach a doctor. There are well-equipped hospitals but no staff! So it is not just Queensland that has a shortage of doctors and we realise how spoilt we are on the southern coastline of Australia where there are surgeries on every corner and in most shopping centres. I have just been offered a 'bushies' remedy for food poisoning or gastroenteritis. Hot water with sugar and a good dose of brandy and it kills all the germs. I have a bottle of brandy in the van which has never been opened! If only I'd known.

We walked around Barcaldine this afternoon and it is really charming and so peaceful. John said that he could imagine the staff at the Council offices saying 'Shall we do that form tomorrow and go and buy a cake for afternoon tea?' but I suppose that they do have some work to do. It's just that it feels so relaxed and laid back. The streets are wide and the houses appear to be on land of approximately a quarter of an acre apiece. Some are so old that they are almost falling down with the odd new or the renovated home here and there.

We saw the 'Tree of Knowledge' and I bought a postcard with the words of the 'Ballad of 1891' from the Tourist Information Centre. The tree is a Eucalyptus tree and it commemorates the gathering of the shearers when they decided to strike in 1891 which led to the formation of the Australian Labour Party. Thirteen of the strike leaders were sentenced to three years hard labour and there is someone else I would like to see serve the same sentence because it has been headline news recently that someone has poisoned the old tree. Whatever anyone's political agenda there is absolutely no excuse for such ignorant vandalism. It is beyond me how stupid people can be at times but perhaps the person who did it had a mental problem. I'm not sure what the person intended to gain either but the tree has my sympathy and I think a little more deeply about the bravery of those first Unionists and hope that they realised what they achieved.

The caravan park that we are staying at has super clean amenities and several en-suite units that apparently came from the Olympic Games village. The washing machines are top of the line and are there is no charge for using them. One night they had billy tea and damper and the local bush poet entertained and he is apparently very entertaining. Unfortunately I was not well enough to attend but I had heard of this bush poet over two years ago from a friend at the Gold Coast. The park only charged us $14 per night even though it is a very busy time for them as the 'dry season' has just started. You do not travel to certain areas of Australia in the wet season because of possible floods. Indeed this year, we had the cyclone in the North when Innisfail, Mission Beach and the Tablelands and all areas between suffered so much damage and some people are still living amongst the ruins of their homes.

Chapter 4

LONGREACH – June 2006

This is our second night of free camping by the river. We are allowed to stay four nights and it is certainly very popular. However, it is a large area and there is ample room for everyone. Just as we arrived at Longreach a shock absorber collapsed on the front of the bus. We were so lucky to get it welded so close to where it happened and despite it being a difficult job which took an hour and a half, we were only charged $60 for which we were very grateful. So we arrived at this site late in the afternoon and today we have looked around the town centre. Jack has not been well and we realise that he has suddenly lost most of his hearing. Last night John had to pick him up and put him in the back of the Ute as he didn't appear willing or capable of moving but tonight he seems a little better. Tomorrow we are going to the Stockman's Hall of Fame. We have actually experienced a little rain on and off today and the temperature has been perfect at around 22C.

Yesterday, prior to our realising there was something wrong with the bus, we had driven in the Ute into the town centre to visit the Information Centre, leaving the bus on the edge of town. We called into one of the nicest coffee shops I have ever visited opposite the Information Centre, just as you walk into the main street and it was called the Coffee Pod. It is down an alleyway behind a shop called House of Kanandah which, for colour starved travellers, is a wondrous place to visit. Both are a feast for the eyes and soul but for different reasons. The coffee shop has tables in a garden, the meals are home cooked and the shop is one of the most exotic I have seen and the perfumed air is a delight. One shop leads into the other. Check out the different mustards, pickles and sauces etc. I wanted them all! Even the bottles are lovely.

WINTON - ARNO'S WALL - 8

If you read my last diary you will know that I was questioning how I would know if I was in the 'outback' and what did the term really mean. Well, as we saw the 'Welcome to Longreach' sign on the side of the road I actually saw it in writing! 'Longreach. Gateway to the Outback' (or something similar) so it seems we have reached that 'gate'!

WINTON - ARNO'S WALL - 9

I am so happy to be in **Winton** at a caravan site with full power and water instead of having to take care not to use too much of either as we did when staying off-road. Our priority on arrival was to shower and wash our hair – bliss. Then we put on the electric kettle and plugged in the electric toaster – we like our mod cons! Did I tell you that we travelled from Barcaldine to Longreach and only one car passed us on our side of the road – a distance of 107 klms. We did see traffic coming the other way - two cars, a few trucks and the rest four wheel drives. I also saw my first wild boar and it was enormous. Luckily it was also very dead, unless it liked sun bathing, because it was lying on its back with its legs in the air, a bit like Callie does.

Today we travelled 180ks from Longreach to Winton and one car passed us and we passed a very slow mini-bus. The majority of the time we had the road completely to ourselves and couldn't see any vehicles for as far as the eye could see both in front nor in the rear view mirror. I discovered a button to open my CD recorder which is new and had not yet been used. The machine gobbled my Bob Dylan CD I then returned to my usual practice of playing Dire Straits Brothers in Arms. Thank goodness I don't have to pay them royalties every time I play one of their numbers as my old tape wore out on our last trip. I think I'll start with The Kinks next time, just for a change of pace although I did consider Silver Chair today as I love it and John loathes it! The Kinks seems appropriate as I like my comfort (as I'm realising more and more on this trip) and will enjoy listening to Sunny Afternoon ('I love to live so pleasantly. Live this life of luxury...' and 'lazing on this sunny afternoon'.) I also like their 'Dedicated Follower of Fashion' – so bitingly sarcastic about the Carnaby Street fashions of the 60's.

What a pity that Carnaby Street has changed so much. It's like Byron Bay here, where we went recently. It's lost its magic and there are no dingle/dangle scented shops full of hand dyed sarongs and T-shirts with Byron Bay emblazoned across the front. The shops have all metamorphosed into up-market coffee shops or sports shops.

When we were in the Stockman's Hall of Fame yesterday I saw the men's shirt collars which used to be detachable and remarked to John that I could recall Dad wearing them and John said that he had worn them and this young guy near us looked at John and exclaimed 'You used to wear them. Really?' It's odd to be looked at as though you are a living antique. I told John more quietly that I used to enjoy using the plug and switch telephone boards when the Manpower agency used to send me out on temporary jobs!

I have trouble understanding the Australian language although having been here now for 25 years! I read in the paper today that half a pint of beer is 285ml in our metric system. In Queensland we call that a 'pot' of beer. I had no idea that in New South Wales it is called a middy and in South Australia a schooner. I thought that was only for sherry! Can you imagine me asking for a schooner of sherry and getting half a pint of it? In the Northern Territory it is called a handle and in Tasmania it can be called a pot, a ten or a handle! As we will be travelling to all these places except Tasmania this information might be useful for John. Apparently a couple of pubs in Brisbane have been selling their beer in 250ml glasses which look the same and it is not against the law but the bottom of the glass has to have the exact volume so look under your glass next time you order a pot!

Here at Winton we drink bore water which comes from the Artesian Basin about 4000 feet underground. As it comes up at a temperature of 83C it has to be cooled before distribution. An information booklet tells us 'Don't Despair' but I read it after I had filled the dog bucket on arrival and smelt this awful 'aroma'. The booklet says it is 'distinctive'. They are not joking! It is a hydrogen sulphide gas and we are advised to let it stand or to boil it prior to chilling and then it is magnificent, very pure and it is their best kept secret. I got all that and we have two glasses of boiled water prepared for bedtime. However, I wanted a shower in our motor home. In Australia you cannot have an electric exhaust fan in the ceiling of a shower cubicle but we do have one in the adjoining bathroom area in the van. I had a rather quick and very unpleasant shower because I found I was holding my breath because within the confines of the shower cubicle, which has a solid glass door, the smell was almost overwhelming. I must admit though that once the water is poured into a jug the smell dissipates very rapidly. I wonder what it might do to our electric kettle as it apparently tarnishes silver and the sinks in the public facilities are stained brown!

Tomorrow we will hopefully collect our post from the Winton GPO, which the postie at Gracemere failed to deliver and returned it to Helen saying 'insufficient address' despite the postmistress there having written out the address, postcode included which was diligently copied by Helen. There is only one post office there anyway! We will have a look at some of the fascinating sites around town. There is a musical fence and Arno's Wall which is made up of every type of household item imaginable apparently, including a kitchen sink and motor bikes. I was told about it by a girl in a newsagent in Longreach. There is also an open air picture theatre and although we have one between the Gold Coast and Brisbane which still operates, this one still uses the original projection equipment. It is near here that Banjo Patterson wrote Waltzing Matilda and it was first performed on April 6 in 1895 at the North Gregory Hotel in town which we intended visiting anyway as the owners are members of our motor home club and allow us to camp there for free so we intended to check out the facilities and pop in for a drink and say g'day.

Post Office shut, as were most of the shops because it's a public holiday for the Queen's Birthday! England doesn't normally have a day off work but we do, even though it's not her Birthday today. John and I obviously hadn't realised that it was a public holiday for her and I wonder if she knows!

Before going into town we went to play with the Qantas Cairn and Musical Fence. John enjoyed playing with it more than I did. I am going to quote from a leaflet now: 'The Winton Shire Council became the first local authority in the world to support an airline with its contribution to the acquisition in 1920 for Qantas' first runway. The first plane landed here on 7th of February 1921 and a memorial cairn marks the site.' That is really something to be proud of isn't it? We took photos of course! However, Longreach lays claim to building the first hangar and the country's first purpose-built landing field. Gets confusing because today I read that Qantas was 'conceived' in Cloncurry which is 253 kilometres away and that 'their' hanger is still at the airport. Whatever, it is a great airline and whatever their contributions they have the right to be proud.

Now where was I? Oh yes, the next stop was Arno's Wall which required many photos as it is quite extraordinary, many strange household items and bric-a-brac embedded in the wall at odd angles. From there we walked through the beer garden of the North Gregory Hotel and out into the main street and next door was the Corfield and Fitzmaurice Store which was a general store and opened in 1878. You can pay to see the dinosaur exhibition, including casts of fossilised bones found locally. The latest find is apparently of the Sauropod. We didn't go into that but I did look at the displays of locally made craft and purchased a cookery book named 'Country Cooking' which is made up of recipes supplied by parents, teachers and children of the Longreach School of Distance Education. I fell for a chocolate cake recipe apparently made by Nana Miller because underneath was written 'Nana makes this every day for shearing and there is a child's drawing, presumably of herself beside it and if it is her, her name is Bonnie. Because John is six foot tall he saw the Sauropod anyway by just looking over a partition!

We returned to the hotel and I had a free (make your own) coffee placing a donation in the tin for the Royal Flying Doctor Service. John bought a beer because we felt we had to buy something and were not hungry.

It was time to look after the dogs needs so we took them to the **Long Waterhole** and there we really felt like we were in the 'outback'. There is also a **Pelican Waterhole** which was the first settlement here (by white man anyway) but we were advised that the water is not drinkable and we should take the dogs to the former one for a swim. Apparently the locals swim in it. I wouldn't because I'm not into mud baths and the dogs didn't think much of it either. Jack came out as soon as he got his paws wet! However it is scenic and close to town and worth the trip.

We returned to town and found the **Banjo Patterson** statue outside the Information Centre which is also the **Waltzing Matilda Centre** and a museum. There was a show about to start but as we have so recently been to the Longreach Hall of Fame we decided to give it a miss. There sure is a lot to see and do, if you want to, in and around Winton. The people next to us have been out to the **Lark Quarry Dinosaur Track ways** which is the world's only site of a dinosaur stampede. Lots of small dinosaurs (Coelurosaur and Ornithopods) were having a great time next to a billabong and minding their own business when a great big dinosaur (Carnosaur) approached and scared the living daylights out of them. Because old Carnosaur was looking for some dinner we are left with the legacy of thousands of footprints for us to look at in awe. Our neighbours have a four wheel drive vehicle and it took them an hour and a quarter to get there on quite a good dirt road. It apparently inspired Steven Spielberg when he was dreaming up Jurassic Park and he thus incorporated a stampede scene.

124klms from Winton **is Opalton** and they have the record for the largest piece of opal ever mined and recorded, being more than 3 metres long. Don't rush there because that was found in 1899 and I reckon a few people may have searched the area since then! They have a shop at Opalton and mail only on Thursdays which is more frequently than we are getting ours.

Our next stop will probably be Kynuna about an hour and a half along the road. We can stop for the night there. The following day we will pass **McKinlay** and the **Walkabout Creek Hotel** has apparently gone walkabout and is now by the highway! Why? Because it featured in the film Crocodile Dundee so they obviously want to cash in on its short period of 'fame'.

I've been so-o-o confused over the television programs as one channel calls itself 'Imparja' but I believe I've cracked it! It seems to be a mixture of both Channel Nine and Channel Ten! So we watch the Channel Nine daily current affairs program after the news, albeit that it is on at a different time and we watched Sixty Minutes (the same channel) last night. However, tonight we have Big Brother on the same channel which is a Channel 10 program! We do not have a magazine which tells us the T.V. programs though! Every time we stop we have to tune the T.V into the local reception. Luckily, the T.V has automatic tuning when you press a few buttons. I have just found out that the program we thought was channel Two is really channel Seven! As we leave tomorrow, all this will start again unless we skip T.V altogether which is happening more and more frequently recently as it's just too much bother.

Yesterday I was a ratbag and today John has been too. It's not all married bliss for us when travelling. Some people appear to manage to keep talking sweetly to each other despite being with each other 24/7 but I'm afraid both John and I are just too independent and need time to be on our own. This is where driving separate vehicles becomes very valuable as it releases our pressure valves. After John had insisted on using the kitchen area to make coffee, just as a whole heap of rice was ready for draining for the dogs dinner, a silent truce was called as we had to work together to get the rice out of the saucepan!

Jack will not drink so I have devised a plan which I hope works or he'll end up on a drip at the vets because he is continually passing water from the wrong place! I bought a big pile of rough mince from the butcher which I've cooked in a heap of vegetable water. The vegetables were a small can of peas well washed and drained tossed in the pot with broccoli and two large carrots. Having mixed the rice, vegetables and cooked meat together there was about three quarters to one litre of vegetable juice left and I mixed that through. He's going to get fluid whether he realises it or not. A quick trip to the vet might be easier but there isn't one here so I'm learning 'bush medicine' (of a sort) very quickly. The dogs loved their dinner and keep asking for more.

We are, of course, heading to Alice Springs and we saw on the weather forecast last night that it was to be zero last night. Tonight it's even better at minus two!! It is winter of course and we were warned it could get cold but that's a bit much with dogs in tow. I think we'll stick to powered sites for the time being so that we can have our fan heater on.

Kynuna

Before heading for Kynuna, John went into Winton to collect our post at last. He then went to look for bread but there was none in town at all and the bread shop does not open on Tuesdays albeit that it was a Public Holiday yesterday and they therefore had Monday off work! Then he went to the garage opposite the van park to buy gas for the van. Someone had filled up and left their vehicle and John reckons that whoever it was, had gone to the loo with the newspaper as we had such a long wait. Eventually John got the bus into position only to find that the vehicle before had used up the last of the gas! Welcome to the outback towns!

Something happened to me today whilst driving. I fell in love with the outback. It is so serene and beautiful in its vastness and emptiness. It is the first time on this trip so far that I've actually been glad that we left home! We overtook two slow moving cars towing caravans and one car passed us. Other than that there was only the odd traffic on the other side of the road so for most of the time we travelled for many kilometres without seeing any vehicle. We only had to slow down once when a house approached us on the back of a truck and as the load took up most of the road we had to get partly off the bitumen! We have still not seen a 50 metre road train although we have seen the signs warning us that they could be on the road. We have seen cattle trucks and when full of cattle or sheep it is enough to turn you into a vegetarian. I haven't yet seen quite enough of them though.

Anyway, today there were no visual pollutions such as cattle trucks, billboards, houses, and petrol stations and the only sign of civilisation other than the road, were the wire fences. I realise it has been colonised and therefore cleared and is not the same as the Aboriginals knew it eons ago but to me it seemed pure and untouched. Occasionally a ball of dried grass would roll across the road but much of the grass was green, the soil beneath red and where the grass had dried out it was also red and set against the clear blue skies it was just so beautiful to look at. The only reason I wanted to stop here was because I know we are heading towards more populated areas and I am certainly not in a hurry to reach Mt Isa.

We stopped at the Kynuna Roadhouse for petrol and had lunch. We then decided to stay here the night and have the place to ourselves and it is great. The dogs love being off their leads. There is a stand-alone bathroom with hand basin, toilet and shower for us to use. We have to share it with the odd truckie who calls into the roadhouse for a meal but it's a nice touch. It only costs $8 per night and we have the power and water and oodles of places for the dogs to romp about plus a covered area with table and benches if we want to sit outside.

We are further away from the main road than we were in the last caravan park which was terrible because right behind us was the road train stop and they came and went day and night. Jack got very upset with them as to him they appeared like monsters roaring up in the dark with big flashing 'eyes' and although he might be going deaf he couldn't avoid hearing them! However, he's already getting better and is now drinking again.

There isn't any telephone or T.V reception of course but if you're desperate there is a good one on in the Roadhouse. John walked the dogs down to the hotel where there is also a caravan park. I had tried to book into it by telephone this morning but was told that he didn't take bookings as people booked and then didn't turn up so it was 'first come, first served'. If he had booked us in we would have felt obliged to have gone there and I'm very glad he didn't! John told me on his return that the vans are crammed together like sardines and that they do not have a view like us and for that they pay two dollars more per night. Another guy in the hotel having a drink, overheard John and asked if he could get petrol at the Roadhouse as he was going there for dinner and he has booked in as well so there are now two vans in this park and we have so much space around us.

Prior to Mt Isa we will reach Cloncurry where you can branch off to visit the **Boodjamulla National Park** – if you have a four wheel drive and no dogs. As to Mt Isa, John reckons we should park the bus, get to Woolworths (or whatever) and stock up with essentials and get out of town as quickly as possible. He speaks from experience as he has been there before. Mt Isa is a mining town - silver, lead, copper and zinc and you can tour underground if you like that sort of thing. There are things to see and do with a couple of dams to visit, exhibitions of fossils, visit the Royal Flying Doctor Service base or The School of the Air for the children who live on the outback stations but to me at the moment, in my frame of mind, it is a town and should be avoided at all costs!

I think of a conversation I had with my friend in Tasmania this morning. We went to High School together so many years ago and when we went to Tassie a few years ago, it was the first time we'd been together for 29 years and it was so good. Well she is about to depart Tassie for the mainland and she and her husband will catch the ferry tomorrow morning and they will travel up to Queensland and here we are about to go into the Northern Territory. I'm sad that our timing is so wrong. She said that she couldn't sleep last night as she and her husband are so excited and it will be the first time he has been to the mainland for many years. He too was originally from England and they first lived in New Zealand prior to moving to Tasmania many years ago. I wonder what they'll think of the mainland as it is so very different. Oh well, we'll just have to go back to Tassie to see them!

Chapter 5

Cloncurry –June 2006

In 1928 the first flight by the **Flying Doctor Service** took place from here and that is something the town can be very, very proud of. The pilots, doctors and nurses who fly around the outback of this vast country have to face incredible dangers at times and have to be prepared for any kind of emergency. The pilot may fear the sunset in case he cannot get to some outback station and find the dirt runway before it gets dark and get the patient stabilised, on board and be able to see the runway to take off again! There may be dust storms or other bad weather and they face every kind of medical emergency you can possibly imagine. It's not exactly like the Casualty area of a hospital where you can call on a team of people to help! Like our Surf Life Savers and Firemen in this country – they are just amazing. There are many volunteer fire-fighters here who may be at work when they get a call to leave immediately so here's to those bosses who accept these employees!

We are at a caravan park that we wanted to book into but thought we couldn't because one book said no dogs. However, there are new owners who do allow dogs. We are in a lovely position right at the back end of the park with fields and horses around us and a very steep, high red hill to look at. It's lovely. We do seem to find some lovely positions in the parks we visit but we always ask if we can drive around first before booking in.

We've already checked out the town and I had a chat with a Scottish woman in the craft shop, visited the chemist who ordered what I needed. Actually she handed me the phone so that I could speak to the wholesalers myself and it will be delivered for me at 10am tomorrow! I have also bought some fresh bread from the bakers and have been to the Information Centre to get street maps of here and Mt Isa and I took the dogs for a free run in a park. Jack is completely well again after three home-cooked meals. Isn't rice a wonder! I thought of it only because when Callie had pancreatitis on our last trip that is all she was allowed after five days of fasting. I was then instructed to cook chicken breasts, chop it up finally and mix that in for the next week or so. I was spending more on her meat than I was on ours for a while there!

Whilst I was running around town, John was filling up the bus at two different service stations – one being for gas and the other with discount docket for petrol. We both noticed that there is a Woolworths but could not face going in. Considering we didn't leave until lunchtime we haven't done too badly and we were on our site by around 3pm. Tomorrow I have to face the washing and I will be using my machine because the cost of the machines here is $2.40 per wash which we haven't paid since we were on our last trip and that was at Mission Beach. I had done one lot of washing there at a cost of $2 and when I went to take it out they were changing the mechanics so that I would have to pay $2.40 for the next load. I still cannot fathom the cheek of it especially as I told the park owner that I didn't have the other 40 cents and he wouldn't even lend it to me! From thereon in, we took our washing next door to the back-packers laundry and did it for $2 and they had hot and cold filling machines instead of only cold. It was approximately 12 steps further to walk!

Note: By the time we had completed our trip around Australia I was telling park owners who only charged two dollars that they were daft as three dollars is the normal price and four dollars the highest!

A vehicle towing a caravan passed us today. So from Barcaldine to Cloncurry four vehicles have passed us and we've passed three and that is a distance of 639 kilometres! There has also been the bonus of no 50 metre road trains although we've seen some fairly large ones coming the other way. A French couple beside us have been complaining to John about the wind and the difficulty of driving against it. John told them that they are going around Australia the wrong way doing "The Big Lap" as it is called. We have been travelling the correct way, anticlockwise, with the wind behind us and it cuts down on our fuel use. We were told that there was a 'correct' way to travel around Australia many years ago because of the winds and now that we have experienced them, we can appreciate the advice.

Today we saw our first large ant hills standing on the ground as well as beautiful yellow gorse-like bushes and most of the grass was green. Approaching Cloncurry the scenery was really pretty. Tonight we can hear the cicadas which we haven't heard since leaving home.

However, I felt sad today and found myself crying whilst driving which is really not advisable, especially when you can't find a handkerchief, nor odd serviette pinched from a coffee shop or fast food outlet. Luckily I found a little toilet paper left on a roll but the car swerved from one side of the road to the other whilst I searched blindly through 3 compartments. I was going further and further away from my friend Barbara and I think more of people than places so where we were going was totally unimportant to me, as was the scenery for three quarters of the journey. I wanted to see my kids and Barbara and husband John, stuff this trip! However, John is also important to me and as I'm pretty committed to him I am here and not there. How I longed to have a hug with Barbara though - just for a moment. I spent the rest of the journey wandering how much it would cost to fly to Cairns and see them when they get there so that kept me occupied and stopped my tears!

I've occupied the rest of the time with overdue phone bills, setting up our van again, eating and writing this and sending a lot of text messages as my free ones, being a special promotional offer, end tomorrow! This offer was for new customers until I phoned up and complained that I had been a customer for umpteen years and deserved to receive the same offer or else I'd have to cut my phone off and only use their main opposition (I have two phones with different companies) and then rejoin to gain the benefit. Realising it would cause them a lot more paperwork they immediately agreed that I should get the benefit. It pays to complain sometimes.

An information leaflet tells us that Cloncurry has a friendly heart but they forgot to tell the lady at the Information Centre who was abrupt and rude. Whilst we were talking to her she thrust a couple of town maps at us and spoke to a man over our shoulder at the same time. However, other than the girl who took John's money at the petrol station yesterday everyone else we have met in this town has been charming and really friendly which makes shopping a pleasure for a change. For example, they tell us about themselves and I now know that the lady behind the service desk at one grocery store comes from Currumbin and when I said we did too we became more deeply involved in conversation. It's not that they are not busy but that they show a genuine interest in their customers and smile and laugh a lot.

The lady in the chemist yesterday (where I was getting my nicotine replacement therapy) told me how she had quit smoking 'cold turkey' thirty odd years ago and I told her that was not a good idea in my case because we are travelling around Australia and unless I get my nicotine hit, plus at least two mugs of coffee inside me, I am completely unable to talk or see for more than a metre in front of me, let alone walk as far as the car parked outside. Even if I did stagger to it I wouldn't have remembered the keys and would be wondering why I felt cold not realising that I only had my knickers on. I cannot understand why they have places for heroine addicts to go where they are monitored and assisted and where they can feel relatively safe whilst going through withdrawals but do not have them for smokers who are as bad as I am. I have honestly been frightened when trying to give up as the side effects have been so weird and so unexpected. I am off the cigarettes but still totally addicted to the nicotine inhalers.

I took a photo of our washing machine at work, outside on the concrete pad along with our rotary washing line. Now you must think that we have gone completely loopy but we are – or rather were – inordinately proud of having our own that we can set up anywhere. Having taken the photographs (yes, I went so far as to take more than one) the washing machine packed up and the washing line started tilting precariously and I just caught it in time from blowing over and taking off down the road. This happens to me every time I boast about something or take pride in something, even when I only think these things. I always get taken down a peg or two and I never need anyone to admonish me as 'Pride before a Fall' is my middle name.

To cap it off, just as everything was happening, the park owner turned up to say he had found Callie down the other end of the park and we had agreed to chain them up when we arrived. We hadn't actually, but that is beside the point. We both believe he was exaggerating because it's a heck of a way to the other end and a moment before Callie had been asleep in the back of the Ute. I think she took off in fright when I screamed for help with the washing line! I had said to John this morning that they had not asked us to tie our dogs up nor given us any rules and because there were absolutely no vans within several hundred metres of us and our patio faces the fields, I didn't see why we couldn't have them off their chains for a while because Callie likes to sunbake and Jack likes the shade. It is difficult to please them both and the ground is so rock hard that moving tent pegs that hold the chains down is tedious work.

Just after John had righted the washing line with all the jumpers and jeans on and hand-rung out the last of the washing for me, the machine decided to work again whilst empty and started spinning merrily! Murphy – please take a holiday will you and leave us alone, I promise I'll try to remember not to be proud again.

If your calves start to get loose stools and there is no vet available, mix up a couple of eggs and add it to their milk. How you add it to the mother's udders I have no idea but I thought you'd like to know that.

A lady suggested we do the same with Jack because as soon as he went back on his tinned dog food it started again (you know what I'm talking about). I wasn't sure that it was such a good idea – the milk part of the recipe I mean, so I have just 'cooked up a storm' for them which should last them for the next four days. I also have the name of a vet at Mt. Isa, albeit that tomorrow when we travel through the town the vets may not be open apparently because it is a Saturday. It is Friday here but the local vet is at the annual Show Day and on Saturdays she likes going to go to the races so won't be available. We had no idea that it is a public holiday here at Cloncurry. I do wish that Jack could be ill on a normal working day. The last time we were anywhere near a vet was when passing through Emerald on a Sunday.

CLONCURRY - CHINAMAN CREEK DAM

Anyway, the dogs have had a nice morning as we took them to a very picturesque area called **Chinaman Creek Dam** where they romped in the water and as Jack drank quite a lot of the water whilst barking at Callie who was catching sticks, I am not that worried about him. We also went up to the lookout and could see a distant view of the town and the beautiful surrounding outback and I now have a heap more photos to download.

Cloncurry was founded on copper in 1867 followed by gold being found not long after. The museum has a mineral and gem collection and you can still go fossicking here in particular areas so bring your shovel. Another important fact that you might like to note is that it can get to well over 40C in summer so do plan when you visit and be glad you were not here on January 16th in 1889 when it got to 53.1C as that is actually Australia's highest recorded temperature – so far anyway! It's certainly worth while stopping here and having a look around.

MT ISA - FROM TOWN LOOKOUT

MT ISA

We arrived yesterday and it was a nice surprise as it is a very pleasant city. The journey from Cloncurry to Isa is absolutely beautiful and we only had to pass one vehicle and let another overtake us. We had left late as usual at around 11.30am and everyone who is in a rush to get anywhere had obviously already gone so we virtually had the road to ourselves yet again.

We parked the bus on the main road, just before the Tourist Information Centre and we spent ages in there as it is so interesting, returning later for our lunch. It is actually called Outback at Isa and it is a huge complex with a mining tour and fossil centre and the Isa Experience Gallery has exhibits and films. The café is run by people who need work experience and I had the best toasted sandwich that I've ever eaten with a pretty sprinkling of very finely chopped, fresh parsley over the top. I asked for a glass of tap water and the girl served me and as I took a sip she looked very concerned and said 'I wish you wouldn't drink that. You are obviously not a local are you?' When I said we'd just arrived in town she rushed off and came back with some more water which she had taken from the coffee machine and to which she had added ice. She gave it to me with the comment 'No-one drinks the tap water around here'. However, everyone else we have spoken to tells us it is fine. I cannot agree as it has a bitter taste and we have pulled out our 12 litre container of spring water which we were saving for emergencies as I have started to get stomach pains again. The girl in the café did tell me that it had too much of some mineral in it but I have forgotten what it was called.

We had pre-booked into a Top Tourist park and John suggested we drive first in the Ute so that he could check out the route and the site. We didn't get chance for that because when we arrived he **was** told that they did not have a site for us after all and that they had booked us into another park! We thought that a bit of a cheek and went to look at our preferred park, which was right in the town. Anyway we liked the one out of town so we booked in immediately.

Today we had a drive down the road to see the town dam. It is called **Lake Moondarra** and we stopped at various places, allowing the dogs to have a swim at the Warrina Park Picnic Area. We were limited from driving further because it is a reserve and dogs are not allowed but we did look over the whole area from the lookout and the dam is huge and beautiful. At present it is apparently 84% full according to a local man who John was talking to.

Having washed my hair I am now about to undertake a job I usually detest but today I do not mind doing, so I must be relaxed! I am about to cut John's hair as the last hairdresser he went to made such a mess of it. The same thing happened the last time I went to a different hairdresser and I had to recut my own only two weeks later!

Tomorrow is Monday and it is 'stock up with food and other necessary items to last us until we reach Alice Springs'. It will be a busy day visiting some major stores, chemists, Post Office, two Banks and Vets. We also want to go up to the Lookout in town and I want to visit an Aboriginal Enterprise where they make paper out of grass, gun leaves, Emu feathers and other natural resources. I also want to go to an Aboriginal Tribal Centre where apparently descendants of the Kalkadoon tribe are available to talk to them. I also need to find a good craft supplies shop and I think I saw one on the way into town as I am loving my new hobby of making greeting and special occasion cards.

Well Monday didn't turn out quite as expected because we took 'Cracked Cranium Callie' (CCC for short) to the vet as her head has been caving in on one side. I also wanted them to cut her nails as she won't let me do them. Then there was Jack. One of his legs has been collapsing and he still has a bad stomach and he and I come out in sympathy with each other every time on the same days.

Callie was easy because it has been decided that when she crashed into Jack on the beach and knocked him over back near Rockhampton, she damaged nerves in her head and it is nerve/ muscle wastage that has caused that. Her right eye was checked but it is not droopy and we hope the nerve damage doesn't spread to her eye. The vet asked me if it would be better if she took Callie out to the back room, away from me, to cut her nails and I agreed immediately. When she returned the vet looked rather dishevelled and mumbled about Callie not liking her nails cut! I was relieved not to have witnessed the struggle.

Jack was given a seven day dose of tablets to relieve inflammation to his leg which was hurt when Callie ran into him and more tablets for when needed. Then we were given a sample pot and told to get a stool sample from him. To add to the cost we bought another tub of Sasha's Blend which is supposed to keep their cartilage fit and healthy and the vet marvelled at their fitness considering their ages. She then told me that I must go to the Mt Isa Hospital immediately and tell them she had sent me as she believes that I have caught a bacterial infection off Jack. We then received a bill for over $200 and staggered out of the office wandering if we could afford to eat this week.

The Hospital turned out to be interesting as it was spotlessly clean, the staff were wonderful, super efficient and what impressed us most is that they smiled at everyone with friendliness despite being very busy. We watched a stream of Aboriginal families come in with various ailments but it was mostly their children that needed attention. John and I both marvelled at the care and concern they showed because the whole family would turn up and want to be totally involved. As an example, a grandmother came in with her grandson who had split his lip and as she relayed this information tears were silently slipping down her cheek which she managed to hide from the child. Mum turned up having parked the car and they both went with the boy for immediate attention. The grandmother came out again so that she could weep in private and by this time her husband and other family members had turned up. I doubt that this would happen with other races. Then a teenage girl arrived with her boyfriend and she was taken through and her young boyfriend insisted on accompanying her and the Sister, who was laughing, told him he was welcome if he really felt he needed to go with his girlfriend to the toilet where she was to supply a sample of urine! He went through with her. There were no young Mums on their own as they were always accompanied by family members to provide support and assistance to both the mother and child. It made for a very packed small waiting room but as everyone was processed so quickly no-one minded. Right outside was a café and people were popping in and out of the door buying hot chips or cups of coffee. When I went in I was told that I should not be travelling with all my symptoms and should be under the care of my family doctor and not visiting different doctors and I was also given a sample container which we were able to return today. I now have to wait four days for the results of the cultures so we are stuck her in Isa.

However, we have spent a lot of time stocking up on tinned and dried food products and I have been told to only drink bottled water so we have bought huge containers of spring water and I am already a lot better and so is Jack.

There is the most awful smell here at the park, particularly some evenings and I believed it was during the rush for showers early evening when the men come back from work. We are right next to the shower block and toilets. I asked the new Managers of the park and I was told it was the Gidgee trees which surround the perimeter of the park which give off a pheromone at night particularly in cold weather. The nights are cold here at present and although I wandered at the 'pheromone' statement as it is only animals that do this I believe, I went along with it until the following day when it was bright and sunny and we were on our way to the local dam. When we went over a bridge with water running beneath there was that smell again and it was very warm. I became convinced it is the water. Anyway, tonight I met our neighbour who is a very interesting lady. She is a nurse and has spent the last six months visiting all the islands and Aboriginal settlements in the far north and she has spent time here over the last ten years. She tells me that the water should not be drunk without being triple filtered as it has far too much sulphate in it. She said that the Gidgee tree story is ridiculous (I was later to find out she was wrong and the Gidgee trees are more commonly known as 'stinking wattle') and that it is the smell of sulphur which is so foul. John reckons it smells like rotten cabbage and I say rotten cauliflower but it is a gaseous smell. We have smelt it at various places on our journey and she tells us that we should never have drunk the artesian water on the way here and to stock up on bottled water for the rest of our journey through the northern Territory as it is mostly artesian unless you are in major towns like Darwin, Alice or when we get to Broome. She believes that it is my drinking of this water that has made me so ill and I do drink a lot more water than John. We found that we used the first 12 litres of water in just over 24 hours! Luckily it is not dear here with 15 litre plastic containers of spring water costing just over $6. We are not giving it to the dogs but it would be a lot cheaper than going to the vets or my buying mince and vegetables for the dogs and cooking it for them so we might have to consider carrying some just for them.

This lady I chatted to also told me that when she was at University she did her thesis with a group of other people on leukaemia and Mt Isa has the highest rate per population of childhood leukaemia in the world and that nearly every second child has it. I suggested that it has nothing to do with the water but more to do with the tailings from the mining and she agreed. If it wasn't for Colin (my son) I wouldn't have known about the dangers of tailings but we have received so many diatribes from him over the governments and councils stupidity when it comes to our environment and the big corporations with their monetary deals with governments at the expense of people's health and land care that I can fully understand why this is happening here. Of course, I could be talking out of the back of my head but there surely has to be a connection. We are particularly lucky because the mine is closed for three weeks for maintenance so we won't see nor smell any of its sweet aromas! Apparently all the children in Mt Isa are to be tested for lead in their blood!

She and her husband have a couple of flats in Cairns and another property in Townsville but have returned here and have worked for six months of the year doing security fencing and have earned enough money in six months to be able to have the other six months off travelling each year. However, they have just bought a fencing business here so will be staying for some time. Her tails of life on the Aboriginal settlements was disturbing and she has no answers because she says that even where grog (alcohol) is banned to stop the violence, they always manage to get it, even if it is from Papua New Guinea which is so close to Australia. Apparently the sexual abuse of young children is rife and many suffer from malnutrition because the money from the government is spent on grog and gambling. The answer has to lie with getting the children educated but the parents do not encourage schooling and I recall one Minister suggesting that they would stop money going to parents who did not send their children to school and it seems a sensible solution.

She told me that they were feeding the children at school and in one place keeping the schools open until 6pm so that the kids were safe for as long as possible. So here in the city I've seen well cared for children and parents who seem to dote on the children but in the settlements many of the children are suffering terribly. We saw a program on television saying much the same thing and that was about some settlements outside Alice Springs. It is the sexual abuse that I find so extraordinary and so abhorrent. Very young girls are still expected to marry much older men in arranged marriages and then their husbands control them and they are not allowed to go out of their settlement without his permission. It seems unbelievable in this day and age in Australia. Many women are still treated very badly by their men but there can be violence instigated by both men and women against each other and the kids witness this. There is now a generation of glue and petrol sniffers, smoking 'gunja' (marihuana) literally by the bucket load who do not work and do not expect to work but who live off their grievances of the governments past mistakes with the 'stolen generation' being their main grievance and which affected their grandparents. I am beginning to wonder if they should bring back the removal of children – what a controversial thought! The Aboriginals have their own 'Tribal Law' and the Government is loathe to interfere with their culture but when human rights abuses occur then the Government should step in.

Some of the lucky kids do get an education and succeed and some go on to university. We need so many more succeeding and integrating with the general population. Apparently where our neighbour was, they don't even bother to fish, they go for the shells which will get many thousands of dollars. They then go to the casinos and gamble it all away returning to repeat the process. I admire those Aboriginals who follow their traditional practices of being self-sufficient and I have always believed that we have so much to learn from them but some communities seem to be casting that aside and latching onto the gambling, drug abuse, sexual abuse and violence that most sensible people want to eradicate! It is so sad!

We went up to the Town Lookout today and back to the Information Centre for advice as to which vegetables and fruit we can take over the border into the Northern Territory from Queensland. There are not too many products that we cannot take although I was surprised to read it includes lettuce along with fruit and some vegetables but it will be a different story going from the Northern Territory into Western Australian border where we won't be able to take in any fresh fruit and vegetables, nor honey and all sorts of other products which I have yet to get a list of. Apparently we can take vegetables and fruit over if it has been cooked first but we are winding down on the fresh products and only buying what we need for the next couple of days.

Last night on television we saw yet another program on the plight of the Aboriginals and a RAN (remote area nurse) was saying much of what I have already said above and it was suggested that the councils and government are so afraid of being accused of creating a 'stolen generation' again that they are not removing the children who need to be removed from their immediate families. There is a problem finding people within their extended families to look after those children at risk and foster parents are needed. We are unfortunately talking here of predominantly twelve to fourteen year old children contracting sexual transmitted diseases via sexual favours in return for petrol for them to sniff but even worse, there are the odd cases of children as young as four or five being seen at the clinics who have been sexually abused.

Yesterday John enjoyed a round of golf and today I went shopping and felt so guilty at my bill at the craft shop that I refuse to buy any more bits and pieces, however pretty they may be. It's time to go natural and start drying out some grasses and leaves and designing my own patterns! Jack and I are both ill again so it definitely is not the water as all I've drunk is bottled water and he has had the tap water and we both became ill on the same day yet again. We both await the hospital results.

Chapter 6

Saturday 24ᵗʰ June 2006 – NORTHERN TERRITORY

Yes, we finally crossed the border today having found out my results showed no bacteria yet they gave me antibiotics for a bacterial infection 'Just in case you have traveller's tummy'. Outside we met a nurse who told us that the dogs and I obviously have Giardia Lamblia which is caught via bad water and I need a specific antibiotic to kill that and so do the dogs. Back to the vet before leaving this morning but he refused to give the dogs tablets without samples. It is very frustrating as Jack has been suffering badly today and I have apparently useless antibiotics. The dogs and I will just have to wait until Alice Springs to get sorted.

Back to that yellow 'gorse' (which is what it looks like to me). It is called Mimosa and is flowering at the moment because they had a lot of rain not long ago. As for the spinifex – I have now seen it and as I thought its stems are covered in spikes and apparently if you brush a bare limb against it, it will itch very badly so it is to be avoided at all costs.

There was a guy who cleaned the toilets at the last park and he loved to impart words of wisdom. He showed me his 'office' which is a store room and I believe the most important items inside are his coffee, mug and kettle. However, he pointed out large containers of Hydrochloric Acid and told me never to call a plumber if I have blocked drains but to pour one litre of this acid straight down the toilet bowl and it will clear it every time. Thought you might like to know that. We've never yet had a blocked toilet but he assures me I'd be wasting my money if I called in a plumber when I could do it myself so easily.

He also told us to be careful of the White-tailed spiders but added that he thinks he has them under control and he lets them die a long slow death. Yuk. Apparently when the previous owners of the park lived there the wife got bitten by one and there is no anti-venom. I asked how they treat the bite and he said with maggots because the flesh rots. He reckons that the road signs are covered in this spider's webs and he's waiting for a Council employee to get bitten because the Council just doesn't seem bothered.

He also warned John about 'grasses' on the hill just as John had arrived back from climbing it with the dogs! He told John it would cause him problems. I think he was referring to spinifex.

Jack completed the climb with John, even with his limp but Callie apparently sat down half way up and waited for them!

The road from Mount Isa to Camooweal is called Tojo's Highway built by the Americans during the 2nd World War. After a brief stop at **Camooweal**, only a small town and realised that we were going over the border into the Northern Territory because there were a heap of young people wandering all over the road. I wondered why they had cameras when there is absolutely nothing to see but grass for as far as the eye can see! Then I saw the sign. I nearly missed it because I was playing 'dodge the students'. Just prior to the border I had read a sign at a garage, obviously facing the way we had come, which said 'Welcome to Queensland. Put your clock forwards 5 years and 30 minutes'. Cheeky! However, I realise now that it is no longer 6pm but 5.30pm! I believe we are going to go through several of these time changes.

There are no speed limits here and I'm very tempted….just once eh? Find out how fast I can go with my foot hard down? Perhaps not, petrol costs too much here. There are some speed limit signs as you approach towns in the Northern Territory of course and there are a few others such as on the way to Uluru but most of the time you see these round signs with a black line drawn diagonally across the white background, which means that there are no limits. (Note: This has changed since time of writing.)

We crossed a creek called **Shakespeare's Creek** and I wondered where on earth that name had come from way out here. Was a swagman sitting reading Shakespeare? I cannot believe that this scenery reminded anyone of Shakespeare or any of his writings. It is flat and endless. However, we are now parked in a free camp spot, along with a lot of other vans, called **Avon Downs**. John went for a walk to take a photo of a creek with lily pads flowering on it and walked up to the 'Driver/ Reviver sign and helped himself to free coffee and biscuits. It is only on the other side of the road but he had nothing else left to investigate. I suppose he could have gone to visit the Police Station!

It is when you are crossing country like this, seeing the huge cattle stations, that you really do realise the need for the Flying Doctor Service and School of the Air. I would feel more comfortable having a satellite phone as neither of our phones has a signal.

The road just goes on and on and on and signs such as 'We like our lizards frilled not grilled' or 'Belt Up' when leaving rest areas makes me giggle endlessly! I recall that I used to say 'Belt up' to friends when I was a kid (meaning 'shut up') and wander why they cannot write 'Buckle Up'. These small things occupy one's mind for an inordinate length of time out of sheer boredom.

John and I start to have silly conversations. I turned on my two-way radio half an hour after leaving our previous stop and concerned that John might have been trying to get hold of me I called him up and told him that I had forgotten to turn it on and before I could ask him if he'd tried to call me he said 'Did you? Have you got it on now?'

One car passed us which woke us both up for a while. Then we approached a road train which John overtook and I had to do 138 kph to pass it so I ponder what speed John was doing as we were going up a slight hill at the time. Gee, our bus is good, it's a 7.5 ltr V8.

Stopped for a break at **Barkley Homestead** where they rely on generators for all their power and they have a sign up apologising for their high prices. They must hate these fuel price hikes! Not far now before we hit a T-junction and turn left for Tennant Creek.

TENNAT CREEK GOLF CLUB - 1ST TEE

Tenant Creek

Well we managed to cover over 400 kilometres today and arrived here this afternoon. The dogs were fantastic and just lay down and slept except for the three times when we stopped so that they could stretch their muscles. Jack actually ran around the second time and his back legs only gave way once. We're in a caravan park so that we can recharge all the batteries (two mobile phones, computer and two-way phones), get some washing done and when we first arrived, we even needed the air conditioner on for a while as it was so hot in the van, even with the windows open. It's nice to use the water without checking our levels and now that we have some 240v lights as well as the 12v ones, we have more lighting options and we do not have to pay the power bill! The cost here is the same as at Mt Isa at $20 per night for us all and John always uses the park showers. If it is as hot tomorrow I may even discard my cardigan and don a bikini and go and find the park swimming pool.

The dogs love the balmy night air and will get a shock when we get to Alice. It's just over 500ks down the road but has vastly different night temperatures than at Tennant Creek. I'm becoming very Australian because Alice is now 'just down the road'! When I first arrived in Brisbane someone told me that where I wanted to go was just down the road and I put Helen in her push chair and started walking, not knowing that it could mean anything from about 10ks upwards.

All we saw today were endless flat plains with a few shrubs and the odd patch of trees but the scenery changed quite dramatically as we approached Tennant Creek. One section of the highway has been cut through a hill and either side were sheer walls of various shades of red and rust and the range was covered with green trees, all of which shone in the sunlight. It was quite beautiful.

TENNANT CREEK TO ALICE SPRINGS

First afternoon in Alice and John has just gone off to explore the town but I need a day out of the car and the time to download photos and catch up on this diary. With a glass of Black Douglas Whiskey and lemonade I am sitting under the awning surrounded by other vans and trees whilst my little washing machine works for me. I need the whiskey – that journey was endless!

I left Tennant Creek with tears in my eyes but not because I'll miss it. Most of the people we saw in town were Aboriginal and we heard terrible arguments at night and saw far too many males of all ages with nothing to do. There were also some women just hanging around the town to see who they would meet up with presumably. People were walking from here to nowhere to pass the time away. I saw a little girl of about three trying to keep up with older females with no shoes and mucus pouring down from her nose and into her mouth and men who were so obviously either alcoholics or drug addicts. I saw an older, quite handsome Aboriginal man walking jauntily along the road with a fabulous red shirt on, a drovers (cowboy) hat and pointed-toe shoes or boots and he looked so dapper. With him was a very handsome younger man. They seemed to be walking to their required destination quite quickly. However, within a few minutes they were walking back on the same route they had just taken and the next day I saw them doing the same again! They were literally walking backwards and forwards. As we left town there were a group of males gathered in a back street but for some reason or other it was one old man who tore at my heart strings. He may not have been that old but he seemed beyond help as he sat slumped against a wall and all I could think of is 'What a waste of a human life'. I realise we see this all over the world but this was predominantly the picture every time we went through town.

We visited the Golf Club which was closed and the biggest signs were the security signs. I took a photo of the first tee which was a mound of dirt but it was difficult to see where the second tee was! We also went to the Information Centre which is beside the **Battery Hill Mining Centre.**

We went to the **Bill Allen Lookout** and the **Nyinkja Nyunyu Culture Centre** where we had coffee and cake and where people get experience in the hospitality industry. The Indigenous people were the Warumunga tribe but there are members of many tribes living in the town now.

LISA PUSHING A DEVILS MARBLE OVER

Having departed Tennant Creek we went approximately 100ks further south and stopped to look at the **Devils Marbles** and they were amazing. They are granite rock formations that are rusting away into boulders of various dimensions and colours (of rust) and some are balanced so precariously upon others that it is an amazing vista. We may camp there with the dogs on our return journey. Almost everyone was having a photo taken of them trying to push over a 'marble' so John suggested I did too! The Indigenous people believe them to be the eggs of the Rainbow Serpent who laid them in Dreamtime.

We continued through **Wauchope** to **Wycliffe Well** where we stopped for whatever is the opposite of 'brunch'. It was about 3pm by this time and I asked what kind of toasted sandwiches they could offer and was told 'Any kind'. I asked for chicken and pineapple and ordered John a steak sandwich and a few chips. I received the most perfect toasted sandwich with beautiful sliced chicken and not soggy with pineapple and John's steak sandwich included salad and then a huge platter of perfect chips were put on the table. They were piping hot, very crisp and the potato inside melted in my mouth. I ate far more chips than I normally do! Our total lunch bill was $15 and we were also vastly entertained.

The building was the reception for the attached caravan park, a restaurant, a shop selling good Aboriginal paintings and canvases along with didgeridoos and other artistic and hand made gifts such as bead necklaces. There were also a few jars containing preserved snakes and more to the point it is also a **UFO centre**! As it also has one of the largest selections of beer in the Northern Territory one wit has written that perhaps that is why so many 'little green men' have been seen. The place was full of newspaper articles of sightings and people's personal stories of having received mysterious markings to their bodies (one to a little girl), of space craft and even one article from a scientist of his discoveries and he was asked to assist with work in America. We were kept amused for far too long so stopped at the next rest stop at **Taylor Creek** for the night along with quite a few other travellers.

Then it was back onto the endless road. As we were travelling along I saw a huge dead bull with its legs in the air and it struck me as amusing and totally hilarious that I was even doing this trip and I started laughing out loud. I'm getting outback fever or something similar. The scenery never seems to change unless you get a slight bend in the road or slight incline or another vehicle appears in the distance and that becomes the focus of your attention. We saw very little traffic again despite the fact that we were not the last to leave the rest area – there was one other van still there. I realise that they may have been staying there for two nights or may have been waiting for friends but it was a first for us to not be the last to leave!

We stopped at **Barrow Creek** for auto gas but the proprietor said they didn't have any despite there being no sign on the pump to say it was out of order. We tried again at **Ti-Tree** and although he didn't have any either, he was kind enough to telephone the road house at **Aileron** and it was confirmed that they had some. We went out of Ti-Tree and stopped at the **Ryan's Well** rest stop for a late lunch and eventually arrived at **Alice Springs** late afternoon. We have booked in for a week and have caught up with a few phone calls and text messages now that we have communication again.

Having looked at the price of various tours and having spoken to other people in the park, we have decided that we are going to drive on to the Ayers Rock Camp Ground. When we take into account the cost of kennel fees and petrol versus tours there is little difference and we will be more relaxed if we go on the tour (despite the tedious driving) Tours leave here at 6am and do not return until something like 11pm and that is not what this trip is about for us. We do not need to cram a visit to Uluru into a day trip and the cost of entry gives you a three day pass anyway. Also, you can see the sun rise and set from the viewing platform at the camp ground and that sounds just fine to us.

The following day we found a local kennels and went to check it out and booked the dogs in for Sunday so that we can visit the West MacDonald Ranges which is National Park. Jack and Callie will spend the day together in the large pet kitchen and I warned the owner that Callie will probably try to get into all the bins of biscuits and treats. She did not take me seriously and does not realise that Callie turns things over and will use her claws to get to food! We also pre-booked for the van site at Yulara at the Ayers Rock Campground as we had been warned it could be full. We will be here for a full week first and then will have a couple of off road stays en route.

We went up to the Lookout and then took the dogs into the town centre and had a coffee in the Mall. Naturally we were approached by people of all ages who wanted to pet the dogs and talk to their owners and I had to say that they could not have food scraps although Callie had her tongue lolling out of her mouth at the aromas. Callie particularly likes all the attention from the children and Jack checked out a couple of other dogs and every lamp post. There are some lovely shops in town, particularly the art and gift shops and some excellent clothes shops with quality merchandise. I also found out from a signpost that we are now only 15,030 km from London and that doesn't seems very far to me because on our last trip we did nearly 20,000 km in the Ute and that was a much shorter trip than this one. Perhaps we should drive to London!

5th JULY 2006 – WE'VE DONE ULURU, THE OLGAS AND KINGS CANYON!

We changed all the above plans but I'm leaving it in this diary as it demonstrates our confusion which arises out of the cost of everything here. Instead of the quoted cost at the caravan park being for two people per night which is normal, I was warned that it was 'per person' per night which made it a ridiculous option as it was more than the cost of a normal motel room! Everything here is expensive (if your income is in Australian dollars) and the trip we did included all our food. We had phoned the caravan park at Kings Canyon and found out that we couldn't have a powered site and the temperature at night has been dropping consistently. Combined with the problem of the distances that we had to cover, the time involved to do everything, the cost of the fuel and site accommodation at parks plus the fact that we had no idea who would look after the dogs resulted in us getting the brochures back out.

Now, having done a two day package trip, we both agree that it was a very wise decision. Even with kennel costs it was cheaper than us driving ourselves and that is without the fact that we didn't have to pay for any food. The dogs survived and we had a ball.

We managed to be outside the gate for pick-up by 6am and I had two jumpers plus a lined anorak on and was still cold! Then it was a two hour drive in a warm coach to the **Mt Ebenezer roadhouse** where we had coffee, enjoyed the roaring log fire and picked up some more people. Then it was back on the coach to head for **The Olgas**. Whilst eating our pre-packaged breakfast en route we played the game of who would spot Ayers Rock first and naturally it was a trick because everyone thought that Mt Connor was it.

Mt Connor is much older than The Olgas and Uluru but there is no public access as it is on the Curtain Springs Cattle property and they will not permit it to be used as a tourist site. We stopped briefly to look at the **Lake Armadeus** chain of salt lakes. As we drove along we were given lots of information about spinifex, marsupials, the wedge-tailed eagles, black cockatoos, budgerigars, dingos and the wild cats. There is a ratio of wild cats of about one per kilometre out here and they can survive without water so long as they can catch small birds and marsupials. Here I will mention that spinifex does have some uses other than holding the sand stable as it also protects some of those small marsupials from those wild cats. We were told about the trees – the ones with yellow flowers being the wattle and cassia – the desert oaks, mulga trees and mallee trees and others.

ULURU - AMAZING PLACE

We were also given a brief insight into the Aboriginals beliefs and their culture. Approximately sixty-seven percent of the land in the Northern Territory is now Aboriginal land under the Lands Rights Act. There are some big communities with 200-300 people but the majority are small with only 10-15 people with approximately 800 of the communities having less than 50 people. The problem is that where they live there are minimal facilities so in some ways these land rights have not assisted their communities. They may have a generator and a bore but no educational, health, or police facilities and no opportunity for employment. They rarely get fresh fruit and vegetables and eat mainly only kangaroo meat or bustard (bush turkey) which today they hunt with rifles and vehicles and they do limited gathering of bush tucker. They purchase Western food which does not store well, such as soft drink and chips.

We were told that the boy's initiation to manhood takes many years (unlike Australian law which assumes that kids become adults on their eighteenth Birthday for some reason) and that the circumcision is just a small part of it. They need to learn the ancestral stories which can take 15-20 years and some are passed on by songs. In the beginning the ancient ancestors (being people, plants and animals) travelled around having adventures, both good and bad ones and they created the hills and the creeks etc and formed the world as it is known today and it is now the present generations responsibility to look after all these ceremonial sites. Uluru is a place where many song lines meet as the songs reflect the journeys.

Reading the booklet given to visitors at Uluru, you come to realise just how complex the Aboriginal customs, beliefs, laws and meanings are. We had been told it was complex and that there are certain things that we will never be told as we are not of Aboriginal descent. There are things that Aboriginal men know that they do not share with women and the women also have their secrets. So, as the boys grow older they are taught more and more until they eventually become 'men' and are highly regarded. Usually when a man marries a woman it is she who joins his tribe but not always. Today they teach with stories, songs, dances, ceremonies but only to those who have inherited the right to the knowledge because with knowledge comes responsibility.

In the booklet, Barbara Tijikatu, a Traditional Owner says that Tjukurpa (chook-orr-pa) is the foundation of their culture and is their religious heritage, explaining their existence and guiding their daily lives. It provides rules for behaviour and living together.

'It is the law for caring for one another and for the land and the relationship between people, plants, animals and the physical features of the land.'

Barbara says that it does not seem right when some people refer to it as 'Dreaming' or 'Dreamtime' and this is because to them it is very real now as well as the being part of their past and their future. I am only touching a seed of a huge tree here in trying to explain that I now realise that the Aboriginals who do still hold their beliefs and live according to them have a depth to them that is usually not apparent to us and that the majority of us are so very ignorant of their culture.

Tjukurpa is not written down of course. I particularly love a quote by Kunmanara, Traditional Owner as follows:

'The tourist comes here with the camera taking pictures all over. What has he got? Another photo to take home, keep part of Uluru. He should get another lens – see straight inside.

Wouldn't see big rock then. He would see that Kuniya living right inside there as from the beginning...'

AMAZING FEATURES OF ULURU

There were many people climbing Uluru (and about 35 are known to have died with one man in a coma at the moment) but Kunmanara, Traditonal Owner asks us not to and continues,

'That's a really important sacred thing that you are climbing….You shouldn't climb. It's not the real thing about this place. The real thing is listening to everything.

And maybe that makes you a bit sad. But anyway that's what we have to say. We are obliged by Tjukurpa to say. And all the tourists will brighten up and say, 'Oh I see. This is the right way. This is the thing that's right. This is the proper way: no climbing.'

Both of these above quotes come from the Visitor guide and maps booklet entitled 'Welcome to Aboriginal land' and you should be given one when you pay your entrance fee. If not, ask for one because there is a lot of information in it.

If you take one of the tours from **Uluru** and do not climb the Rock, you can get a certificate to that effect rather than the other way around. Their belief system penetrated my thick skull enough that when I found out that I had taken a photo of a sacred place of the Aboriginal women which I shouldn't have done, I deleted it when I got back to our van and before John could see it!!

We were told by our guide that there are not many ceremonies held at Uluru any more but there are at Kata Tjuta (Olgas) which means 'many heads'. There are 36 steep rocks and we were restricted to certain areas as it is sacred under Anangu men's law. According to their laws the details of the stories cannot be revealed. Women come to the site to help prepare for the initiation ceremonies but then turn their back as a mark of respect. We went on the Walpa Gorge Walk and John found great delight in calling out whilst in the Gorge and hearing his words echoed back to him! It was interesting but we had been given a time limit of ten minutes in and ten minutes out which was a bit off-putting to say the least! We seemed to spend the whole day being given time limits along with food and fruit. If we had eaten less we may have got more done!

We then went to the **Cultural Centre** at Uluru and this we can both highly recommend. The problem we had is not having enough time again. If you find yourself with a time limit (we only had 25 minutes in a place where you could spend the day) then get along to the dome with the film running and the circular seating because that film is amazing and you will learn more from that than any guide will tell you. I reset my watch to one of the guide's watches but according to the other guide (who did not smile or laugh all day) we were late and he had been hooting his horn to hurry us up. It was all so stupid because later we had time to come back for another 'ten minutes' and we literally ran back to that theatrette to see more of the film! Almost everyone loses their bearings at the Centre as it is made up of a series of buildings which together resembles two ancestral snakes embracing. There are two toilet blocks – both by exits and if you know which is which you should be able to get your bearings again!

If you have the time then stay a while because when we entered a courtyard there was a demonstration going on that captivated us but the horns on the bus seemed to be getting louder and louder so we couldn't stop. You can do tours, enjoy the meals in the café, see art and crafts and buy some and watch that film which must be quite lengthy as we only saw parts of it. You really could spend the day based from there and it's free once you have paid your park entry.

We drove all around the Uluru and did a couple of walks. I think it was the first walk that I found boring but I think we were supposed to be doing the Mala Walk of about a kilometre. I honestly cannot remember! The 'unsmiling' guide wanted us to do a PhD in geology I think as that seemed to be his speciality and he stopped in one place for so long that I got bored. John stuck it out and says he found it quite interesting. A French guy and I slipped away for some time, until we began to worry that perhaps they had all gone back to the coach as the group still hadn't caught us up but there they still were and the guide was obviously still loving the sound of his own voice. I called out 'How long have we got?' and he looked at his watch and he suddenly got everyone moving and to think that he had been the one hooting at us!!

I think we did the **Kuniya Walk** because we certainly went to a waterhole and that was a pleasant walk with the other driver/guide. He was surprised that we hadn't been showed more 'bush tucker' on our first walk and tried to show us as much as he could. We were lucky because we did a tour the next day where we were shown a great deal.

So after our second brief stop at the Cultural Centre, we set off for the viewing area to watch the sun set over Uluru and as it became colder and colder the highlight became the aroma of the sausages and onions being cooked and the sight of the containers of all sorts of different salads. With my plate piled high with lettuce, tomato, beetroot, potato salad, coleslaw, two slices of bread, two sausages and fried onion (thank goodness I had my gall bladder out and ulcers dealt with!) and a glass of wine I sat down with all my jumpers and anorak on to watch the sunset and eat. There were all sorts of other salads of the bean or corn variety which I could not fit onto my plate!

A lot of other coaches arrived and some people were given their nibbles and drinks and I gloated as I filled up with such a lovely barbecue. Sunset over and it was time for the long journey back to the **Mt Ebenezer roadhouse** where we immediately purchased hot drinks and stood in front of the log fire. John and I and a Frenchman and his fifteen year old son stayed there overnight in the motel units and we were delighted to be able to because we felt exhausted. With the reverse cycle air conditioner set at 27C and the kettle on, I jumped into a hot shower and we sat in bed and watched the late evening news revelling in the warmth.

Chapter 7

KINGS CANYON

We both slept solidly and were packed and back at the adjacent roadhouse for breakfast by about 8.20am so we had an hour before the coach arrived. We then discovered that we were to set off in a small group in a mini bus for our Kings Canyon tour and we had a wonderful lady guide who was a mine of information and who had infinite patience. As she has two sons of 21 and 17 she obviously has to have patience of course but she was wonderful.

On the road to the Canyon the vegetation is not dense like the Mulga bush to the north-west of here but there are Mallee and Desert Oaks. It has been said that if the nuts of the Desert Oak are crushed they taste like chocolate. The Oaks start off growing very narrow and tall and it takes many years for their roots to find water but when they do find it the trees spread out and form a canopy providing shade – although one explorer complained in his diary that they all had bull ants nests underneath so he couldn't rest for long! We heard a lot about the explorers and poor old Gibson is still out there somewhere.

We were particularly lucky with the people who made up this group of nine. There was one Italian man who did not speak a lot but everyone else got along so well together. There was the Chinese Mum, Dad and son of seven from Hong Kong and their beautiful boy already speaks three languages. There was the Frenchman and his son, (a different Frenchman than the one we had toured with the day before). The son was a beautiful young man of fifteen and he spent most of the day with the seven year old Chinese boy following him around. He played and talked with the little boy the whole day and they caused us a great deal of amusement. I kept getting the French boy to say things back to the Chinese boy in French and the little boy had such a wonderful ear that he repeated the French with perfect pitch which I found fascinating.

Then there was an Englishman from Leicester who sells pottery at the Stamford and Oakham markets which thrilled me as my sister-in-law lives at Oakham and I used to live there and we spent a fair bit of time chatting together. He has taken a year off to travel the world. John and I made up the number, other than our tour guide.

Kings Canyon is approximately 440 million years old (give or take a few years) and when the ice caps melted there was a shallow sea over the Kings Canyon and we were to be shown the water ripples in the rocks during our walk. Apparently the word 'canyon' in the dictionary means 'crack in a rock' and that is what the Canyon is here, whereas the Grand Canyon was formed by water! The Kings Canyon is formed by two types of sandstone and when the softer sand underneath erodes, the rock above collapses and gorges are born. Vertical cracks to the East and the West allow water to seep into the porous sandstone and it is the thick vegetation which holds it together. I can confirm that there is spinifex as it wrapped itself around my legs and I could feel the spikes which had pierced my jeans and were trying to pierce my skin! Ten percent of the plant species is prehistoric. Wind, rain and time have formed the formations on the Canyon and whilst there we saw a huge slab of rock that was breaking away and will collapse to the canyon floor below so let us hope that when it does there are no tourists beneath.

Kings Canyon is absolutely beautiful – stunning – awesome. If you can get there do so.

However, do not take the advice that we had seen written down by going up the way you come down as I have mentioned earlier in this diary. There is no way you could do it that way as it would be far too dangerous and our guide was horrified when I told her I had read it and said that the rangers would be very angry. You go with the directions of the arrows and you take care. A girl recently got lost up there for three nights as she had strayed from her group and believe me it is so very easy to do so. We had gone through a narrow gorge to see one vista and as I walked back I realised that I might be walking the wrong way because there was more than one gap in the rock which hadn't been evident when we entered. I stopped and turned around and walked back to our group and realised that I had indeed been heading in the wrong direction! It is not that easy descending but it would be far too steep to come down with an even steeper descent, especially when you are already so tired having walked right around the canyon rim plus having probably descended into the **Garden of Eden** which is a rock pool surrounded tropical plants.

KINGS CANYON - LOOKING DOWN THE DROP

You need to be fit to do the Kings Canyon tour. Ha, ha! Everyone knows that I'm not fit and can think of nothing worse than walking just for the sake of it but give me some rock pools on a beach or a mountain to climb and there I am raring to go and so it was this day. One word of warning – this was the coolest time of the year and it was hot climbing up and very hot up there and there is no shade at all so take a lot of water with you.

Another word of warning – the walk commences down a little winding path and then you look up at what is commonly known as the 500 steps of 'Heart Attack Hill'. This is not a staircase – the steps are rocks, so you have to watch where you are going and decide for yourself which rock to climb onto next. I am glad to say that I was not the last to reach the top! When you get to the top, it is not the end of climbing as you spend most of the day climbing up and down and even up and down wooden steps when going to the Garden of Eden. There are several paths you can go on off the main path and we chose to do most of them. We had come a long way to see this and didn't want to miss anything. So the walk itself around the rim is 6ks but as we kept shooting off 600m to see something else and back again many times over we would have walked much further than that. There is very little flat ground to walk on so you need good walking shoes with good grip, especially when you come down.

That was quite hilarious because I saw a white arrow pointing to over the edge of a cliff. I actually stopped and said 'No' out loud. I then went a little further forward and stopped again and said 'No. This is stupid. This can't be right'. Everyone else was behind me and they were standing about talking not quite knowing where we were going next. I edged even further forward and low and behold there were the rock steps with a sheer drop to our left hand side. I immediately grabbed the seven year old who had followed me and said 'Where are your parents?' and I turned around to find the constantly smiling Chinese mother behind him.

We were told which trees the Aboriginals used to get water out of the roots, which ones they used for boomerangs (some are made to return for small prey that they may well miss such as birds and others are made not to return) and which ones were used for spears. Some sap was put on my sore finger to make it heal quickly and we were warned about some of the berries which looked quite edible! I started to get totally confused between my Mulga and my Mallee and which was used for what!! On this trip we were also told about the Acacia Bloodwood trees and Gum trees.

There has apparently been an increase in the population of the Wedge Tail eagles due to the amount of road kill and that it is feared that they may be losing their natural hunting skills. We were warned again not to drive at night. We were also warned to slow down if we saw road kill because if there were eagles there, they are very slow taking off because of their size.

The communities out at Kings Canyon are 'dry' (no alcohol) communities although they get their problems with drugs or glue sniffers and apparently they are kicked out of the community if they do not abide by the rules and they are some of the people living in Alice Springs today - not all of them of course! Apparently Alice Springs is the murder capital of the world and it is mainly

Aboriginals killing each other for retribution for some grievance or wrong doing, possibly allowed in their law. There are four distinct languages in Alice Springs and women remain subservient to their men.

Actually, most of the Aboriginal women and children we saw in Alice the other day were better dressed than John and I! They seemed bright, happy, healthy and prosperous in stark contrast to those we saw in Tennant Creek. We still saw many hanging around or walking and who didn't appear to have work but at least there was a 'mixture' as there is with any nationality in any city. From what we were told there is more of a problem in the outlying communities and were warned not to stop if we saw a vehicle at the side of the road and the bonnet up because if the vehicle had an Aboriginal owner we could well be asked for money rather than for help with the vehicle.

On the way to Kings Canyon we had stopped at the **Kings Creek Station** and we returned there for what was supposed to be a brief stop on our return journey. Our guide/driver had been concerned about a tyre and went to get it checked out and it needed changing so we were there longer than expected. We set off again only to have the whole vehicle shudder and had to return again so this time we did some tourist shopping, stroked the camels and had a very good, hot coffee whilst she sorted the problem out. Thus we arrived back at Mt Ebenezer where our lasagne and salad had been ready for us for an hour but at least the chips were freshly cooked! A glass of red wine and we all piled into the coach that had been out to Uluru that day and our guide headed for the back of the coach to lie down for a sleep. She was exhausted.

I was wide awake and after half an hour got up and stood by the driver for an hour and a half talking about cars (he imports and collects American cars), the tourist business (he is a shareholder in the company), real estate (of which he has plenty and is still buying in areas that I am very familiar with around Brisbane) and all sorts of other subjects including cows and kangaroos. The latter was particularly pertinent as they were everywhere, lit up by the coaches' bright lights and they kept running across the road trying to commit suicide. We managed to avoid all but one and it was one of the biggest 'Skippies' I've seen! The car behind hit one of the ones we missed and he went off the road most likely with most of the front of the car smashed in. Apparently if you read the small print, with two pairs of glasses on, along with a magnifying glass, you will read that cars are not covered by your insurance policies in the Northern Territory if you drive after dusk, so beware if you hire a car here!

Anyway, I asked the driver if he was going to say anything to the passengers and I was expecting him to assure them that everything was okay and no damage had been done to the bus and he gets on the microphone and says 'It's okay, the Kangaroo didn't get hurt' and I collapsed with laughter. There must have been blood spattered all over the front of the bus and one of the lights had broken!

ALICE SPRINGS - SNAKE TREE AT STANDLEY CHASM

We were the first to be dropped off so on went the kettle and fire and I unpacked whilst John went for a hot shower and we were in bed by about 1am. John picked the dogs up this morning and albeit they survived, apparently Jack did a lot of howling. John reckons it's a good job he didn't hear him or he would have gone back for him but I said 'Rubbish. You are too much the accountant and you'd paid the money for the trip. You would have gone on the trip'.

3RD JULY - KATA TJUTA (the Olgas)

It was a wonderful trip and in the two days we saw so much, met so many wonderful people and had such a good time and we did not want it to end. We enjoyed being driven about and fed and it turned out cheaper than had we driven ourselves. The only thing I would have liked is more time at the Cultural Centre and a hot drink instead of alcohol or orange juice whilst watching the sun set over Uluru. And perhaps a different guide to the grumpy-bum that one of them was!

WALPA GORGE AT THE OLGAS

Chapter 8

6th July 2006

So yesterday was a day of rest except I exhausted myself downloading photographs and writing in the diary! Trying to recall so much information scrambles my brain. Today we had to drop the dogs off again at the kennels and by tonight they were glad to see the back of Jack who apparently barked so much that they had to separate our two dogs from the rest! John became a hero (he has a habit of this) as he rescued a woman who was walking her dog back to this park when he found her and her dog being attacked by two dogs, one particularly vicious. Very sensibly he drove the Ute towards the dogs and they moved away. I would have got out and screamed along with the woman. She thought he was going to kill the dogs and her husband wished he had! John bundled her dog in the back of our Ute along with our dogs and drove her back to the kennels where the woman in charge phoned the authorities. John then drove this lady and her dog back to our park and tonight she and her husband visited us and gave John a card and a gift.

ALICE SPRINGS - ARRIVING AT STANDLEY CHASM

John told them that it's not often he gets the opportunity to be a hero and come along like a knight in shining armour to rescue a damsel in distress so he didn't mind at all. However, she was very distressed today because fifteen years ago she had had to defer her wedding as she had been badly attacked by a dog and today is their fifteenth wedding anniversary! She said that she's not going out again on her anniversary. Action will be taken and she has had to make a statement.

ALICE SPRINGS - PEOPLE WAIT FOR NOON SUN STANDLEY CHASM

So today we went to the **West MacDonald Ranges** which stretch for 161 kilometres. There are also the **East MacDonald Ranges** but we won't get around to visiting those. John set off at a leisurely pace and veered the Ute towards the Alice Springs Desert Park which is another attraction and I was getting stressed as I knew how much we had to see today. Later on during our trip he realised that we would probably run out of time and we only had time to have one cup of coffee all day and lunch on the run! He became like that ratty coach driver. We would drive to a Gorge and he would rush me along and say 'Right. Got photos? Seen that, let's go' so it became quite ridiculous. However, we saw some beautiful places.

We managed to visit **Standley Chasm** at midday when the sun is overhead and it was awesome but we spent rather too long chatting to another lovely couple who are well travelled and who have a daughter in Shanghai so they have visited China and had so many interesting things to tell us. We then travelled the length of the sealed road to **Glen Helen**, saw wonderful views from the **Mount Sonder Lookout**, came back and went to **Ormiston Gorge** which again was overwhelmingly beautiful and then on to the **Ochre Pits**. This is where the Aboriginal men dig out the different coloured ochres for various uses, not just to paint themselves with. They are also used for medicines and at one time berries would be wrapped in ochre to be kept for when food was scarce. It has to be crushed of course and it is mixed with water or animal fat for painting and they would use goanna for the animal fat. I had ideas of getting some of it but there were signs warning of hefty fines, so I left well alone.

ALICE SPRINGS - ORMISTON GORGE 1

We then moved on to **Ellery Creek Big Hole** which was far more beautiful than it sounds. It was also very peaceful there and the colours of the rocks were amazing. We have seen so many beautiful natural colours today that it would inspire anyone to have a go at painting. You feel like getting an axe and cutting yourself a slab of it to take home! The colours of the rocks range from light sand tones through every shade of pink and red to deep brown and then some have white lines running through them or in the case of the Ochre Pits which had been cut out, there were yellow and white colours as well as the red. Contrast these colours which were predominantly of different reddish hues, with the very deep blue, clear sky and the various greens of the vegetation and you may have just a small idea of the palette of colours we experienced all day.

Our last stop was **Simpsons Gap** which we enjoyed but we were too rushed as by this time it was nearly 5.30pm and we had to pick the dogs up by 6 o'clock.

ALICE SPRINGS - ORMISTON GORGE 3

John dropped me off as we passed our van site and I was able to get the water heater on and prepare dinner before he got back with the dogs. It was a wonderful day but there is just so much to see and so many walks to do that you could easily spend three months in Alice Springs and do something every day and you would still not have done everything! If it wasn't so cold I would want to stay on but John is getting fed up with the cold evenings, nights and mornings especially as he is the chief dog-walker!

I phoned a park at Darwin today because I have been told so often that Darwin and Broome get completely full at this time of year. I started with a preamble about booking ahead and the girl at the other end said 'What do you want?' so realising I was holding her up I said 'A powered site next month'. When she found out that we had an old American R.V. she sounded really interested.

'What's the weather like there?' I asked.

'About 35C today'.

'What! I'm sitting here at Alice Springs with two jumpers on and directly in front of the fire'.

'You'll love our pool and don't you worry, we'll get you in somewhere at any time. Just phone us a couple of days before and ask for me because I manage this place and I'll look after you'.

Isn't that nice? I was also told that some parks segregate those people who have dogs but she doesn't and also that they are probably the cheapest park in Darwin and considering it has several stars in the rating system that is certainly good news. I feel much more relaxed about our visit there now and am no longer concerned that no-one will have room for us.

When we get to Katherine we will probably want to visit Kakadu National Park and there is so much to see en route that we could easily spend another three months travelling before arriving at Darwin. However, we have to limit what we can cover because of the weather being too hot further north and because we have to do the north during the 'dry season'. We have many thousands of kilometres to cover in the north because we are also going to Broome and Western Australia and it will be a long, long way before the temperatures drop to what we are used to back at the Gold Coast.

I have until Monday to relax as that is when we will leave to head along that long road north once again. We will miss the camel races which are on next weekend and it sounds like a lot of fun. I was listening to a guy on the radio and he was saying that most of the camels from Alice are 'working' camels and they might well be carrying tourists around the day before the race. If they don't have enough camels then some are brought in from a couple of the stations around Alice. When asked how they are trained he answered 'Well, I give them a serious talk' which indicates the humour of the conversation. They start from a sitting position and we saw a segment on T.V about them. Sometimes the camels don't feel like getting up to race so they just stay where they are! However, the first 'race' was held on the land our caravan park now sits and although there are camel races in other parts of Australia, if you win the race in Alice you apparently have serious 'bragging rights'. I think the boat race is due too. The driver of one of our buses said that the only time it wasn't held was when there was water in the river. With these boat races the competitors pick them up and run down the dry river bed. We've walked down one around here and it was sandy so you can imagine how hard it must be in a team with your feet sinking and slipping. That too we will miss unfortunately.

We did get to the markets in Alice Springs which are held fortnightly on Sundays. I was disappointed that there were no stalls with clothes other than one with imported oriental ones as I wanted a skirt for Helen with the colours of the Red Centre, meaning the browns and reds, stone and sandy colours. However, I saw a stall with some craftwork that I've never seen before. This guy was selling figurines that he had made out of material and they were largish and amazing. Every figure was different and when I asked him what the bodies themselves were made of he told me that they were made from material, as well as the clothes and then they were 'hardened'. They almost felt like paper. He said I could go to classes in Alice and make my own. Oh, how I wish I could.

I could have stayed on in Alice quite happily so I left with very mixed feelings. I had met so many wonderful people and I love the town and area and I felt I had 'unfinished business to attend to'. I was so relaxed when we drove away that I forgot to pack the water filter and it crashed to the floor apparently but John just ignored it. He said he knew something had crashed but nothing was going to stop him!

Chapter 9

Mataranka ('The capital of the Never- Never' apparently)

I know it is Thursday because I just asked John but the only time I become aware of what date it is, is when I turn this laptop on. I now also know that it is 13th July. I've seen it written that people who come never want to leave and I also read that Jeannie Gunn wrote the book 'We of the Never- Never' which I have heard of but never, never read. Nor have I seen the film.

We stopped here because of the **Thermal Pools** in the **Elsey National Park** and we have already sampled the **Bitter Springs** ones as we can walk to them from this caravan park. I didn't think much of them though and did not like the green slimy rocks beneath my feet but we are in a lovely park that allows dogs and have been separated from other vans again because of our big rig. What an advantage as we have so much space, a lovely view and can walk to the en-suite amenities. We can go and feed the Barramundi tomorrow if we wish and that must be quite something because those fish are so big. We can hire a canoe, go bird watching, visit the art gallery, museum or to listen to the Talking Termite Mound. As it's man-made I think we'll give that one a miss but we will go to the other thermal pools where we apparently have to restrain our dogs in the 'private pet parking bay' which sounds interesting! I wonder if they line them all up.

So we've been staying off road on our way here and have done over 1100ks since leaving Alice Springs. I was ready to catch the nearest flight home yesterday. John asked me to be 'brave' which is an interesting word to use as I'm not ill or hurt, nor was I facing any major hurdles. It was just one of those days.

The fridge isn't working properly, I tried to knock a moth or similar from my face and scratched my ear which was still bleeding in the evening, I found the source of a smell that John thought I was imagining (said I was 'hypersensitive' which I found rather insulting) and the triple wall cupboard with all our crockery, glasses and mugs came away from the wall. It appeared to be falling and I called out to John who was chatting to someone by a neighbouring van and then called again and said 'It's urgent. I need your help now'. I was holding it up and it's very heavy.

He sauntered over to the bin and slowly wandered back with a look on his face like 'the missus is nagging me' and somehow I kept calm! Of course, everything needed emptying out and he thought he couldn't do much with the cupboard but as we couldn't drive with crockery all over the floor he found some brackets and I put the stuff back minus anything that is breakable.

The source of that smell that I mentioned was a dead mouse under John's bed and it had been there for some time. I had isolated the source to the bedroom by shutting the doors from the living area to the bathroom and the door on the other side of the bathroom to the bedroom. I had had enough and couldn't decide if we had a gas leak or there was a rotten cabbage camping out in the van with us. Even he could smell what my 'hypersensitive' nose had been picking up for days when we lifted his bed base up to look in the storage area beneath.

'Oh yuk, a dead mouse. Oh the smell. I feel sick. That's what that terrible smell was last night in the bedroom that kept me awake and it's under YOUR bed. You'll have to get rid of it. Oh dear, I've had enough. I'm not cut out for this.'

A small voice responded 'Oh go on, be brave'!

He was brave as he got rid of the mouse. Well he didn't have much choice really because I wasn't going to do it and was still muttering 'Hypersensitive nose, eh?' just loud enough for him to hear. However, he's still my hero.

I do have a rather too sensitive nose though. I passed wind in the supermarket the other day and I didn't just look over my shoulder as if to see who did it, I actually ran away from myself as I couldn't stand being near me! I have heard it said that once you give up smoking your sense of smell recovers and I'm dreading the fact that it might get even better as I can smell things from so far away. It's the same with my hearing and last night a guy in a van some distance away was driving me nuts with his snoring and I told John I'll divorce him if he gets that bad. I'm always asking John 'Did you hear that? What is it?' and he hasn't heard a thing. I was screaming 'Can you hear me?' the other day whilst driving as I was getting no response from him on the two-way and then I realised that I was up to my old tricks and had been screaming into my tape recorder.

(John's just said to me as I'm typing this 'It should be a nice day tomorrow, shouldn't it'. It wasn't really a question, more trying to get me to think that this is a wonderful trip!) We've hit the hot weather and it was 30C as we ate tea. We now need the air conditioner on instead of the heater and tiny bugs and moths fly around the lights at night inside our van. As soon as we open the fly screen door they hurtle in and dance about with delight. Perhaps they are enjoying the air conditioner too. We haven't seen T.V for days and have no radio or T.V reception here and only CDMA phone coverage. I went out to the car to hear the news as that works with the aerial right up but this is the first time that radio has picked up a signal since we left the Alice Springs area.

So far, the only bonus out of this trip has been the Kings Canyon and that day will stay in my mind for life. Uluru and The Olgas were okay but I don't think about them at all. My point to John was that we have spent hundreds and hundreds of dollars on fuel, food and accommodation and we could have flown to Alice and have had a holiday in a top class hotel for a week for the same cost! I have to remember – life is supposed to be about the 'journey' and not the 'destination'. Between you and me, I could gladly have missed out on some of the kilometres we've covered! Especially the bit when we stayed off road at **Renner Springs** and there was a road train with cattle parked most of the evening and into the night. By the time we went to bed the cattle had had enough and because of the sounds they made, so had I. Even John admitted later that they had disturbed him. We felt so sorry for them.

I love cows. I find them so endearing, especially when you watch the mothers with their calves. That same morning I had watched a calf run away from its mother and not only did the mother run after it but four of her female friends went with her! Five big cows all chasing this one calf. The calf seemed to think it could do an about turn and dodge Mum but got surrounded by five irritated women!! Back at Gracemere I had watched a mother wash her calves face, ears and neck and like all kids the calf got kind of fed up with the face wash long before the ears or neck had even been touched. It was wonderful to watch the battle that ensued but Mum won of course. So they love playing and they love lying down and the cows in the truck were packed in standing up and couldn't move and I'm not sure how many hours or days they had been like that. It was pitiful and they were very distressed.

At another stop there was a dam (big pond) and Callie looked at it with joy envisaging a swim but three geese perpetually followed us about and claimed the dam as their own when we went anywhere near it. As we walked around the dam they followed us.

John saw two of those big road trains we had been looking out for yesterday but I had missed them. I finally saw the third one and shouted out loud "I saw a four, I saw a four.' That is four trailers hitched together with a prime mover, a very long beast. They aren't anything to worry about unless you are trailing a caravan or boat that might sway so I'm not sure what all the warnings have been about from other travellers. John says if a large one is coming at you, get off the road into the dirt because they must keep on the bitumen and cannot get onto the soft edges.

At **Elliott**, where we stopped for gas, a whole gaggle of peacocks suddenly appeared (I know it's a gaggle of geese so that word will do). They were beautiful and they strutted about in front of the bowsers and the cars just had to wait.

After Elliott I tried to take photos through the car windows because trees covered with pink blossoms had suddenly come into view. I had already seen the yellow bushes again and some wild flowers which turn from purple to white depending on their age and at one place some small pink flowers that looked like miniature roses amongst the grass by the side of the road. It was really pretty with a mixture of trees, some with dark green foliage and some with light and suddenly at one point a stand of trees which were a light grey colour. Along the side of the road was dark gravel which contrasted with the red sandy soil behind and the sky was very blue again but this time with fluffy white clouds here and there. So, although the journey was endless there was a lot of natural beauty to enjoy and I had a CD on which complimented my surroundings and when I wasn't singing, my mind was wandering from one subject or memory to another.

In Australia, we tend to make the most of what we've got when it comes to history. That's fine when it is Aboriginal history but when I read that I should visit a town and a certain pub because it used to be an Officers' Mess in World War 11 I find it unbelievable. This is an attraction that is suggested you could do from Katherine and it would be a 384km round trip! Mind you, you can also visit an old Police station and have a cup of tea so that might add to the attraction!

We stopped there for petrol and if I recall correctly they didn't have any fuel left so you could get all the way there from Katherine and then not be able to fill your tank to drive back again. Now that's what I call the 'Never Never' meaning 'You'll never be able to leave.' John's taken to looking at Obelisks out of boredom I think. So now, every time I spot one I call out 'Obelisk' and people look at me as though I'm demented. When we saw the first one commemorating John Flynn (founder of the Royal Flying Doctor Service) it was a little interesting but by the time you get to the third one in his honour, you're really getting over it.

Our next stop is Katherine and from there we will be able to visit the Katherine Gorge and perhaps even arrange a trip to the Kakadu National Park. We have heard it said 'Kakadu! Kakadon't' but we wish to find out for ourselves. After that we head for Darwin which is only about 290ks. No wonder it's hot. I started to cut Jack's hair off last night whilst we were parked off-road and filled up two plastic bags but haven't yet finished so he looks rather odd.

I just had to stop and clean the ceiling. It all started because I had a bug in my computer. One went down between the keys of my laptop. I looked up and the ceiling was covered, as was every surface in the lounge/kitchen area. As fast as I wiped the table, more landed – blast, another one on my computer. I've had to use spray twice and everything has been washed but they still keep coming. With all our fly screens I have no idea where they are coming from – ah, one's on my back! Welcome to the tropics!!

John has just returned from the park toilets and he was laughing. Apparently a small green frog had been watching him go to the toilet and when he moved, it moved its head round to keep tabs on him. John carefully moved the door to go out and when he turned the light off the frog was so startled that it leapt off the door and landed on his nose!

MATARANKA THERMAL POOL - 30.5M LTS A DAY

We drove to the **Elsey National Park** near here today and as it said nothing about dogs being banned we took them in with us. It's pretty ordinary but we went to have a look at the river near the boat ramp and it was quite pretty. On the way back we stopped where the road was slightly flooded by a stream so that I could cool the dogs down. I had changed into bikini and sarong whilst John had been driving but when I bent down to splash Jack with water my bikini top fell off just as John was taking photos! With the dogs now cool we parked our vehicle in the designated area near the **Mataranka Thermal Pool** and left the dogs in the back of the Ute with water. The short walk under the pandanus and cabbage-tree palms to the pool is so beautiful and the pool area itself absolutely stunning. Apparently the Aboriginals had known about it for years but when the soldiers found it in World War 11, they dammed the flow creating a bathing pool. It now has a wall around and steps and an underwater seating ledge and is a bit like the Roman baths. It is artesian water from rainwater collected by sandstone and we are told that it flows from Rainbow Springs at 30.5 million litres per day and is constantly 34C (although it did not feel that warm to us). It is so clear you can see the bottom of the pool quite unlike the one at Bitter Springs. Having said that I must add that a lot of people we spoke to prefer Bitter Springs as they feel it is more natural. We walked around a man-made track (to protect the ground from human damage) and decided to go and buy a coffee. Just as we approached the café I saw a dog that looked so much like Callie that I was surprised until I realised that it was her! She had pushed the side window back and had climbed out. We were fuming with her and when we got back to the Ute poor Jack was so hot with stress because she had disappeared. We had to calm him down and have decided that in future she will be kept on a short lead in the back of the Ute, attached to one of the metal hooks in there because now she has done it once she could do it again anywhere and we could so easily lose her. We obviously have to leave the side windows open, as well as the back between the cab and the driver's cab but she has broken the fly screen off one side just after we bought it a couple of years ago. She cannot be trusted for a minute. She is so inquisitive and always wants to explore.

There appear to be a number of Aboriginals who live in or around the parkland in the centre of Mataranka and I saw some children with blankets there today. In the general store the freezer displays housed bags of corn chips and crisps instead of frozen vegetables and deserts. When I went to pay for the cheapest 2 litre bottle of milk I could find and one tomato, the bill came to $4.75. I asked how much the tomato was and she checked and it cost $1.

No wonder some Aboriginals don't eat enough nutritious food – nor would I at prices like that! If you haven't got a fridge you obviously cannot keep milk so I know I would pop in the shop for a hot meat pie, a bag of chips and a cold can of drink. It makes sense as you are hardly going to carry pots and pans around with you if you haven't got a home and you could not afford to rent anywhere and pay for electricity and eat on the money you get from the government. I couldn't anyway and I'd choose food first. It's warm enough to sleep out here all year around so that's what you do, so you can eat!

It strikes me that the government needs to spend their money on long houses with fridges provided and shelter to sleep under in rain or when it's too hot. I suggest long houses because they are so family orientated that they like to live with their relatives and many months later I was to hear a highly educated Aboriginal man who was discussing housing say that 'They can become prisons'. I realised what he meant. Not all Aboriginals want to be segregated into three bedroom brick houses where they cannot live communally. They need co-operatives and a water supply and assistance with growing their own food and someone to organise communal cooking. It's probably the way a lot of us should live but it seems senseless what the Government does now and just throwing money around does not solve the issues, nor give the Aboriginals pride in their own abilities. The elders have so much to teach us and the younger generation don't need to learn it because they can just collect their cheques and not work for the money unlike the rest of the population in Australia who have to adhere to mutual responsibility.

I have been told so much that I won't write down because it would fill a book but there is a huge wastage of money and little done towards the future of the Aboriginals and if I were of their family I would think 'If I don't want to go to work today, why go? What for? I'll get money anyway so why bust my gut for the same money?' Aboriginals also claim long mourning periods when a relative dies and they can't go to work then anyway.

When you are not used to work it appears complicated with clothes and shoes to worry about and times to keep to and not being able to please everybody. If you could be in the park with your mates or family instead and still get paid, what's the point of being someone's slave? If you have freedom and you have native title to the land you live on and perhaps you get royalties once a year (for example the tribes around Uluru) which is enough to replace the car each year, then why bother making life complicated with houses and bills and work. That's what I'd think anyway and I guess many Aboriginals probably think the same way. Many don't even bother to maintain their vehicles and run them into the ground because they know that they will soon be buying a new one with the royalties they receive from visitors like us visiting their land and there are cars littered all over the place.

What they may not realise is, is that the prices they are paying in the shops here is criminal. We've been much further away from major towns before in Queensland and the prices were still nothing like they are here. We savoured our one tomato and made a big deal over it when eating our lunch! Luckily our fridge has started to behave itself again and has adjusted to the sudden change in temperature. Of course, it didn't help that I had turned it off for a few hours yesterday instead of switching it from 'Normal' to 'High Humidity'.

Chapter 10

Off again tomorrow and have already booked into a park at Katherine.

KATHERINE - DEFINITELY THE BILLY

KATHERINE

Well the prices here are the same in Woolworths and I stood in the fruit and vegetable section absolutely stunned. Tomatoes brought all the way from Roma in Queensland were the cheapest out of all of the tomatoes which makes no sense at all and they too were very expensive. Woolworths did not sell any bread without preservative in it either so I had to go to a bakers shop to buy it which meant I paid more than I usually do for that as well. We don't keep bread long enough to warrant preservative! We are trying to do as little shopping as possible because of the high prices!

We went for a walk at the **Katherine Low Level Nature Park** today, blissfully unaware that the dogs weren't allowed there at the picnic area. We didn't stay on that side of the bridge anyway, preferring to spend most of our time walking along the sandy foreshore on the other side. We had a problem tonight with the photos as we couldn't delete any of them as they were all just so beautiful! We also stopped on the way back to talk to some goats and the big Billy stood up on his hindquarters, placing his front legs on the wire fence, in order to have a closer look at John and they spent some time together having a natter! There was a mother who appeared to have two kids as they were both trying to suckle from her but she wouldn't let them as she was far more interested in inspecting us. They were quite a lot of them and they were so inquisitive.

We have been spending far more time than we usually do talking to neighbours in the caravan park. John spends more time next door than he does in his own van! We have met some lovely people here who are going the same way as us but are not sure if we will meet any of them again as we travel at different paces! Tonight it has suddenly turned very cold which is really annoying as I have just packed away all my winter clothes and the winter quilts off our beds.

KATHERINE GORGE - HOLE FORMED BY WATER

KATHERINE GORGE

Unfortunately there is only one tour group that you can go to the Katherine Gorge with so you do not get a choice! The land and touring operation is now fully owned by the Jawoyn people (Aboriginal) who are the traditional owners of the 3000 square kilometres of parkland and they lease it back to the Northern Territory Government.

However, the sandstone that makes up the gorge is apparently 1650 million years old so they didn't own it then and as it is so old there are not even any fossils to discover! The gorge itself was formed when the sandstone cracked open and is apparently only about 25 million years old – comparatively young. The traditional owners prefer the gorge to be called by its original name which is Nitmiluk Gorge (Nitmiluk meaning 'cicada dreaming' and at the Nitmiluk Visitors Centre there is a wealth of information so it is well worth a visit. You can buy a 'do-it-yourself' coffee or pay too much for half a cup of excellent coffee with a lot of froth – which is what we chose! There is a huge outdoor balcony to sit and relax as well.

In the information centre I saw pictures of the Jirrup tree and I was quite taken with the fact that the Jawoyn people used to use its leaves for plates, the fruit is edible and the wood can be used to make canoes or carved, wooden dishes as well as the fact that the trees provide shelter and shade. That really is making the most of a natural resource.

There was information on the kinds of birds, insects, trees and plants that we may see and we were later told that there are fifty-six species of fish in these gorges but I can only remember the barramundi. All I can recall of the former are frogs, skinks, echidnas, snakes, dingos, hooded parrots, common finches, bower birds, falcons, quolls, bats, turtles, water monitors and of course, the crocodiles! However, these are fresh water crocodiles rather than the 'salties' so not a worry – take a dip and enjoy your swim. The Katherine River becomes the Daley River further down and ends up in the Timor Sea.

So we went on the four hour boat trip although we could have chosen a two hour or eight hour one. There are thirteen gorges and the Gorge is twelve kilometres long and we were to see three of them. I don't think any of the trips do the lot so you'd have to take a helicopter flight to see them all.

We were packed together like sardines in a low level tin with one dubious toilet which I would not recommend. Remember to bring tissues with you! Our guide was informative but he was also rather rude or as John so kindly put it afterwards 'He had something lacking. He didn't have any empathy with his passengers and you need that if you are going to take people out for the day'.

I would have put it rather differently because he was extremely sarcastic to me and he made a public announcement about my asking if there was 'afternoon tea as it said in the information leaflet'. He told all the passengers that if anyone had been told that then he'd like to know who it was and he carried on in that vein until I gave him the leaflet which he ripped out of my hand whilst saying 'I am f….ing fed up with this!' and then added 'There hasn't been any tea or coffee served for at least twenty years. How old is this leaflet?' I queried and added 'It must be over twenty years old according to you'.

He was so angry that he was unable to read it, so I calmly pointed out 'Inclusions' and it still seemed to take him an age to settle down enough to uncross his eyes and then he actually read it and proudly boasted, using the microphone, that I had made a mistake as it did not say 'tea or coffee' but 'refreshments'!

Now I can only suppose that he was angry because someone else had also asked because I hadn't made a fuss about it but had simply asked if coffee or tea was going to be served. We had our own food and water with us anyway. It could also have been because he had made such a fool of himself earlier in the day.

We had got back onto the boat and he was drinking a plastic cup of water and he was in an awful mood. He told us all to wait because 'Someone has filled our container using a rubber hose so I am going to pinch someone else's water'. He then proceeded to run our boat straight into the side of another boat that was moored, which bounced against a third boat and there was a loud cry from within the galley of that boat. We heard 'F…k you!' and I think it must have been one of the girls who had been clearing away wine glasses from their boat where lunch had obviously been served. I dread to think what had happened within the galley but my mind pictured smashed wine glasses everywhere. Another guide stood in amazement watching our guide ram the boats but rather than say anything he tried to help to diffuse the situation by finding some iced water. We know it was iced because the container fell off the edge of our boat and ice cubes tumbled into the water which caused an outburst of laughter from some of our passengers who witnessed it happen. He then got off yet again and collected some water from somewhere else as a female staff worker came out onto the deck of the third boat meekly offering a little water in a bottle! As we took off at last, our guide said something to the effect of we'd had our laugh for the day.

Now, in Australia, when anyone talks about morning or afternoon tea, they are not talking about cucumber sandwiches and a pot of Earl Gray. Usually it is a cup of tea or coffee and biscuits or cakes to go with it. On a cruise like this the word 'refreshments' usually means the same but can mean a cold drink such as orange cordial so it's best to check beforehand.

Another odd thing that you might come across is someone asking you out for tea when what they really mean is for dinner. Another words it means an evening meal which you pay for yourself unless it is at their house.

Anyway his public display of sarcasm left me feeling flat and confused so it put a bit of a damper on the trip for me. However, as I said to John 'You gotta do it though' meaning that if you are in Katherine it is usually for one thing only and that is to visit the Katherine Gorge because there are many hot springs in the region so there is no need to stop in Katherine for them in particular.

At the end of the first gorge we all trooped off the boat and walked over some rocks to the next gorge and clambered into another boat and repeated this again for the third and then we reversed and repeated the procedure and stopped at the first one again for half an hour so that people could have a swim. It was there that the guide produced fresh oranges, orange cordial (make your own) and some fruit cake. Most people were well ready for any type of food and drink by this stage. I quite enjoyed a weak orange cordial which I don't usually drink. The guide seemed to offer everybody but me some cake. He kept looking at me and then turning to someone else so I ignored him as I wasn't that bothered. Standing there with two whole cakes left he finally offered me some and I took one piece. 'You can have more than one' he said, as he had been saying to one and all but one was quite enough for me because we had already eaten. We had left after the 11am departure time but had had to pick up the tickets by 10.30am and we had been hungry long before we got that cake. Of course we got back on time so we didn't get our full four hour trip.

It cost $63 each it and it would probably have been better to have hired a double canoe for the day for $71 which you can have from 9am to 4.45pm. John envied those who had some peace and tranquillity and could do what they wanted. It would be hard going upstream but you'd probably see the three gorges that we did and you would be carried back with the flow of water when you are tired at the end of the day. There are a lot of places to stop and rest and sunbathe or swim. It was certainly very pretty and I particularly enjoyed getting out of the boat and clambering over rocks again to get to the next gorge as it reminded me of our Kings Canyon rock climbing day. (We later met many middle aged people who had hired out the canoes and they had enjoyed a wonderful day.)

KATHERINE - EDITH FALLS - ANOTHER BEAUTIFUL VIEW

LEILYN (EDITH FALLS)

As the falls are also in the Nitmiluk National Park I have given them their rightful name above. John reckons that I haven't been raving about Katherine Gorge and the reason is that I do not like feeling like a sardine! A fellow traveller agreed with me today and said "Get on. Get off. Get on. Get off' which is what it was like and we all agreed (there was a group of us by this time) that there is rarely a more beautiful sight than the Upper Pool at the Edith Falls and that it was far more enjoyable to spend the day there than to go up the Katherine Gorge in a sardine tin.

We started our visit by admiring the lake at the base of the falls near the car park. It is described as a 'large pandanus-fringed plunge pool' and is a popular swimming place. Apparently the water becomes very deep very near the edge of the lake so it is not good for little ones who cannot swim well. It was really pretty and there was a large lawned area with free barbecues supplied and seats. There is also a kiosk there, a caravan and camping park, toilets and showers.

This is where the bus tours arrive so that you can have a quick look at the falls. Don't do that. Drive there yourself from Katherine and enjoy a full day in this area because there are so many walks including a couple of loop walks and you simply cannot miss the climb up to the Upper Pool which is along one of those loops. It is steep and rocky in many places and we were advised to go up behind the car park and do the hard climb first to get there quicker, which we did.

By the time we arrived at the falls, after so many stops to take photographs of the stunning scenery around every turn, we were ready to go into the crystal clear water however cold it might have been. We realised only afterwards that if we had gone over the bridge there, as if we were leaving the area, we would have seen the sandy beach on the other side and it would have been much easier to have entered the water there. There was a small sandy beach on our side (and remember we went up the 'wrong way') but there were also so many rocks under the water that were slippery that it was difficult to get out far enough to swim without banging your knees on the rocks as the water is quite shallow there. You could see the rocks because the water was clear but their height was very deceptive. You might think a rock was small and low and then you'd walk into it!

However, we didn't know about the other side of the bridge and we are glad we stopped where we did because we met some lovely fellow travellers from all over Australia and enjoyed some interesting conversations. It was glorious, sublime – I cannot think of enough adjectives and we stayed there a long time. We should have taken our sandwiches up with us though, but we had taken water which is imperative. Someone said that you shouldn't drink the water in the pool but it tasted wonderful and a little girl collected some at the edge of the sand where she was stirring it up into a muddy mass and it was crystal clear in her bottle. A couple of us tasted it and it was lovely. All that sifting through the limestone rocks had left it sparkling.

It was quite a long walk down but after the initial stage which was a bit difficult, it was easy walking. We finally got our lunch at about 3.30pm and our coffees had never tasted so good! We had a wonderful day and it is the second highlight of our tour – the first being Kings Canyon. I loved Alice Springs town centre too but it wasn't stunningly beautiful!

Chapter 11

LITCHFIELD NATIONAL PARK

We arrived at a caravan park with a Banyan tree, which I thought was a fig tree. Anyway, it has roots growing from its branches which hang down to the ground but they've put a notice up asking people not to swing off them. Spoilsports – I would have liked to have played Tarzan. We had turned off the main road heading towards **Bachelor** and then continued on towards the National Park where we found this caravan park. John was happy to have seen an area named **'Rum Jungle'** on the way as he had heard the name many years ago and has always wanted to find out where it was. There are lots of places here with the name incorporated but I'm not actually sure where Rum Jungle actually is! For example, there is a Rum Jungle Recreation Park in Bachelor and a Rum Jungle Recreation Lake which is on Poet Road, off Litchfield Park Road and it is popular for fishing, picnics, canoeing and has toilet facilities. We went down that dirt road today and turned around because we weren't sure how far we would have to go to get there. Someone told us 900m but we had done more than that when we turned around. It sounds like it's not too far so perhaps we'll have another try at finding it. In Bachelor you can also stay at Jungle Drum Bungalows (not sure why they added the 'D') but we haven't actually found a place called Rum Jungle if you know what I mean.

We have a lovely site overlooking a paddock, with trees on the other side of it and to our right there is another field which is sometimes visited by some cows and the sunsets are glorious, complimented by the sounds of the birds as they fly in here to roost overnight. Last night there was a free 'sausage sizzle'. Bread, sausages and fried onion and you were not allowed to bring your own beer or wine which I found really odd until I found out that they expect you to buy their alcohol and John tells me that a small bottle of beer cost him $4.00! John was told to take his beer and my glass of wine back to the van so I asked him to get me a bottle of water. I was a little surprised that there was no lettuce or something as at other parks but with the price of fresh vegetables around here I suppose it is hardly surprising!

Anyway, the company made up for all of this as it was attended by practically everybody who was staying here and there was live music. However, when they started to do the 'chicken dance' I slipped away to check on the dogs and did not go back. It was a good decision according to John who found himself flung about for various dances to the point that he became dizzy and he'd only had one beer! At least I did not have to cook dinner.

I'm not going to give you a rundown on all the information on this National Park because you will find it in any guidebook or on the internet but I will tell you that we were advised many times not to miss out on seeing this area.

Today we went to visit the **Buley Rockhole** and its name is misleading as it is a series of waterfalls and rock holes cascading down the hill and it was beautiful. There were a number of people in the water despite the fact that the water is so cold that it takes your breath away. There is a walking track to the **Florence Falls** but it was too hot for that so we drove there and went to the viewing platform. There are two waterfalls beside each other surrounded by rainforest and that too was beautiful.

We are running the risk of getting almost blasé now, having seen so many beautiful water features and forest, so we doubled back and drove past our park and went to visit the 'town' of Bachelor. There is a sign which tells you that you are in the centre of town, which was good or we wouldn't have known. There are a couple of petrol pumps in front of a shop and adjoining take-away food shop. We bought a newspaper and went next door for home-made apple pie and coffees so at least we've done our bit to support the local shops!

Bachelor is so well laid out and in the centre there is parkland which is really pretty. We went to the **Coomalie Cultural Centre** which sells art made at the local Bachelor Institute. Apparently there are usually a couple of artists in residence and you go there to watch them at work. We didn't go to the **Bachelor Bird and Butterfly Farm**. We were only out for about three and a half hours and it was a test to see how the dogs would get on being looked after by the musician who had played for us the night before and his wife. Callie did well but Jack fretted and it soon became apparent as to the cause of his unrest. They had taken Callie for a walk without him! They'd pinched his wife/playmate/soul mate and I don't doubt he will not trust them again despite the fact that they brought her back to him! Tomorrow we'll stay here at the park but on Monday they will be left there for longer as we have to go a bit further afield.

I forgot to mention that we took photos of each other standing in front of the 'Magnetic' termite mounds today! Now anyone who knows of the problems that we had with termites eating one of our houses will know that it is more than odd that John and I would treat a termite mound as a tourist attraction. The ones that ate our home probably had their home underground because we never saw their home in any of the nearby trees. These termites are different however. In fact they are amazing. They build their mounds with thin edges pointing to the north and south and with the widths facing east and west for temperature control. The least surface area is exposed to the sun and they move around inside according to whether they want to cool off or warm up! They have my full admiration. I saw a 'For Sale' sign on a spare block of land and took a photo of the termite mounds just behind the sign! I realise that they are not known to like Cyprus pine but I'm not going to be tempted to test out that theory albeit that this is a lovely area.

I read in the newspaper that we are experiencing unusually cold weather at the same time that Europe is experiencing a heatwave. 37C+ in Surrey – it's hard to believe and must be awful. There was a photo of someone carrying a surfboard into the sea with a heading along the lines of 'No, this is not Darwin, its Skegness'. We were surrounded by people from Europe last night and there are many English accents around us. Even the park owners are from Europe as is their musician friend who is here on a visit. Today, whilst out, we predominately spoke to British backpackers. One young couple had been in Asia for six months prior to coming to Australia for a year. That's one heck of a holiday albeit that they do have a work permit for Australia should they need some extra cash. They told us that we would love Western Australia and we're the ones who have lived in Australia for 25 and 39 years respectively!

The Territorian people are beginning to drive me batty. I had phoned a park in Darwin and after a very terse initial conversation the girl became very chatty and told me just to give her a couple of days notice and she would fit us in somewhere. I also phoned another park here, very close to the National Park and the guy who answered told me that he would look after our dogs for us. On the day we came here I phoned Darwin and the Manager of the park answered the phone – the very same girl I had spoken to before and she was more than terse this time and told me she could never fit us in and she wouldn't have said such a thing! John phoned the caravan park here that we were supposed to come to and was told that they definitely would not look after the dogs. On top of this, the caravan park information is abysmal. You have to collect every leaflet and book that you can get a hold of and even then you will miss out on the names of some of the parks! We have heard of parks that are not in any of the guide books and we are now totally confused. Most of the parks in Darwin are out of town and those that do take dogs often segregate you if you have them so that there are a mass of dogs in one section which seems like a recipe for trouble to me being that dogs are territorial and pack animals to boot!

Many times we see a sign denoting Information Centre only to find it is a board with a map or, as was the case today in Bachelor, an unmanned office with some leaflets and a visitors book to sign. So, if you are coming here I advise you to do all your research on the internet before leaving home. The only phones that seem to work here in this park are the CDMA phones and they work intermittently. As CDMA phones are being phased out I suggest that you buy a satellite phone if you are going to tour Australia so that you do not have to worry about telephone reception all the time. Mine only works with the aerial extended which I've never had to use before. We are only about 100ks from Darwin which is relatively close to a capital city in this country.

Every time we get somewhere John is looking at leaflets for the next place or the one after that. I keep suggesting that he looks at the leaflets for where we actually are so that we know where we are going to go today or tomorrow. He's already decided on his trip to Kakadu. I say 'his trip' because I'm not particularly interested in floating on the wetlands in a sardine tin again or seeing more rock art, nor getting up at 5.30am and spending a lot of money to do the trip from Darwin. With fees for looking after the dogs for two days, if I go, then we can add $200-250 for my trip and their costs and that kind of equates to what I've spent on my new hobby of making cards. I have now made about thirteen, although I will use one soon for personal use. However, I have felt a bit guilty as I am too shy to show anyone the cards and I'm therefore not getting rid of any of them! So, I can look after the dogs and if I am alone I will take the opportunity of getting my paints out which I haven't yet touched. I wish to have my first go when alone so that no-one is looking over my shoulder, not even John!

24 July 2006

It is our last day before moving to Darwin so we went to see the falls that are accessible for a non-four-wheel-drive vehicle. We met a couple who had flown to Darwin and it had cost $79 each and as I said to John, it costs me $70 just to fill my petrol tank up once in this part of the country and I have a very economical vehicle! John added that there were two of them so I said 'O.k. that's two tanks of petrol'. To be fair though, they are paying for the hire costs of a small motor home which is probably costing them about $1000 a week.

Our first stop was at the **Tolmer Falls** as we thought that we had a long walk there so decided that we would get all hot and bothered before going on to Wangi Falls were we knew we would be going swimming. We saw the sign for the walk and set off climbing and stumbling over the rocks until we came to a beautiful view of the falls. As we were coming down another couple told us we were doing the 'long walk' and when we got to the bottom we saw this concrete path which led to a similar view and which was only a short distance from the car park! However, we both enjoyed our rock climbing experience again and were certainly hot enough for a swim.

Wangi Falls are the most popular and we could see why when we got there. There are two waterfalls which tumble into a huge circular pool and there are steps to enter. It is only a short distance from the car park and there is a large lawn area for picnics or sun bathing, a kiosk and toilets.

WANGI FALLS

This national park has monsoon rainforest, streams, waterfalls, the termite mounds and historic ruins and we have seen all but the latter. With a four wheel drive vehicle you could see a lot more and I would have loved to have seen the **Old Blyth Homestead**. What a family they were! Harry Sargent was originally from England but he and his wife Alma had lived in Canada and Queensland before coming here. When he bought the land here they, along with their eleven children, dismantled the house they had at Stapleton about 40ks east and transported it by cart. He used 32 horses and the teenagers, then rebuilt the house! They ended up with fourteen kids and the whole family worked from dawn to dusk whether on the property or in the Mt Tolmer Tin Mine. Harry started with one square mile and ended up with a 1,100 square mile property. They were totally self-sufficient and I wonder what sort of life Alma had as she schooled the kids herself and they grew all their own fruits and vegetables and any excess were dried for future use. They had their own grain which had to be ground and cattle for beef and milk and most of the time the older kids and Harry were away from the home itself. They didn't go to the doctors as the kids were taught that to look for help was cowardly. It seems unbelievable to me today with my easy life and I try hard to imagine what it must have been like but fail miserably. Only those who experienced life like that would know what it was really like and I can only imagine how incredibly hard it would have been.

Aboriginal people have lived here for thousands of years but until 1986, when it became a National Park, the tourists hardly knew about it and now the coaches pour in daily from Darwin, Katherine and elsewhere and we are just a couple of the quarter of a million people who visit the area each year.

Copper has also been mined here and it had Australia's first uranium mine 'White's Mine' which closed in 1971 but we were reading in the newspaper the other day that it will probably be reopened and at least one caravan park is thinking of expanding, to house the influx of workers to the Bachelor area.

John and I had both had a swim and lunch at a picnic bench near Wangi Falls when a tour guide from Darwin, with a small group in tow, asked to share our table. He sent them all off to the waterfall so that he had time to make them lunch and I had the time to quickly get changed before they returned and we chatted together relating stories.

John had been stunned when swimming to see a guy dive into the water with his hat and sunglasses on and they didn't come off and then his companion did the same. Anyway, we noticed that the lunch was particularly varied and inviting and yet there was no margarine or butter which surprised me. It was the same the other night at the barbecue. I wonder if it is peculiar to the Northern Territory that they eat their bread without margarine or butter. There were so many different kinds of meat and salad and mayonnaise to choose from but when I asked him about the margarine he looked perplexed and said 'We don't have that'.

After leaving there we stopped at **Table Top Swamp** which was obviously a wet area of land with water lilies on. A couple we met there had been to Kakadu National Park and said that if they knew now what they had not known then, they wouldn't have bothered as Litchfield National Park is much better. We have heard this so often and another complaint is that it is so far to drive to each point of interest. It has further cemented my decision not to go there but John feels he will regret it if he doesn't. Likewise, everyone also says that if you are going to go, you have to go for more than one day or you won't see anything which doesn't make a lot of sense if there is nothing much to see! John will be going for one day and he will take the camera so I can see some snapshots!

Chapter 12

DARWIN - 28th July 2006

We are parked in an area that is called 'outer Darwin' and we are 26ks out of the town centre. However, that is not as bad as it sounds because Darwin is so big and when we leave we have to return the way we came so the bus stays here and we travel in and around in the Ute.

On our first day we ended up in Darwin city centre as that is the only place you can find an Information Centre. I find it absolutely amazing that a city as big as Darwin has only one Information Centre. Even small towns have manned information centres and in other states they are often manned by very enthusiastic volunteers who know the area well. The one in Darwin is apparently manned by young people who are so badly paid that they don't stay long, preferring to find work with higher wages. There should be information centres on all major roads approaching Darwin along with ample parking space. We couldn't find anywhere to park without paying for a parking ticket so beware if you have a motor home and think you will find a parking area outside! Most information centres cater for buses and coaches and many provide refreshments and toilet facilities but not here. Their season here is predominantly only for four months of the year so you'd think the Darwin Council would make an effort to support the Tourist Industry wouldn't you?

So there we were having found out where it was and it was blazing hot and we had almost given up when we found a Woolworth's car park but still there was no under cover parking, so we just did a bit of shopping in Woolworths, bought a local paper and left without getting the information John wanted! The next day we tried again as we had to go into town anyway to try and get our printer repaired. This time we found a Coles supermarket which has undercover parking. You collect a ticket on entry but if you are not in the shopping centre for more than three hours, it is free to park. This was invaluable to us as John was able to go to the Information Centre and get some cash out of our bank whilst I went into Coles.

I couldn't find a dentist under my health care scheme and the doctors' surgery over the road from the caravan park was closed and I felt that we were getting nowhere fast. John was still trying to make up his mind about which trip he should take to Kakadu and was driving me batty with his thoughts. One tour company would pick him up but returns to Darwin on a different route and drops everyone off at the Transit Centre in Darwin at 9pm! I'm sure that many people must get caught out by this (I have already met four people already who did not realise) and I have never heard of it being done before. Usually you get picked up from your accommodation and returned to it.

We went to see a slide show of a tour, promoted at our park and we liked the look of the tour so much that we've booked for tomorrow. We are going up the Adelaide River with a small group (maximum of 10 people) and it is an area where vehicles cannot access. The full day costs less than all the other tours and instead of being in a coach for hours going to Kakadu we will be on the river all day as the access to the river is nearby. We get off the boat for a barbecue, which includes steak as well as sausages, rissoles and salad and get off again at a small island where a guy has built himself a home powered by a generator and he has set up a bar under his huge verandas. The island is surrounded by crocodiles and we will not be able to swim anywhere up the river because of them. However, we will see as many as 50 species of birds, perhaps wild boar and buffalo as well as the crocodiles and will spend an hour fishing for Barramundi. As I have never fished in my life and have been wishing to learn, I thought I'd try my hand at the best fish! It should be a pretty interesting and wild trip and he has a gun if we get into any difficulties with the wild life. I think I really got hooked when he said that it is a trip with personal service because it is such a small group and if we want three cups of coffee instead of one he's not going to throw a fit. Cups of coffee! We've never been offered a hot drink on a tour yet unless we've bought our own from an outlet! We've only been offered water, cheap orange cordial and horrible wine so far in the Northern Territory.

The company is run by two brothers and their wives prepare the food and take the bookings. After many years of taking backpackers into Kakadu the men decided that they needed a change as they would either collapse from exhaustion or their livers would pack up as the backpackers wanted to stay up all night drinking and partying! So John has now put Kakadu on hold but I'm not sure if that is a permanent decision. We keep getting told by other travellers that the trip is not worth it and the people who live here tell us not to do the day tours as they are rubbish and if we want to see it properly in a day then the only way is to fly over it.

Yesterday we also went back into Darwin but called in at **Palmerston** on the way which is a suburb of Darwin with shopping centres. I was reading that three-quarters of the 25,000 population is under 35 years of age which is probably why they have forty recreation and sporting groups apparently. There is also a lagoon, many parks and a leisure centre with an Olympic-size swimming pool.

We had also been told that **Casuarina** had a 'huge' shopping centre (undercover mall) so we went to see that later in the afternoon but, to us, it was not very big. Compared to the ones in Brisbane and the Gold Coast which we are used to, it is quite small. There wasn't even a departmental store, just the usual brand-named outlets plus a jewellers and a shoe shop that I hadn't heard of. So why are we suddenly 'into' shopping centres? We are not and never have been but Darwin is 'so spread out' according to a fellow traveller who had warned us before we arrived. If you want a

Target store then you go to Palmerston – it is the only one in the whole of the Northern Territory! If you want the Information office then, as I've already mentioned, you have to go into Darwin city centre, likewise my dentist through my major health fund.

So yesterday we spent the whole day running around in the car but it was also a sight-seeing day. A local man gave us some advice in a coffee shop. He said that the 'real Darwin' is firstly the city centre and that then we were to drive around to East Point and the coastline of Nightcliff.

We started in the city and because it was our third day we are beginning to get cocky, nipping to the bank and the Post Office to collect our post and knowing the places to park! I saw even more shops that I want to visit and I need a day in town without the dogs.

Next we set off for the **Cullen Bay Marina** and then to **Mindil Beach** where the dogs had a run on the beach and we had a coffee break. Our next stop was **Fannie Bay** which had a beer garden set on the edge of the beach right next to the boat ramp. The dogs went straight down to the sea again and then we sat in the adjacent park and tried to photograph some huge birds that were swooping overhead, without a lot of success because they were flying so fast.

We went to the **East Point Reserve** but could not go in because it does not allow dogs so continued on to **Nightcliff** and had lunch on the foreshore near the jetty. All along this drive we looked at the houses as well as the sea views and at one point John commented 'I can see the money dripping off the trees around here'. Most of it is pretty modern of course because Cyclone Tracey destroyed so many of the older homes but there were a few old homes left. We continued along until we reached the **Casuarina Beach Reserve**. We walked the 500 metres to the beach (further along there is a nudist beach) and we had the whole beach to ourselves.

The day so far had been what our dogs would term 'a dream day' with woodland paths, barbecue tables with their wonderful smells, grass and sand and endless beaches to run on and water to swim in. Their next stop would be an underground car park at the Casuarina shopping centre! I don't think they really minded because they were so exhausted. We only went in to exchange something at K Mart, have a quick look as we'd been told about it and on finding our favourite coffee franchise we just had to stop a little longer.

Refuelled, we set off again and drove out to **Lee Point** as I wanted to see a caravan park I had heard about. It was further away from the Centre of Darwin than I had expected and it seemed that we were almost out in the countryside. However, at the end of the road we found a lovely park where we stayed to watch the sunset. It was amazing because we could actually see it sinking as we watched, or as John said, the earth moving as we watched the horizon! There was a Caucasian guy (to be politically correct as the media no longer says 'white person') who spoke politely to several people but who had obviously only one set of clothes which were pretty threadbare and boots that looked like they were about to fall apart. A woman asked us to watch her car because it had been broken into the week before and she wanted to go for a walk on the beach with her dogs. Everyone's antennae were up! We were all watching this young man as he darted around looking at cars and he appeared rather agitated and obviously wanted 'something'. He even approached two cars with people in them and they drove off very quickly. He asked me how long I was staying and I told him until sunset and I kept one of the dogs off the lead at all times and he kept looking at them. He left us alone after that because we were obviously going to stay too long and then a man gave him a lift but told him to get in the back of his open Ute with his two dogs and we all finally relaxed! We stayed until the sun had disappeared because we were chatting with other people.

On the way back, between the beach and the caravan park, we noticed an air strip on one side of the road and cars dotted along the side of the road with young people hanging around. One car screeched out in front of us without warning and broke the speed limit to get away. Our guess is that the area is a drug pick up point but we may be wrong. As John said, it would be easy to land a light plane there from Indonesia and there was no other apparent reason for those people to be there and they did not appear to know each other.

John also commented on the way back through the Casuarina streets that the area is like a huge 'Robina'. Robina is on the Gold Coast and there are hundreds of 'Robinas' in south east Queensland. Rows and rows of very nice brick and tile homes with neat gardens and the divided roads have shrubs and trees down the middle. Of course there is the shopping centre with all the same shops in every suburb and we really could have been back anywhere near home as they all look the same!

The **Mindil Beach night markets** were on and having now seen them I can understand why they are so well known and why are a tourist attraction. We went back there to have dinner as we had been told that there are food stalls of all description. Indeed there were, whether you wanted hot or cold food. There were many Asian outlets as well as Australian or you could go for the pancake or fruit platter stalls and we became totally overwhelmed. We laughed when we saw one Australian stall called 'Road Kill'. I saw a Chinese stall which advertised 'No MSG' and stopped to buy a small meal (as opposed to medium or large which we were offered) of sweet and sour pork and fried rice. The fried rice included every type of vegetable imaginable and the meal was too big for me! It was also lukewarm and stuck in my gullet like a load of hard bullets. We should have looked further because some of the other Asian stalls had piping hot food on offer. John's food was so hot and spicy that his mouth was on fire. He spoke of an iced cold beer and I promptly offered him a bottle of cold water from my bag! Aren't I a spoil sport?

We commenced to look at the stalls, the fire dancers and to listen to the Asian musician but I was gripping John's hand as the markets are so huge and so packed with people that we could hardly move an inch and could have easily lost each other. It was just too much for me and certainly was not fun or relaxing. We had been told to take our table and some chairs and to sit, like hundreds of other people were doing, around the edges of the market and to keep going back to taste small samples of different foods. How anyone could eat more than one 'small' sample I can't imagine.

The idea is that you go there to watch the sunset first with a nice bottle of wine or some beer and make an evening out of it. As we had watched the sunset on a beach with only our two dogs for company (they would not have been allowed at Mindil when the markets were on) I found the vast crowds overwhelming. It was like the radio was on full blast with thousands of voices babbling away and you couldn't turn it down. I asked John if he minded leaving and I couldn't get away fast enough. I was also disappointed that there was no lighting on the beach as it would have been a good place to sit to eat.

However, we had enjoyed a lovely day and one of the highlights was seeing Callie on the beach at Casuarina chasing a live ball. It kept running away from her and then turning around and running back towards her again and she was totally entranced, just as we were. It was a crab and it was about the size of a tennis ball. Naturally I took too many photos! Jack got bored of running after it fairly quickly but the only thing that drew Callie away from this delight was me asking her if she wanted the 'water' and she rushed off down to the sea and promptly lay down in it whilst she waited for us. All the way back across the sand she searched every scrap of seaweed or stone for her 'ball'. The other highlight was the speed of the setting sun and we also enjoyed almost deserted beaches the whole day long.

Today is the Darwin Show Day, a public holiday and this show has followed us all the way from Rockhampton. We keep trying to get away from it! So today we stay at home and get the chores done. We have been placed in the centre of the park and we do not actually have a site number. It is a huge open area with very few caravans on it and a couple of tents and our water is piped to us through long black irrigation pipes. This is causing us some concern but had its advantages today when I did the washing. The concern is that the water is hot, as it is being solar heated inside the black irrigation pipes and we should not be drinking it. The advantage today was when I did our washing in my machine as it washed and rinsed in hot water and I will never, ever agree with the soap manufacturers again who say you can use cold water and cold water powder and get a really good result. I have never rinsed my clothes in hot water before but today I did five loads in my small machine and it all washed and rinsed in hot water and my washing has never appeared this clean before. I'm quite stunned by it actually. Stains on towels have disappeared and socks that I thought were destined for the bin suddenly look new! You must remember that we are in the 'red dust country' area of Australia at the moment and everything gets covered in red dust. I wear a pair of jeans for one day and they need washing. I've had to wash a pair of slippers I accidentally wore outside back in Litchfield. I've had to wash shoes regularly. We also do not need to put the gas hot water heater on to have showers or to wash up but we are going to have to buy some water for drinking as soon as possible because I've virtually stopped drinking and I usually drink several bottles of water a day. It was hard washing my hair over the bath with the shower rose because I was using only the cold water tap and the water was so hot that it was nearly burning my head!

UGLY BRUTE OF A CROC

Adelaide River Cruise

It was a wonderful day out mainly thanks to Harry, our guide, who is still so excited by the sight of the salt water crocodiles. His enthusiasm was so infectious that we were looking out for them all the time, despite the fact that they are so grotesque! We would be flying along 'out of the water' as he termed it, when he would suddenly swerve violently ninety degrees and head for the river bank. We got very, very close to them and met up with crocodiles over five metres long. He reckons that they are the largest estuarine crocodiles that you will see in Australia and that it is only thanks to the ban on crocodile hunting in the Northern Territory river systems in 1971 that we have the chance to see these big, old crocs because these are the ones that the hunters missed. The five metre crocodiles are about eighty years old and he reckons that one of the ones we saw would have been about 5.4 metres! So, as most of the crocodiles in the river systems of the Northern Territory are juniors and we saw several very big ones today we were very fortunate! He mentioned at one point that we were travelling in fresh water despite the fact that the water ebbs and flows some three metres and then explained that salt water crocodiles are so named because they have two glands that secrete the salt from their bodies which the fresh water crocodiles do not have. He kept imploring us not to put our hands into the water!

We started out day with a visit to the **Windows on the Wetlands Visitor Centre** but we saw more wet land as we travelled along the road towards Kakadu because of the cyclone that hit northern Australia three months ago. It is amazing that there is still water hanging around considering the heat and he showed us how high the water rose in several places as well as along the river. Harry told us that Kakadu is the second largest National Park after Antarctica. This is why John is having so much trouble deciding what to do about going there as the distances are so vast.

Harry told us lots of things and he is quite a character and has been on the travel shows on T.V. He told us about the Whistling Kites that we were seeing all along the river and how clever they are. They can eat 'on the wing' (whilst flying) but they are a nuisance when the bush catches fire because they spread the fire further afield. They will pick up burning sticks and carry them along and drop them from a great height to recreate fire. They do this to collect the insects – cooked meat! However, being meat eaters, the cane toads are killing many of them and a lot in Katherine have apparently died already. A crocodile was even found dead last year with one in its stomach.

He pointed out the Mimosa, an introduced flower which has turned into a terrible weed in the area and showed us the effects of the Government's introduction of a moth to the area which kills it. There were large areas where the Mimosa had died and the natural vegetation was being given the chance to renew itself. I asked what the moths would eat once they had cleared up the Mimosa but apparently they need something peculiar to that particular plant to live and will therefore die once it has all gone.

We also saw eagles but try as I might, I just could not get a shot of them with my camera. There was a guy on the boat who had one of those cameras that takes continuous photographs very rapidly and he captured the most amazing photographs. Harry put a piece of meat on an ice-cream lid and floated it on the river and this man had a close up of the eagle grabbing the meat in flight and it is an extraordinary photograph. Harry asked him to send him a copy and I do hope that he does.

We had already pulled up at the side of the river where Harry had made us tea, coffee and offered juice and cake and now it was already time for lunch and we were still going upstream. We stopped at the most amazing place which I cannot tell you about because it is a secret! Harry cooked up a storm and it was all done on a barbecue without a drop of oil or fat being used. Whilst eating lunch we had a discussion about what we called our swimming costumes, togs, bathers or swimmers depending on where you live in Australia. I'm still learning the Australian language and was quite confused when I was reading in the paper about some girl who had four 'tin lids' all born in the Northern Territory until I realised it meant 'kids'. It's like being back in the East End of London!

Anyway, back to this secret location. There was a flush toilet provided with soap, a real hand towel and flowers 'for the women'. The men were told to go anywhere in the bush! Along with bread and butter and a lot of salad we really did not need the sweets that Harry kept offering to us as we travelled further up the river that afternoon! We were nearly 'crocodiled out' by the time we reached Goat Island which is a story in itself!

A guy from Sydney, fed up with traffic lights, sees an advertisement for an island (the land being about a kilometre long) on the Adelaide River and buys it. When he gets here he needs a barge to get a house onto it but he can't find a big enough barge and no-one wants to make him one so he builds the barge himself and it is an engineering feat on its own. He was able to put the foundation poles into rock and Harry advised him to put the house higher than the termite mound in the tree in case of floods. He was very appreciative of that advice during the recent cyclone as the floods rose up to just under the termite mound – termites are so clever. Along with the house there are also some original rooms that I think were already there but toilets needed to be installed and as they had to be bio-septic they cost $20,000 each!

We could not get the family history of course but the owners appear to be a married couple with another guy that lives there (who could also be a part owner – I have no idea) and this other guy has the ability to craft wonderful pieces out of wood from the island. There was so much to see there, whether it be where a local crocodile, who loves Danish potatoes and gravy but not meat has spent many happy hours having his dinner or the fabulous tables and chairs and the timber railing which is wide and flat so that you can place your beer on it whilst watching the views from the veranda or the ornamental wooden pieces, all made from the island wood. There is also a bar and a menu because a restaurant is also available. You can come and stay in this wilderness and buy your food and drinks and if you are sensible, you will borrow a friend's boat and use it not only to get here but to fish.

I actually got hold of a rod at long last and have a photo to prove it but did not catch a Barramundi. Harry had just got the first two lines out for us, ensuring that no lines would get caught in his propeller or would cross each other, when the guy with the first line got a Barramundi but it was too small so we had to throw it back. I'm not sure we got all the lines out because Harry suddenly saw an eagle and we were zooming off again!

Anyway, back to the bar and the island. Several beers were consumed and Harry told us about his doctor who had asked him how much he drank. Harry knew that if he said twenty beers a day he would be classed as an alcoholic and said as much to the doctor who retorted 'You are not an alcoholic until you drink more than your Doctor'. Apparently this doctor is an Englishman and it is he who has a practice opposite our caravan park where I went the other day and found it closed.

On our return journey back down the river we again stopped for more crocodiles, eagles, wild pigs and for afternoon tea and coffee, this time with a wonderful selection of biscuits. Back in the mini-bus on our way home, Harry pointed out the Didgeridoo Hut/ Authentic Aboriginal Art and Craft shop on the corner of the Arnhem Highway and the Stewart Highway and as it was not far away from where we picked the dogs up, we called in there around 6pm and found it still open. There was one particular canvas which I would have loved to have bought but it cost $3000. This place is owned by Aboriginal people so if you want something authentic it is a good place to call into.

At some point during this journey we were also told about the Gamber Grass that was introduced from Africa in 1931. Gamber grass fires are twenty times as hot as native grass fires and give off far more carbon emissions and yet it is sold as cattle feed and mulch for gardens! It has the potential to alter the Australian landscape if nothing is done about it and it can grow 3-5 metres tall. Later in our journey I stood beside some and it literally towers over you. I saw it in the Northern Territory and in Western Australia.

Chapter 13

1st August 2006

Today was a frustrating day of shopping as we went to **Palmerston** and for a relatively new town it is so badly laid out. We had to get back into the car to drive to another area for different products and after trying three chemists in three different places I gave up on finding a packet of a pretty common dental hygiene product. I have also had to give up on getting a replacement battery for my CDMA phone. In fact we gave up looking for a lot of things! John has gone off to the Australian Aviation Heritage Centre and unfortunately did not have the time to wait for me to clear my camera. I had wanted to go but it's too hot to leave the dogs in the Ute for too long and I had the camera full of photos and my diary to catch up on. However, I'm still enjoying our memories of yesterday when we went up the Adelaide River.

John enjoyed his visit to the **Aviation Centre** and found it absolutely fascinating. He loved the B52 bomber, which has been donated by the USA Air Force. As it was so large it took up all the hanger space and yet the cockpit was very small. Whilst he was looking at the exhibits several fighter planes took off and the whole hanger he was in shuddered. All sound was blotted out by the noise emitted by these planes because of their sheer power, including the sound of the video he was trying to listen to!

The exhibits included a World War 11 Spitfire Mark 111, a Sabre Jet and some helicopters as well as a couple of ultra-lights. He enjoyed reading the accounts of combats by fighter pilots when Darwin was raided and looking at the old uniforms and regalia and bits of Japanese fighter planes that had crashed.

Touring day without the dogs

We dropped the dogs off at the kennels and started our touring day at the **Howard Springs Nature Park** which is not far from our park and there is a beautiful spring-fed creek and swimming area there along with rainforest, lots of birds, fish and it is a really lovely place for a picnic. There are also walking tracks for those who feel energetic and have the time.

Next stop was Darwin where we walked around the city taking photographs including one of **Parliament House** because of its lovely architecture (it's also white and bright), street scenes and **Government House** which is just beautiful, especially as it is on the headland with white picket fences, immaculate green lawns and borders of bright pink flowers. We also had a look at the harbour and started to read some of the many plaques around with information about the bombing of Darwin during World War 11.

We asked a lady where the town 'Mall' was with the 'a' pronounced as in 'apple' and she looked so perplexed I immediately repeated it as 'm-a-w-l' which she understood immediately! When I am in Brisbane I pronounce it the way I said it first. She pointed to another lady and told us to follow her and this second lady told us she would take us there. John asked her what it was like to live here in the summer and she looked puzzled and said 'Summer? We don't have 'summer'. We just have the wet season or the dry season'. She told us that she didn't use an air conditioner and that it was pretty cool at the moment. Cool!!! We were seeking shade!

Then John said that he liked the fact that there are so few rules in the Territory and I told her that we have so many rules now in south-east Queensland that if your cat pees in your neighbours garden at the Gold Coast, you can be fined. She laughed and retorted 'Not here. We're still a bit feral up here'. In the Northern Territory, if you have a driving offence you are fined but you do not lose demerit points from your licence as in other States in Australia and we were amazed by that. Also, of course, there are so many roads where there are no speed limits. You do not have to get a boat licence either and just go and buy your boat and off you go – no licence for the boat and none for yourself. It takes a while before you realise that you have more freedom here and the only thing that impacts on us is having the dogs here. I don't think I'd like to live in Darwin though but many want to as it is the fastest growing city in Australia according to a newspaper report.

The people who do not work in the tourist business are so friendly but you feel that underneath they are as tough as nails and could face anything that life throws at them without a murmur. I've met several people in the tourist business though who leave me feeling that they are sick of tourists and a good example of that happened when we arrived at the East Point Military Museum later in the day, but I digress.

After a coffee and cake in town, we went back to the **Bicentennial Park** along the Esplanade for another look before heading to the **Museum and Art Gallery of the Northern Territory** which is further out of town. We spent a long time there and thought it was a wonderful place to visit as you find yourself in an art exhibition and then a botanical and fossil section or else perhaps in the area displaying photos of Cyclone Tracey. A giant Witchetty Grub caught my attention and it was the first time I realised that they produce giant moths! In that section you can enter a small, unlit room and listen to the sounds of a cyclone and try to imagine what it must have felt like for the population on Christmas Eve of 1974. We also watched a film about it and it was horrendous. Darwin has been so badly hit, what with the cyclone in 1937 followed by the bombing in 1942/43 and then being almost completely destroyed again with Cyclone Tracey. The

Museum does not charge an entry fee and we both strongly recommend it although a museum is not normally a point of interest to us. (Later that night I was looking through a leaflet about the museum and found that we had completely missed three sections so make sure you look at the leaflet you are given on entry!)

It was after this wonderful experience that we rocked up at the **East Point Military Museum** and I got a lecture from a lady, who luckily doesn't usually work there. I queried the entry fee because I usually get a concession (a lower price, as does John because he has a Pensioner Card). 'I get so angry with people asking me about concessions.......' she started and she went on so long that I just said 'I can't afford it then'.

It wasn't the cost at all but the fact that I couldn't stand listening to her going on and on and on any more. I have always paid the higher price before without a quibble, such as on the Katherine Gorge Cruise but there is no harm in asking and she has no right getting angry at anyone asking either. When I said I wasn't going to go in she decided that I could get the concession because my name was also on John's card. Guess what – the concession that caused her such anger was $1!!

Similarly, we phone caravan parks and they won't take bookings and when I phoned one the other day the girl said 'There are five other parks in town'. Now that is rude. I told her that their park is the only one that allows dogs and what would we do if we arrived and found nowhere to stay and she retorted 'Go to the Showground'. Now that means absolutely nothing to me and I speak the language so it would be most difficult for someone who does not speak English that well.

I had the same feeling when we bought two coffees and one piece of carrot cake yesterday. The girl behind the counter repeated back to me 'One piece?' with raised eyebrows and a resigned look. When it arrived I decided that I'd like some after all and ordered some. When she brought it to the table she said she'd get me a fork and I told her not to bother because for some reason John had two forks. It was then that she told me that she had assumed we were going to share the one piece. So I get the feeling that they are sick of nit-picking tourists who are 'cheapskates', if you know what I mean.

Anyway, back at the East Point Military Museum we went straight into the theatrette to watch a short movie about Darwin being bombed and we now realise why there are so many plaques commemorating military sites, air fields, runways near the roads, troop stations and incident sites in the Northern Territory. On the first day that the Japanese targeted Darwin, the two worst air raids of the war took place and twice as many bombs dropped on Darwin that day than were dropped on Pearl Harbour ten weeks before. Darwin received warnings but they were ignored and a lot of people were killed and injured. Direct hits included the Hospital and a hospital ship, both of which had big red crosses on them. An American naval vessel still lies as a tomb on the harbour floor. The Japanese knew exactly where to drop the bombs to cause the most hardship and chaos.

Australia had often employed Japanese topographers because they had so much knowledge of the Pacific region and as they had the maps, they knew exactly where to target. It is believed that the Japanese had been pearl diving and fishing in Australian waters for years. A reconnaissance plane was also seen a week before. Darwin was first attacked on 19th February, 1942 and continued to be bombed until November 1943. There was a great deal to look at inside as well as all the exhibits outside such as an American mobile workshop, gun carrier, anti-tank guns, an amphibious vehicle plus some bombs and so forth! Australia was certainly close to being occupied!

This museum is on a 200 hectare reserve with great views of Darwin across the water. There is also a beautiful area for swimming or a picnic at Lake Alexander and we stopped there for a while before heading back towards Darwin. We drove into the George Brown Darwin Botanic Gardens but did not have the time to explore it as it not only covers forty-two hectares (just the thought was exhausting by this time of the day) but we had to pick the dogs up. What little we did see of it we liked very much and took a few photographs of the area that we could see, which was mainly by the beautiful fountain by the car park!

Tomorrow we leave to return to Katherine and connect to the road that will take us across the border into Western Australia.

Chapter 14

KUNUNURRA, WESTERN AUSTRALIA – only one million square kilometres!

Yes, one million square kilometres in just one State – makes some other countries seems so tiny, doesn't it?

We left home on 17th May and now we are in Western Australia on 6th August and considering we are on what is supposed to be a leisurely trip, that's not too bad. However, I try hard not to listen to anyone talking about distances as it depresses me to think just how many more kilometres we have to do before we reach Perth! Helen is planning to join us there. Yesterday John was telling me how many weeks we had been on the road and I exclaimed 'Is that all?' and he replied 'Oh, don't be like that'.

'Well what does it feel like to you?' I asked him.

'Forever' he replied.

WARNING: In the Northern Territory if you see a road sign which is white with a black line through it, it means No Speed Limit. If you see the same sign in Western Australia it means 110ks maximum. How many people do they catch out by not having signs saying 110ks! To confuse matters more there are some signs with 110ks on them so you have two different signs that mean the same thing. Local people tell us that the Government does it on purpose for a revenue raiser!

The whole time we were in the Northern Territory we hardly saw a fly and I had gone and bought one of those fly net covers to put over my hat and face and it is still in its packet unopened. We had some small insects and small moths around the lights at night but I cannot recall even seeing a fly outside our van. Where have they all gone? I've seen it so often on films where people are swatting them away from their faces.

Now I am going to backtrack a little because when I last wrote in this diary we were about to leave Darwin. On our return journey to Katherine I really enjoyed travelling the section of road between Adelaide River and Pine Creek. I think it was more to do with my mood, which was reflective and peaceful. The Northern Territory has sunk deep into my soul and I can now 'feel' this ancient land. I sort of feel like life is eternal but I'm getting this feeling from the land rather than from my religion. I have the feeling that I can accomplish anything and do not feel insignificant in the vastness of the surrounding scenery. I feel part of it whereas I could feel something like an ant I suppose. It's so hard to explain.

About 9ks out of Katherine I saw a dam with red earth walls and the water was bright red which is something I have never seen before.

We stopped at **Pine Creek** as we had been there before but had not had the time to look around and it is such a pretty place. As it turned out there wasn't much to see anyway but it is a good place for a break.

We booked in for one night at **Katherine** and then I said to John that I felt so exhausted that I needed to stay on another night and did not want to pack everything up again in the morning. However, we were not allowed to stay unless we moved to another site because the site we were on was classified as an overnight site only so we did pack up and leave! The 'rules is rules' mentality. It was utterly ridiculous as there were a whole row of sites and the caravan two doors away was not classed as an overnight site. The park was half empty when we left but the 'rules is rules' mentality could not be broken! I wish there were more Harry's about in the tourist industry in the Northern Territory.

TIMBER CREEK - OUR SITE NEAR CROCODILES

So, exhausted, we set off again and covered another 287 kilometres, with several stops for the dogs, until we reached **Timber Creek** and stopped. The journey was beautiful once we came to the **Gregory National Park**. We saw a couple cycling and this is not the first time. We saw one couple between Alice Springs and Darwin, cycling at 1pm when the sun is at its hottest. They were going so slowly with exhaustion that they would have been better off pushing their bikes. Some people certainly act in extraordinary ways sometimes.

There appear to be two sides to this caravan park and we are on a very pretty site near the creek where there are crocodiles! I'm told they are fed here every afternoon which is good as they probably don't need to eat our dogs. The other side of the park has a lot more trees but the vans seem to be crammed together over there. We are on a very well maintained grass site with a lot of room around us and it is not far from the pool. The water is so cold it takes your breath away and it was bliss to get into the pool that first afternoon.

It had been a very hot day and it had been the first time that I had had to use the car air conditioner continually. This is mid-winter (or 'dry season') and that day was far too hot for me to handle so I cannot imagine what the 'wet season' is like. The next day was cooler with a strong breeze and the night was really cool, so it does vary. This is where we had to use up all our fresh fruit and vegetables and honey as they are not allowed to be taken over the border. However, cooked vegetables are acceptable and I have now found out that celery layered with fresh tomatoes and grated cheese is delicious if cooked in the microwave oven. I had a heap of potatoes so made potato croquettes to use them up and froze them. We also had a shepherd's pie so that I could use up the onion, carrots and any other vegetables that were hanging around.

The journey to the Western Australia border was easy and uneventful and we only saw one car coming the other way all the way to **Kunanurra** which is nearly 200 kilometres. The inspection of my car was magically quick as only a box on the floor of the back seat containing the dog's bits and pieces was checked. I think the guy was overwhelmed by the junk on my back seat and the rest of the floor and just couldn't face any more. John called me over to the motor home and another guy asked me a few questions and had a quick look in the fridge and that was that, we were on our way over the border.

Whoever decided on the boundary line for the state must have lived in W.A. because the scenery suddenly became quite dramatic and the area called the **Kimberly region** is a top tourist destination. Prior to the border we had seen signs for the Keep River National Park which is also popular but unfortunately for us, both of the National Parks require a four-wheel drive vehicle.

We also started to see the Boab trees. Now, if it possible for trees to be called ugly then these trees get the gold medals. They are like obese bottles of beer with giant warts on them and crowned with dead branches sticking out of the top.

So we turned up at the tourist park by the lake that I had phoned and I was asked if I had booked and I replied that I had been told that I couldn't make a booking and just had to turn up. The young girl then told me that I could have booked if I was a Top Tourist member and I replied that I am and had said so when I had phoned. Then an older lady appeared from a back office and said that they did not have the room for our big vehicle as she'd told me this morning. I answered that it wasn't this morning that I had phoned and that she had never before said that they did not have sites big enough. She then went on to say that they only had very small sites and that people were crammed so close together that their doors were almost touching when they opened them! There's nothing like running down your own van park is there? She told us to go to the Show Grounds and I told her that that meant absolutely nothing to me as I had just come over the border and could she please give me some directions. Later in the day we saw the park from the other side of the lake and there was plenty of room and as John said 'We felt most unwanted'.

The Show Ground is basic although we do have a lot of room but there is obviously no pool so I don't think we will be staying for more than a week. I was hoping to stay for at least two weeks if not three but there is no other park that allows dogs unless we back-track 70 kilometres to lake Argyle, which is a possibility as it looks beautiful there and they do allow dogs but will mean a lot of extra petrol and John does not like back-tracking.

When the Ord River was dammed Lake Argyle was formed on what had been a million acre cattle station and if the lake was full to extreme flood capacity it would be about fifty-five times the volume of Sydney Harbour. You get the picture – it's big. However, it is not usually this big as you will see later on in this dairy.

Obviously there are a lot of boat trips to choose from but there is one package deal that includes the Bungle Bungle Range, Lake Argyle, an Ord River scenic flight followed by a scenic bus ride and then a tour of a homestead at Lake Argyle. This trip also includes a fifty-five kilometre trip from the lake, up the Ord River back to Kununurra seeing Carlton Gorge and ending with the sunset on Lake Kununurra. It's not cheap but when you look at all other options it suddenly appears to be the best option unless you have a four wheel drive and a few months to spare. The **Bungle Bungle** range is actually in the **Purnululu National Park** which is heritage listed and the area is very important to the Aboriginals and there is rock art in some areas.

However, there is also the **Mirima National Park** which is apparently well worth a visit, the **Ngauwudu National Park** and the **Parry Lagoons Nature Reserve**. How long do we stay? The Kimberley region covers an enormous area and everything seems to be on a vast scale here including the coastal tides which can vary by 12 metres.

We are now deep into leaflets. We are comparing the costs of tours of the National Park, Lake Argyle, the Argyle Diamond Mine and the Bungle Bungles (sandstone domes, gorges and waterfalls, cliffs, palms, rock pools and one of the outstanding sights in Australia which we must see whilst here) and trying to decide whether to fly over them or take various trips or combine trips which offer a discount. Most of the land tours are for two to ten days or more and cost a fortune. There is just so much to see from here that it is overwhelming and we will start with the local attractions in and around town which is a hundred kilometre round trip alone! We also want to drive in the Ute to Wyndham on the coast, where the five rivers meet and apparently there are amazing views from the Five Rivers Lookout. We have copious pamphlets on the sites to see around Wyndham and now have a heap on Broome even though we are nowhere near Broome yet! Our lounge looks like a Tourist Information Centre at the moment.

The Argyle Diamond Mine provides the world with 25% of its diamonds and it's about 180 kilometres from here and the land is leased from the Aboriginals and over 20% of the workforce is Aboriginal. Six to seven tonnes of diamonds are extracted each year with colours (including the normal white) varying from pale pink through to a purple/red colour.

We went into town this afternoon and found a couple of major food stores and the banks and Post Office along with a lot of other useful businesses and shops and went into the Information Centre where we were made very welcome. We then took the dogs to a lovely park by the **Lily Creek Lagoon** which formed when the Diversion Dam was built and saw the town boat ramp but had a job keeping Callie away from the water and the crocodiles within!

We have gained another hour and a half and it gets dark here at 5.30pm! The dogs will have to adjust to a new dinner time so we'll advance them half an hour a day! We are now two hours behind Queensland and New South Wales which will make it fun when we call my kids. It will get more confusing if Colin is still in New South Wales when they introduce their annual daylight saving which Queensland does not have.

Here they have three seasons, those being the 'dry season', the 'build-up' season and the 'wet season'. The dry season is from around April to September/October so that's all you needed to know! Apparently the 'build-up' season is worse than the 'wet season' because it is hot and humid with the odd thunderstorms but no relief from the heat. The 'wet season' has monsoonal weather with many thunder storms and the East Kimberley region (which is where we are) is one of the most active areas in Australia for lightening strikes! How nice. Apparently some people think so and come to see the spectacular sky shows but I can do without them.

KUNUNURRA LOCALITY

We got off to a late start as we went to bed late as we cannot get used to the time difference. On top of that, I felt so tired that I had to drag myself out of the van and into the Ute but vegetables and fruit called as we had none. We set off first to a place called **Barra Barra** which is a café that sells fruit and vegetables and it had been recommended to us but we were very disappointed in the selection. However, the setting was beautiful and they sold fresh fruit smoothies, banana splits, chocolate coated fruit and home made jams and chutneys. We resisted because, as I said to John, we had spent the extra in petrol already to get cheaper vegetables and if we spent money on treats we might as well have gone to the supermarket. It is a beautiful spot to go to for a treat though. Further along the road was found the **Top Rockz Gallery** and we were entranced by the rocks there along with the sterling silver jewellery.

In this part of the world they mine a rock that is called 'zebra' rock and some of it is has very bold, striped patterns in it. It is unique because it is the only place in the world that it has been discovered and it is here in the East Kimberley region. It has been dated 600 million years old and was formed in the Pre-Cambrian period or the Upper Proterozoic era. It is not known how the patterns formed but there are red spots or stripes upon a light background, each piece being different. This rock doesn't have any fossils in it as it was formed when there were only simple aquatic organisms on earth and Australia was not an island! There's not a lot left and it is weighed in kilos rather than tonnes. It was found back in 1924 near the original homestead where Lake Argyle now is (the homestead was moved when the land was flooded). There may be a lot left under Lake Argyle but there's not a lot above the water.

The second kind of rock mined is Primordial which is another form of Zebra Rock and is petrified Algae. This is about 120 million years old and has fossilised plant material throughout. Apparently 53 colour variations have been found from the Riverine Siltstone. Again, this is the only place that it has ever been discovered.

They also mine Liesengang Weather Rock which has circular rings, some being of a dark iron colour and some light. Most of the white in the rock is silica and I was told that it holds the rock together as it is very strong. Some of the white in it can be kaolin.

KELLY'S KNOB - TOWARDS KUNUNURRA

Ornaments, jewellery and coasters made from the rock were available for sale and there were also some marble pieces. I immediately fell in love with a piece of rock that I cannot describe but it has colours in it from pale pinks through to mauves and it is in its rough form so you can see the cracks that were formed millions of years ago. I bought it because I simply couldn't leave it behind as it called to me – it was my rock. As my rock has the pinks in it and the silica, it is a piece of Liesengang Weather Rock. John believes I will have a problem with people wanting to pick it up and look at it as it is fairly fragile but I will put it on my coffee table so that I can see it all the time as I loathe items that are for display only. If it is low down and can be viewed from all angles then it shouldn't be a problem – so says a mother who has not yet had the joy of grandchildren running around her lounge! Our house is not suitable for children under five years of age. It is far too dangerous! The only item I've ever had that I really valued was one of my mother's pieces that I have inherited and that was her beautiful Wedgwood coffee pot that is saw in constant use and I managed to smash that myself so I would hardly admonish a child for breaking anything I've got!

IVANHOE CROSSING at Kununurra

We went on to the **Ivanhoe Crossing** with its mini-dam wall and it was so beautiful there. It is a popular spot for fishing but there is a sign warning of crocodiles so the dogs could not go into the water. We headed back and were going via the Research Station Road when we saw another fruit and vegetable store housed in a solid building which included in its name the word 'mobile' but how it could be mobile I don't know. However, they had a good selection of produce plus and bowls of different kinds of melon pieces topped with ice cream and more tempting treats which we resisted.

We were running out of time as we had to get to the bank before it closed so headed straight back the way we had come and went to town, booking my car in for a wheel alignment en route. The town centre is a little confusing but manageable if you know where things are. It's a matter of crossing roads but is walkable. We needed the bank, the Post Office, a newsagents and the supermarket and went all over the place and we moved the vehicle three times. We ended up getting back to the van around 3.30pm which was when eventually had our lunch!

We are feeling more wanted! The sign outside this Show Grounds (which we couldn't read yesterday as it was covered up with a 'Full' sign which we ignored) states that the show grounds are only for people with 'Big Rigs and Dogs'. Last night several caravans arrived and were turned away! We found out today that the washing machines are free whereas at most parks you have to pay up to $3 or more for each load. We also did not realise that the town centre is so close that we can walk to it and the expensive caravan park over the road is so full that people are parked so close together that they must be able to hear each other dream! We have loads of room and we can also let our dogs run freely on the sports field inside the Showground area and I'm now grateful that the other park turned us away! The Managers are super helpful and friendly and apparently come here for many months of the year just to do this job although their home is in Bundaberg in Queensland. They told John that they love W.A because the sea is so blue. I cannot imagine it being bluer than some of the places that we have already travelled to in other states but I'll reserve my judgement on that point.

I've just put the news on and apparently there has been a tornado at Bunbury in W.A, a place we will be visiting. It seems that only one person was seriously injured but it has been declared a 'natural disaster' area and the damage is estimated at more than ten million dollars. The winds were travelling around 250mph apparently and between Bunbury and Geraldton they are now getting up to eight to twelve tornados per year. That's over 500ks of coastline, including Perth. We will have to remember this and move inland if there are coastal weather warnings as there have been this week. Prisoners are helping out at the moment which brings to mind something that I read this week. Apparently the first police force formed in Australia was in Sydney, made up of twelve of the best behaved prisoners!

9th August 2006

A new day and a lazy morning as our exhaustion has finally settled in and we are benefiting from staying in one place by going to bed earlier and getting up later. It is because we know that we can't go anywhere for a couple of weeks. I have booked into a dentist in town and was able to make an appointment in exactly two weeks time and they are MBF approved. I also have an appointment made at the hospital for tomorrow to check my ulcer medication as I have stopped taking it and do not know if I am doing the right thing or not! It was so very easy to get both appointments unlike in Darwin. We have already had the wheel alignment done on the Ute and the tyres swapped around and balanced whereas we cancelled an appointment in Darwin as they wanted us to leave the Ute with them all afternoon and it was many miles from where we were staying. The only downside is that we have no Optus coverage from now on and that includes all the way down the Western Australian coastline (with the odd exception) and I had to use a pay phone to pay them their last bill yesterday.

Today we set off to visit the **Hoochery** which is a rum distillery. You could purchase a fair sized sample of rum for one dollar so John sampled the strongest. It was so strong that I took over the driving afterwards! On the way back we turned off to visit **Mulligans Lagoon** and to see the Aboriginal Art Sites. There are no signs advising you of distances and we drove ten kilometres on the dirt road only to find that we then faced a barrier stating that the remainder of the road was closed. So in a twenty kilometre round trip all we gained was a couple of photos for John of a Boab tree, as he seems to love their ugliness for some reason and finds them fascinating.

We topped off the morning with a visit to the **Kimberley Fine Diamonds** shop which was well worth a visit. They do not just sell jewellery but many works of art including pottery and sculptures. They had some ornaments which were around $10 so do not be put off by what is displayed in the windows. It was a beautiful store and I asked about the pink diamonds and the girl was so helpful and informative even though I told her that I did not have enough money to buy any of them. One of the stones I liked, which was a very deep pink diamond, cost more than an average house.

After lunch I went into town on my own to do a bit of window shopping. I purchased things from three shops and spent a total of $2.30! So what did this big spender purchase during her two hours of shopping? A packet of ten plastic file sleeves from the newsagents (80c), four thin tent pegs for our rotary washing line from one of the two camping shops ($1) and some scented oil for 50c. However, when I got back I told John he had a wife who was a big spender and he said 'How much? $50? $100?' I didn't let him sweat for too long!

LAKE ARYLE & ORD RIVER DAM

We drove out to the lake yesterday and once we were off the highway the scenery became quite spectacular and at my first glimpse of the water I exclaimed 'Wow. It is so blue'. The scenery was lovely, the colour of the water gorgeous as it was such a deep, rich blue and we took many photographs. However, I was very disappointed because there is very little roadway with just a few lookouts and the only access to the water was down a steep road leading to the boat ramp. We went down there so that the dogs could cool down but there was nowhere for us to swim from and when a fishing boat came in we had to leave as there wasn't enough room for us all. We found one small parkland area by the river where we could see the Dam wall but there were barriers everywhere you looked, whether at the lake or at the river and it was very irritating.

We went to the caravan park near the lake as it is advertised as having a 'restaurant'. As John says 'It is a snack bar' and the menu was pitiful. They offered fish and chips, steak sandwich, salad, chips, chips, sandwiches and toasted sandwiches, chips – you get the idea? The special of the day were fish vol-au-vents and I cannot for the life of me recall the name that they were using for the fish which is because I was immediately suspicious as I'd never heard of it! As I expected and had already suggested to John, it was cat fish. So I asked what the 'Special of the Day' really meant and it meant cat fish pie! To me, cat fish are the cockroaches of the water and I could not stomach it. We were looking for a 'restaurant meal' and I might as well have taken some cheese and tomato sandwiches and a packet of chips (crisps) with me because I ended up with the same sandwiches, albeit toasted and we shared a basket of hot chips.

However, possibly the highlight of the day, other than the little tiny part of the lake that we could see, was the video that was played at the cafe. The video was about the construction of the **Ord River Dam** which was a mammoth task with the contract being awarded to an American company. The building of the dam wall took place over three years because when the annual wet season arrived they had to stop work. When they were working during the 'build-up' it must have been horrendous and there was superb film footage of the whole construction period.

There were a lot of people watching and you could have heard a pin drop as everyone was so awed by the scale of the work and what it had entailed. The Ord River Dam Wall was officially opened in 1972 and it created a lake eighteen times bigger than *Sydney Harbour* with a water level of 92 metres and a surface area of 1000 square kilometres. In extreme flood capacity it would be 2072 square kilometres!

After watching the film we had a short walk around the caravan park but we are both very glad that we didn't stop there with our van, although you can view a bit of the river from there. Two very bored little girls were delighted to have the chance to play with the dogs as there is absolutely nothing to do there and there's not much point in going to the lake unless you have your own boat. If you do have a boat it would be a lovely place to stay but even at this time of the year you would need a boat with shade as it is so very hot. It was about 31C yesterday and there is no industry to speak of so the skies are clear of pollution and the sun is relentless.

You can, of course, pay to go on cruises on the lake and from Kununurra they cost $125 per person at the moment but are less from Lake Argyle itself, so it would pay to drive there yourself if there is more than one person in the car. You can also do a cruise (for the same price) down the Ord River to the lake or you can do a combo trip and do both trips for $170 per adult. It's an easy 79 kilometre drive to the lake from Kununurra and on the way back we only passed one caravan and saw no other traffic until we were five kilometres out of town. Considering that we were on the main highway from Katherine to Kununurra for the latter thirty kilometres, it amazed us that we had the road to ourselves. I said to John 'What if we were to find that we were the only ones left alive on the planet along with the people in that caravan?' and he agreed that it felt almost weird. He wondered how he is going to manage when we are amongst traffic again. He told me that he was telling another guy that sometimes whilst driving he is thinking 'Please, a road sign or a bend or a hill – anything to relieve this boredom.' He was told we will experience more of this on our way to Broome when we leave here.

John is taking a trip over Lake Argyle, the Bungle Bungle ranges and the Argyle Diamond Mine on Saturday afternoon via a float plane and will be picked up and dropped off here at the caravan park. I have decided not to go. There are various reasons for this but the main one is the cost of petrol here (it was $35 at the Gold Coast and my car is now costing over $90 to fill here), the two rate rises on our three mortgages and the fact that I do not wish to sell the van as soon as we get home to raise some cash but would prefer to modernise one of our houses and sell that instead. I want to cut back on some of our expenditure and in all honesty I would love to do every trip that is on offer but it would mean that at each place we stop we would be spending around $1000. Money is floating out of our bank account at an alarming rate and there are certain things that I want to do that are really important to me and the Bungle Bungle Ranges is not one of them. It would be great but I can live without this trip. I'm not even sure if I can do what I want to do because of the coastal weather but if I can, I want to do some sort of trip out to the islands of the Buccaneer Archipelago and see the Horizontal Waterfall. I've seen a program on television about it and it is wild, dangerous and awesome. The well-known Australian character who made the film was in his element as they are waters that he knows well and even he got into trouble when his boat got stranded and he had to be very ingenious to get it back into the water on the next incoming tide. This is my dream and I also want to go snorkelling at Ningaloo Reef. Other than those two things there is nothing that I really 'itch' to do and if it came to choosing between the two I've mentioned I'd opt for the Buccaneer Archipelago.

Chapter 15

BUNGLE BUNGLE MASSIF 1

John reckons that he is seeing a different side to me than he has seen before and that he saw some of it when we climbed Kings Canyon and I replied that it has always been there but has been buried a lot because I am a mother and I needed to be there for my children. I did a complete flip when I became pregnant with my first child and suddenly became scared of climbing a ladder and felt sick on a garden swing! Prior to that, the more dangerous the better but now they are all grown up and I am free to be wilder at last!

I have a feeling though that we are going to be inundated with wonderful and tempting trips throughout Western Australia and in future, if it is an organised trip, then I am going to think more than twice before spending the crazy prices that some of these companies charge. We did a full day trip up the Adelaide River for $100 with a hot and freshly cooked lunch plus all drinks and snacks and when you compare that with sunset cruise on Lake Argyle with a drink of champagne and nibbles for $85 it is relatively very expensive for such a short trip.

SOUTHERN LAKE ARGYLE

It is often the funny things that you remember the most anyway such as Callie with the crab on the beach, the frog landing on John's nose or for John today, seeing a crocodile on the first hole of the golf course. John does not know who was the most surprised, him or the croc.

The young guy in the caravan next to us had his car bonnet up a few moments ago and John called out 'If it ain't broke, don't fix it' and I added 'Stop listening too hard'. He grinned at us and slammed the bonnet shut and said he'd turn up the volume on his radio and drove off. It's great to be our age and have so much wisdom and advice to offer to the younger generation.

John went to get the weekend paper and was told that they have no idea when or if the newspapers will arrive! Sometimes they do get some on a Sunday or Monday but they are snapped up fast. Is this Australia or a third world country! Ten days for post, if more than an ordinary letter and perhaps no weekend paper!!

John got picked up for his flight over the **Lake Argyle**, **The Bungle Bungles** and **Argyle Diamond Mine**, he thought the view was mind blowing from the air. The dogs and I went back to the **Top Rockz Gallery** because I wanted to buy Helen a piece of the rare Zebra rock. Then I went into town to visit an Aboriginal art gallery and asked why two exhibits were priced at $5,000 when there were others which had so obviously taken months to paint and they were only $1,000. I was told it was like any artist's work and whether their work had been exhibited and if so, the resulting demands for that person's work. I asked how they got their work exhibited and was told it was up to the Aboriginal groups to promote their own work. I pushed even further and asked whether it was to do with government funding and was told that it is. So, as in commerce all over the world it appears to be who you know rather than how good your work is!

I again fell for one piece and it was only priced at $1000 odd. I say 'only' because most were so overpriced that it was ridiculous. However, we have seen some extraordinary Aboriginal art, being exquisite in detail and some of their landscape paintings are wonderful.

WINDHAM - VIEW FROM TOP OF LOOKOUT

Next stop was the Tourist Information Centre again and I zoomed in on information from Derby to find out about the trip I want to do. There was one three day trip with no price listed! However, there is a trip operated by Kimberley Seaplanes which costs $395 (at the moment). Apparently you land on Talbot Bay and transfer to a boat. I had to get a photocopied leaflet as the Information Centre had run out of them so they are very popular and I hope it is not hard to book because the boat does not look as though it can accommodate many passengers. The leaflet tells you to bring 'a sense of adventure' and that's exactly what I want. It also strongly recommends that you arrange your own travel insurance!

WYNDHAM - JOHN ILLUSTRATES THE SIZE OF STATUES

WYNDHAM 15th August 2006

Having done my duty by catching up with this diary, printing photographs for our album and also for my family and having shopped the last couple of days, it was time to do some sightseeing so today we went to Wyndham. The journey from Kununurra to Wyndham is very pretty but the only good thing about Wyndham is that the petrol is 13c cheaper <u>per litre</u> yet it is only 100 kilometres from Kununurra. There are only two good heritage buildings that we saw and they belonged to the Police and the Council. We went to the top of the **Bastion Range** to see the view from the **Five Rivers Lookout** and we certainly had a wonderful view. I wouldn't tow a caravan up there though as there are several hair-pin bends.

ANOTHER OF ROCKS AT MINI BUNGLES

We saw the 20 metre crocodile made out of 55kg of welding rods, 10 rolls of bird mesh and 5 cubic metres of concrete! We also stopped for a while at the **Dreamtime Statues** and they are magnificent. They are located in a park and are huge. They are statues of Aboriginals and there is a serpent, a kangaroo and a family camp site set up as well as a couple of other things.

We had also been to see the **Grotto** on the way which was interesting and we drove to the **Wildlife Park** (I think that's what it is called but cannot check as it is not in the brochures on Wyndham). They have crocodiles there but they shut the park quite early in the afternoon. Our best experience was when we were down at the boat ramp near the **Wyndham Town Hotel** because there was a ramp floating on the water that had been joined in sections for the fishermen to grab a hold of and the tide had turned about half an hour previously and as we were on it we could feel the force of the water as it ebbed back to sea. Jack has not got sea legs and although he ran along it without a thought he suddenly realised that he was rocking and he started to walk very unsteadily back to firm land with his rear legs apart!

We were upset that the old buildings in town are not maintained and will literally collapse if nothing is done about them. The original store, which was built by the Durack family, has just been left to rot. It has also been a Post Office and all the old boxes are still there. It has a 'For Sale' sign on it. Likewise there was a small shop on the other side of the road that caught our eye. It had the old sign writing over the top which told us that it belonged to a Chinese tailor years ago. There were many other buildings boarded up that had obviously been used commercially in the past. It was so sad to see and considering that there was not one coffee shop, nor tourist type shop we cannot understand why the Council has not taken them over and restored them and encouraged the community to lease them for commercial purposes. This area is right by the waterfront and we just cannot understand it. We felt it was a sad town and had already been warned by two couples only to only go there for a day trip and to take our lunch with us!

On our return journey we didn't do the 36 kilometre round trip to see the Boab Tree that was once used as a temporary prison. It's a long way to see a tree that I do not even like! However, quite close to Kununurra we turned off on a dirt road and travelled about six kilometres to reach **Valentine Springs** and it was so beautiful there. John, Jack and Callie had a swim. If you have a four wheel drive you can travel a further 10 kilometres, turn left at a T-junction and there is a track on the left which will take you to **Middle Springs** where there is a beautiful swimming area and waterfall. If you climb up above there you should find some secluded rock pools. Another turn off takes you to **Black Rock Falls** but all these areas are obviously subject to the weather conditions at the time.

Chapter 16

DERBY-25th August 2006

We arrived yesterday and immediately booked a seaplane flight out to the horizontal waterfalls for tomorrow. We will be going through the falls after transferring to a speedboat. The following day we head off to Broome as we want to get further south as soon as possible because of the heat.

During the journey from Kununurra to Derby a flock of Kites decided to attack our motor home and as I was following John I got showered in feathers! However, they all seemed to return to the nearby tree quite safely which surprised John as he thought at least one of them would have killed itself. We declined to stay at either **Halls Creek** or **Fitzroy Crossing**, preferring instead to stay at two of the several off road sites provided. The initial part of the journey was really pretty with all the hills and ranges. Sitting in a car for nearly three days does not help you to keep your weight down though and when I saw a photo of myself the other day I realised that I am getting decidedly tubby! I thought I would be exercising in the pool on arrival but ended up going straight into our shower in order to get cooler. John's right arm got burnt whilst driving here on the third day! Although I have tinted windows, I had added an extra sun shield to my right driving window and I had my hat and sunglasses on in the Ute!

Yesterday we spent an hour in the Information Centre watching films of the beautiful scenery of the **Kimberley National Park** and the rivers and waters of this area and Broome, including the Horizontal Waterfalls. Then we went down to the Jetty to watch the sun go down but there is nowhere that we could find where you can safely swim here and the caravan parks do not seem to have pools so the only choice is to pay $3 (or $2 for Pensioners) and go to the town swimming pool.

Today we had a look around town and then went to find out where the kennels are that we have booked the dogs into and to find the airport. Then we went to find the **Prison Boab Tree** but I did not take photos because the photographs I saw of the prisoners chained together (who sometimes had to walk miles like that) made me feel sick. The tree is at least 1000 (one guide book says 1500) years old and has a girth of 14.7 metres with a fairly small hole in the bottom of the trunk which allowed the prisoners to be placed inside until transferred to another jail. At least they got some shade as even now, in winter, the temperatures have been around 36C or more during the day.

The Gibb River Road is famous in Australia for being one of the most challenging roads to drive in the country and some silly people have tried it in two-wheel drive vehicles, which is fine if you don't mind the car being almost totally destroyed. For a start, even in the dry season you have two river crossings. In the wet season it is very dangerous. I told John he can now say he's driven on the Gibb River Road and just omit the fact that we only went a few kilometres on the bitumen to find the property with the kennels! We were told to take the second turning right and we would find it on the left on top of the first 'sand dune'. The kennels were nestled in a tropical rainforest setting full of exotic pets and was enchanting, we felt that our dogs would be very content there for the day.

I had a funny conversation with a very jolly and somewhat inebriated middle-aged Aboriginal man in the Woolworth's car park. He was an attractive man with a constantly smiling face and he engaged me in conversation whilst his poor wife sat in the driving seat of their car asking him periodically to please get in so that they could go. He started by asking me where I came from and when I said Brisbane he replied 'Oh, the other side of town'. He reckons that we all come here to see the Southern Cross as you can't see it anywhere else and talked a lot about the different star formations. He is actually quite right about the brilliance of the stars here. I stood outside the other night when we were staying off road and it was pitch black outside our van and as I directed my eyes to the sky there was this dazzling stellar display. It was breathtaking. I have never seen so many stars. Anyway, after a lengthy conversation about the stars he told me that our bathwater goes down the plughole the opposite way around to the water in Europe and added for good measure that he knows all these things because of what he reads. He was roaring with laughter about this phenomenon.

John has been approached by a couple of Aboriginal men who have asked for money and he finds it very hard to say no but they get more money than we do from the Government! A couple of men have started to approach me but have changed their minds and I have felt both times that when I looked at them in their eyes they just could not bring themselves to do so. I felt that it was more out of respect for me than because they feel ashamed of begging. One guy held out his palm showing thirty cents in it and asked John for enough to buy a pie. It's a good ploy but we know by the state of them that it will go straight towards more alcohol. I have found some of the Aboriginal women very easy to talk to and laugh with and they are the first to offer help when you cannot find something in a shop. I have the habit of talking out loud in shops when I can't find things and will suddenly say 'Eggs' as I'm looking around. One day I asked a woman if she would do all my shopping for me that day as she kept directing me to the products I wanted and could hardly get her shopping done but she continued to gently smile at me and carried on doing her shopping whilst simultaneously listening out for my next query. The children just want to know what 'make' Jack is (as do so many people every day) and then they want to know his name and Callie's name and before you know it you are chatting with ten or twelve little kids all crammed into one car and there are smiles, eyes and giggles all pouring out of the windows or open doors. I have rarely heard an Aboriginal child cry and most seem so happy. Not all, but certainly the majority.

HORIZONTAL FALLS & 'THOUSAND ISLAND COAST'

We've done it – we've experienced one of my dreams. I was enthralled when I saw it on television and asked John if we were going near there. When he said that we would come here I agreed to come on this long trip. I had been prevaricating about making a decision about this trip for so long and we had talked of John doing it on his own but knew that I had to do it if only to experience this phenomenon.

DERBY - 25

So for once I was out of bed early and actually awake, as I was so keen to go whereas I usually sit around like a zombie for the first hour after getting up! We flew out from Derby Airport in a seaplane and landed at **Talbot Bay** and the camera was clicking away all through the journey as there was so much to see. When we landed there was a floating platform where we transferred to a speedboat to travel around Talbot Bay and through the Horizontal Falls.

DERBY - 2

David Attenborough described them as 'one of the greatest natural wonders of the world'. The sea rises by about 8 metres and the water is forced between two rocks with such force that it creates these horizontal falls. There was only about a couple of metres difference in height when we arrived there but the speedboat ride left us screaming for more. We sat astride the 'seat' of the jet-speedboat and gripped with our legs and the woman behind me was having the same adrenalin experience as me and so we all went back through again.

The plane journey is amazing too because there are so many islands to see and the colour of the ocean is just glorious. We gained a bonus period of time out there because when we arrived back at the pontoon there was a problem with some of our passengers whose boat did not turn up to collect them to go on their deep sea fishing trip. It was eventually decided that we would go and find the boat ourselves and find out what had happened to the skipper so off we all went again in the speedboat. We alighted onto the big boat and spent some time aboard which was quite interesting.

There was a huge glass fronted freezer and similar fridge side by side as well as an upright fridge/freezer. I was interested in how they supplied power to such large appliances and was told by generator. I asked about the fuel for the generator and was told that the freezer alone cost some ridiculous amount to run per day and so went my dream of living on a similar boat! There was a huge lounge and dining room and a kitchen bigger than mine at home, several cabins (bedrooms) and a large bathroom and laundry. A large screen T.V with an ample supply of videos and DVD'S along with big, soft lounge furniture invited you to sit down and nestle in and experience deep relaxation. The men had brought along a vast amount of fresh produce so that must have been pre-arranged and when I asked about the alcohol they told me that there was too much for them to bring out so that had been sent out before in crates! They had flown up from Perth, driven in a hired car to Derby airport and had flown out with us to go onto this trip so they had probably been up all night but their excitement was infectious and it was with reluctance that we left them to enjoy their cruise.

We returned via a different route and as I had the sun on my side I passed the camera to John as we had purposely sat on opposite sides of the plane. We flew over the **Paspaley Pearl Farm** and I wondered what it must be like to work there every day. I suppose you would take the surrounding scenery for granted after a while but it is quite unimaginable to me. Pearl farming is hard work though so I suppose you'd be glad of a break from it and to get back to 'civilisation'. Funny word that because it means different things to different people as I am fast finding out on this trip. Civilisation might mean one shop rather than a town or city. That's the trouble with this travelling because we all adjust like chameleons to our surroundings and when you are continually moving it is quite unsettling. Just when you get used to a town atmosphere you are back in the wilderness or just when you are getting used to being by the sea you are back in the outback. You miss the traffic when you've adjusted to it and hate it when you've been travelling for a thousand kilometres and have only seen a handful of other vehicles. And so it was when we returned to Derby having been out over the 'Thousand Island Coast' that I felt like an alien and wanted to go back to Talbot Bay. My photographs will be much treasured.

We stayed on at Kununurra until I had seen the dentist, who charged so much that under half the cost was covered by my health insurance and usually it costs me nothing! He also did a lousy job so I wish I hadn't bothered. He didn't polish the teeth, charged me for a 'comprehensive check' when all he did was noted what teeth I had got and which were filled but he didn't even know what type of filling I had done in one of them! He did not check any of my fillings and when I got back to the bus I saw plaque around the gums of my lower teeth. The cost of everything up here is frightening.

BROOME 1st September 2006

We've been here nearly a week, mainly because the bus periodically overheated whilst we were travelling between Kununurra and Broome. It is a distance of nearly 1000 kilometres so we broke up the travelling by staying off road for a couple of nights. I had a look at the overnight camp spot called the **Mary Pool** rest area but it was very crowded, the bridge looked past its used-by-date and the water was covered in green algae so I advised John, who was still on the highway, to carry on.

So we passed through **Halls Creek** and the next day stopped at **Fitzroy Crossing** and drove around it in the Ute but decided to move on to the **Ellendale** overnight rest stop. We had been told about the one on the right hand side by a dam but we came to one on the left first and when we saw that we could go right up the hill to catch any breezes that we may be lucky enough to catch, we decided that this was for us. Fitzroy Crossing has been consistently recording the highest temperatures in Western Australia over the last few weeks. We were also too tired to go any further anyway and one of our travel books said that the one a little further on can be noisy. I went outside at about 11pm and it was pitch black except for a camp fire further down the hill which was still dancing with flames. I looked up and felt showered by a million stars.

The radiator is being drained and the thermostat checked as I write and I am sitting inside the bus trying to catch up on this diary. The temperatures have been around 35C or more and we are well ready to get further south and when I phoned ahead to a caravan park down the coast he asked me if there was anyone left in Broome! He told me that he has plenty of room as the rush down there is now over. The motorhome has to get an MOT (Roadwothy) certificate and John had a special form allowing us to get the test done in WA.

CABLE BEACH - 29TH AUGUST 2006

The beach is twenty-two kilometres long with white sand lapped by the beautiful turquoise colour of the Indian Ocean. You can book yourself a camel ride along Cable Beach at sunset and the road signs warn you to watch out for wandering camels.

LIGHTHOUSE - NOTICE WARNS UNSTABLE ROCKS!

You can take the dogs on **Cable Beach** at the end, towards the lighthouse, but if you go to the other end where the rocks are you need to drive around the rocks to the other side. Make sure you know how high the tide is coming in as you can get stuck around there. This is also the nudist's beach so do not let the dogs get too near to the people there because you know how your dog is likely to greet them and you may not be too popular.

Dogs are generally not welcome in Broome though, especially near the beaches and although our caravan park takes dogs this year they will no longer accept them in the future. That will mean I believe that there will be no parks left in Broome that accepts dogs. There is an area that they use for caravans and motor homes when the parks are full but we have been told that it is nearly as dear as our caravan park and you are not allowed to use the electricity for any main items such as air conditioners, toasters and electric kettles etc. I need the air conditioner and so does our fridge!

If you are into crocodiles then you must visit **Malcolm Douglas's Crocodile Farm** and it was he who persuaded me that I must see the Horizontal Falls when I was watching one of his documentaries. I also wanted to visit **Cape Leveque** and the **Dampier Peninsular** but it is four-wheel drive country only and we have decided that we saw some of the coastline from the air and must cut back on some of the trips we are doing, mainly because of the cost of everything here and the fact that the gas and petrol are so extraordinarily high in this part of Australia.

Yesterday we visited **The Shell House** which has an extraordinary display of shells, crustaceans and preserved fish (over 6000 of them) from around the world which are not for sale and many shells and jewellery and ornaments which are. I asked about a ship made of mother-of-pearl that I had seen in a leaflet but it had been sold the day before and I forgot to ask to see the clock which is a large shell. I could not resist purchasing a handcrafted mother-of-pearl necklace set in sterling silver for my daughter for her Birthday. She had wanted to come here and as she can't I will take something from here to give to her.

There are six kinds of pearls here, those being Cultured Pearls, Australian South Sea Pearls, Mabe Pearls, Natural Pearls, Freshwater Pearls and Keshi Pearls. The Australian South Sea Pearls are also called 'Broome Pearls' and can be white or shades of a blue/grey or yellow. Some shine with a green or pinkish tinge. The Broome Pearls are grown in the silver or gold-lipped pearl oyster. We went into a gallery to have a look at some of them but we really had no comprehension of what to look for!

We drove around the coastline surrounding Broome one afternoon (it is on a peninsular with water three sides) stopping here and there to look at beaches and views and when we reached **Cable Beach** we were delighted to be able to drive onto it and along it quite safely in our Ute and we all went for a swim. As you can imagine, we are having problems keeping Jack cool and he went further into the sea than Callie which he has never done before. Mind you, it was at Cable Beach which is supposed to be one of the top five beaches in the world and Jack does have excellent taste.

You cannot jump in and have a swim wearing your normal swimming attire between November and May because of the of the Box Jelly Fish. I read in a publication called Pearl Coast Magazine that you should douse a sting in vinegar and 'if in distress' seek medical advice. Vinegar went 'out of the window' long ago as far as the advice I hear on T.V and my advice would be 'Get to the nearest hospital pronto'! Scream, shout, call an ambulance but do not amble off to the local supermarket looking for vinegar! I have even better advice than that – just don't swim during the months when the Box Jelly fish are around.

Unfortunately we are not here at the right time to see '**The Staircase to the Moon**' from Town Beach on Roebuck Bay when the full moon reflects what looks like a staircase down to the sand at low tide. This occurs between March and October and in the Visitors Information Centre they give you a booklet which gives you the dates for this year and next year and another booklet also give you the dates for the current month. There are also the dates and times that you can see the dinosaur footprints which are 120 million years old and can be seen at low tide at **Gantheaume Point**. There is a cast of the footprints at the top of the cliff if you don't manage to walk out to them. Whilst there, one can also go down to **Anastasias's Pool** (it was full of water when we were there) which the lighthouse keeper made for his arthritic wife.

Riddell Beach is named after a pearling fleet operator called Captain Riddell who was murdered by some of his crew in 1899. The Chinese cook welched on the murderers and they were arrested. A British explorer called William Dampier came here twice in the 1600's and Roebuck Bay was named after his ship.

However Broome only became well known around the world when a new kind of pearl oyster was found in 1861 and it was big. Mother-of-pearl was used for many items such as cutlery handles, buttons and jewellery and it was valuable. The King Sound area was, and is, known as 'The Graveyard' and we saw that area from the air when we flew from Derby. The divers therefore moved to Eighty Mile Beach and Roebuck Bay. Before World War 1 Broome supplied 80% of the world's mother-of-pearl but when the war broke out everything stopped and hundreds of tonnes rotted in the warehouses. Pearling started up again, despite being interrupted by the depression and a cyclone, in the 1930's. There were 500 Japanese divers working here when World War II broke out and they were confined. The pearl luggers were also burnt or moved to stop the Japanese from using them if they invaded.

Broome was bombed which was news to John and I. We had thought that only Darwin had been bombed and then only minimally and how wrong we were about that! On March 3rd 1942 Broome was attacked by ten Japanese warplanes. They destroyed 16 flying boats in the bay and seven aircraft at the airport. The flying boats had women and children on board and although they do not seem to know the exact death toll it is believed at least 100 of them were killed. On days when there are negative tides you can see some of the flying boat wrecks.

After the war the Japanese pearling fleets were not operating so Broome did not have to compete with them as in the past. When plastic buttons were invented in America the mother-of-pearl industry became worthless until it was realised that Australian cultured pearls mature in two years instead of the normal four years and that they are twice the size of those in Japan. By the 1970's Broome was producing 60-70% of the world's large cultured pearls. Pearls are back in fashion this year too and I cannot recall them being so popular since I was a small girl.

Chapter 17

Sunday 3ʳᵈ September

My brother's Birthday and I've forgotten it again! I'm on the hunt for two pesky flies is our motor home. I was thinking whilst we drove the endless boring kilometres from Broome to this Roadhouse (petrol station) and caravan park, that we have seen very few 'real' flies. By 'real' I mean the big black, horrible flies that like to vomit on your food before they eat it. I find it odd that we've hardly seen any and that I can recall seeing more in the U.K in summer and that reminded me that the worst time there was a very hot day on a farm enjoying a wonderful family reunion. So, I decided that when we see all those flies in movies and it looks like you cannot open your mouth in Australia, they must be scenes taken in stockyards and on cattle stations etc.

Well having driven over 300ks to **Sandfire Roadhouse** I pulled in to see peacocks, then chickens, some camels and a magnificent bull! As John said, it felt more like 450ks as it was such a boring journey. Anyway, we now have some flies! I had bought a hat with a fly shade over it on the day that we went to Kings Canyon and I haven't had the opportunity to test it yet. To be honest it is hardly worth getting it out just because we have two flies in the van!

It has been so very hot and we were so happy to leave Broome. John reckons he was disappointed with Broome. I had no expectations so I wasn't exactly disappointed but you can see Broome in an afternoon. As I've mentioned above, there are things you can do but unless you have the money to come to a resort at Broome for a fully-catered holiday where you want to laze around by the pool or on the beach and take the odd, short excursion I wouldn't bother! I'd rather spend the money going to north Queensland and sailing around the islands on a yacht. There is far more to see and do and the weather is better – usually. It's been rather wet up there this year.

I burst out laughing the other night when they said on T.V that it was the first day of spring and said to John that if the temperatures are in the high thirties in winter then what on earth is spring like? On T.V they say the temperature has reached 35C or whatever but I have no idea where they get their records from because it was a lot hotter than that on some of the days we were there and it was getting worse by the day.

During the journey I saw a cyclist and he looked fairly elderly and he would have been about 100ks from Broome, heading in that direction. We have seen many cyclists with heavy loads who are obviously travelling around Australia this way. One couple were cycling away from Alice Springs and it was 1pm and blazing hot and they both looked ill. I still feel that I should have stopped because I wouldn't have been surprised if the girl collapsed. They were cycling uphill but were so slow that they could have walked faster and they were wobbling all over the place. It's beyond my comprehension – not the cycling but cycling in the middle of the day under a blazingly hot sun. Also, most of the roads we have seen the cyclists on have been hundreds of kilometres from the next town and the scenery has been endlessly boring.

I've just had a look at my photos of Palm Cove and Port Douglas, not far from Cairns and the Hinze Dam at the Gold Coast (all in Queensland) just to get some beautiful water scenes and green hills in my mind instead of the endless flat plains that we've seen today.

John learned a hard lesson on stopping off- road for coffee stops. After we left Broome we pulled over as usual for a break after driving for an hour or so, then carried on the journey as usual. John noticed a dead cow with legs in the air on his left, funny he thought I saw one on my right on the way to our last coffee stop! To his horror he realised we were going back the way we had previously travelled. 40-50 klms back the other way, the bush looks much the same in these parts and he had turned the wrong way on leaving our last stop for coffee!!! 100+ klms for nothing, always remember which way you turn off after a stop.

Tomorrow we will stop on the main road and John will jump in the Ute so that we can drive together down the eight kilometres of dirt road to Eighty Mile Beach. We had intended to stay there at the caravan park and my RACQ book states that dogs are allowed but when John phoned the park he received a very emphatic 'No dogs' response so we will move further south where we are more welcome!

We will come to the town of Port Hedland first which doesn't thrill me much because I have heard so much about the detention centre which used to house refugees who were seeking sanctuary in Australia. Because they were called 'illegal immigrants' instead of 'refugees' by our Federal Government they felt they had the right to lock them up. Some little kids couldn't remember what it was like outside because they were there for four years and had been very young on arrival. They could see the sea, I'm told, but weren't allowed to go in it or play on the beach. What they did witness were people who had sewn their lips together in protest and despair to try and get attention, and people who were on hunger strikes and hopefully they didn't have relatives who committed suicide there. What I do know is that one teenage girl, pleading for help through the wire, told my son that if he wrote to her he would have to write to a number, not address it to her name. Just like the Nazis our Government numbered them.

I am so ashamed of some of the actions of our Federal Government, like trying to convince us that those people were the type that would throw their children over a boat and into the sea, which turned out to be more lies, that I really don't want to go anywhere near Port Headland. I think I'll let John go and look for himself and then we can get well away from there. It does not matter to me that it is no longer used to house refugees because it will just remind me that they have been put somewhere else instead. There are those refugees of course who gave up applying for entry and agreed to return home and some have received further violations or even death. A Chinese woman who was sent back when eight months pregnant had said that her Government would abort her baby and they did.

Our Government needs to be tough on security issues but it severely lacks compassion. Actually it is not tough on security issues because unless you arrive and leave from a major air terminal, there will be little or no security checks on you or your baggage. I landed at Maryborough airfield once from a light plane seeking a toilet and it was closed and there wasn't a sole to be seen.

I've just had a visitor and he wouldn't go away. A beautiful, very large peacock and he displayed his plumage to me so I think he fancied me. I tried to shoo him away because I thought John would arrive back with the dogs at any moment but he didn't agree and pooped in front of me and then sat down again. I came into the van and tried to ignore him but he kept watching me through the windows. I sat down to eat my dinner and he saw my head move and his head slowly rose like a crane lifting up and he peered at me through the window. When I hid, he eventually left!

Meanwhile John was talking to a young couple on a month's holiday. They had flown up to Broome, collected a small campervan there and were driving back down to Perth. It was their first day of driving and they feel the same that we do about the journey. You'd be better off travelling by coach because at least you can move around and read a book or something or even have a nap. It is early days yet but we wouldn't return to this northern part of Western Australia again. If you do come then ensure you do not have a dog and that you do have a four wheel drive vehicle and make the National Parks your destination. We met many people at the caravan park in Broome who came for one night only and left, not because they had to but because they chose to.

I wonder sometimes whether people take holidays on their own doorsteps. For example, I have been looking at the photographs between the Southern Highlands of NSW down to the coastal town of Kiama and onwards to Melbourne and the variety of beautiful scenery still astonishes me. Whether you like rural scenes or rivers, lakes and sea or perhaps quaint old villages, that stretch of land has so many outstanding places to stay and when we were there we were swimming in the sea in Autumn. There are little spots like Gorilla Bay (which isn't on our map) where you can camp right by the beach, or look south along the coast from Broulee Headland and be awed by the layers of waves rushing towards the long, beautiful sandy beach, or visit Lake Conjola and watch the sun set or drive through Kangaroo Valley and up to Moss Vale in the highlands and visit the beautiful villages around there. There is always this mass exodus from South Australia, Victoria and even from Queensland to escape the winter months but when we were in New South Wales we met many people who stayed within their own State and just went a little further north to another beautiful part of their State. Some Queenslanders do that too but my point is, is that so many of the people we have met from South Australia and Victoria go north once a year but don't seem to holiday in their own State or if they do, it's only to visit a friend or for a weekend. Australia is so big that any time not spent on the roads seems a good time to me! However, if you do need to go on the roads then you need to stop and visit the places en route which are so beautiful and get off the highways yet the people we talk to seem to go straight to the inland highways and high-tail it up to Queensland in under a week and see nothing of their own wonderful coastline. We had nowhere to visit en route today and I now realise the value of having the choice.

No doubt there will be a lot of people who will disagree with me and perhaps they belong to caravan and motor home clubs and go away every month to a different place but I'm sure they often visit the same old places too. So here's a challenge. Everyone who has the mobility and the time and money should visit every town and every bit of coastline within their own State prior to leaving it to visit another. I won't do this, but I should. I'm just as happy to stay at home all year around and not go anywhere as I love being at home but there are those who are restless like my husband and there are so many places he hasn't really visited properly within hours of our own home. Has he been to Kingaroy and tasted Flo's scones? No, of course he hasn't. How much of the area surrounding Toowoomba does he know? Very little. Would he even consider going to the Toowoomba Flower Show? No but if there were cars there instead you might tempt him there but somehow I doubt it. That reminds me. For the last two nights at our caravan park at Broome we were blanketed by the noise of the speedway racing which was happening almost alongside the park. John went the first night and loved it but didn't go last night. We had to keep all the windows closed but still had difficulty hearing the television and on both nights they did not stop until midnight! When all had gone quiet last night John coughed and I jumped as I felt so jangled and kind of nervous. It took me a long time to settle down to sleep. However, if you have a boat and like fishing then Broome could be your oyster – quite literally and you may even be lucky enough to find one with a pearl in it.

Most Australian baby native animals are called Joeys. Thought you might like to know that because John and I didn't! We thought the name was only used for baby kangaroos and wallabies. Apparently we should all check, if we see a dead Kangaroo, that there is not a Joey in the pouch and if we find one we can take them to any vet because all Australian vets will look after native animals free of charge. We didn't know that either.

We left the roadhouse around ten o'clock and went 45ks further along before we turned off the road for the 8ks to **Eighty Mile Beach.** There was only one entrance at the end which stated that no dogs were allowed and it was the caravan park, so we ignored that and drove towards the beach because they cannot possibly own it all! They had kindly put up a notice by the beach saying that day visitors were allowed! Anyway, we took the dogs with us and nobody minded at all. As we walked over the sand dune we stopped as the vista took our breath away. It is so very beautiful. The white sand and the stunning turquoise ocean with a darker blue line in the distance and the sky yet another shade of blue on the horizon. It was a clear, bright sunny day and everything sparkled. The seashells sparkled and we collected some because they had patterns on them and holes at the top just ready to be threaded and made into necklaces. John was as fascinated as I was and he was collecting them faster than I could find them. We had left the bus back on the main road and were glad that we had as the corrugations under the sand road shook us about a fair bit and when we got back to the bus we had a quick cup of coffee and set off again. It was achingly boring until we came across fire on both sides of the road and thick, black smoke from grass fires. I can't call them bush fires because there was nothing growing as high as a bush anywhere and it has been like that for the last two days. The fires were extensive and flames were leaping about but I was fascinated rather than scared. I recalled that when we were having coffee John had casually said that if the grass caught fire it would be hard to stop it spreading. He's saying things and they are happening just as it was doing on our first long trip.

John had also mentioned breaking down or something so of course that had to happen too. He blew a rear tyre and we were very lucky that it happened 45ks out of Port Headland because when I put the phone on I found that at last we had phone reception. I also managed to locate quickly (and quite by accident) the names and phone numbers I had written down about a year ago of the major tyre companies. I phoned one of them and the recorded message kept asking me for my postcode and again, luckily, I could lay my hands on a postcode book and frantically look it up whilst the recorded voice kept saying 'Sorry, you did not give me enough digits' and I found the four digit number and keyed it in before the call was cut off. I was put through to Port Headland and the young girl there gave me a mobile telephone number for the guy who does the trucks and he was with us within half an hour and the spare was put on in 10 minutes. He departed with our tyre (what was left of it) and didn't even ask for any money! John's jack would not budge the wheel nuts as they had been tightened by pressure tools. Also he had not realised that the outboard tyre was left hand thread.

Then came the fun part as we had to find somewhere to stay in **Port Hedland** and one park did not take dogs, another had closed down a month ago and the other park said they were full up. It got progressively worse from then on because as we came into Port Hedland we were both struck dumb with the horror of the place. We have both agreed tonight that neither of us can think of another place we have ever seen in our lives which is so ugly and there is this weird smell everywhere. Between us we have seen a fair bit of the world and some places that we had thought before we pretty awful but this place takes the cake. A man we spoke to said that nobody comes here unless it's for the ore. We are at the caravan park I was told was full but that's a story in itself and too boring to write about. However, we spent an hour running around this place and ended up seeking help at a park that I knew wouldn't be able to help us as it is a group that never allows dogs but the receptionist there got us in here. That park was by the coast and even that area was not pretty. When I told the receptionist here that we would probably be here for more than one night because we would have to wait for a tyre (ours are very hard to get hold of and our last two came from Perth to the Gold Coast) she insisted on only booking us in for one night in case we changed our minds! She's quite right because we don't want to stay another night and have decided that we may even just pick the old rim up and move on down the coast and just pray that we don't get another flat tyre between towns!

Chapter 18

W.A. APPROACHING FIRE

What a day of contrasts. John said he wanted to see Port Headland and we've certainly done a fairly big tour of it already and several times got caught with a red light at the railway crossings which means that you turn off your engines because the ore cars can be over three kilometres long. They also mine export salt here, ninety percent of which goes to Asia. The engineering works which stretch so widely that you see little else except for the roads, along with the salt mines equates to a very ugly panorama. I thought back to this morning when we were on Eighty Mile Beach and the difference within a few hours overwhelmed me. I was also very tired and by the time we were setting up the van it was 6pm and the dogs were wondering if we'd forgotten to give them their 4.30pm dinner.

ROEBOURNE (KARRATHA)

Having settled into a caravan park at Roebourne, which has some lovely old buildings and having visited the town of Karratha today to get shopping and organise our van inspection, we have decided that we will probably stay on here as we do not like the park that we could stay at in Karratha. We have limited choices elsewhere because of the size of the bus and the dogs. It is also nice to be outside the town albeit that we are thirty kilometres or so north of Karratha. Here we have the river and wildflowers and space and it is so relaxing.

We went into the village yesterday, thinking that we would travel further but got caught up in the Museum and Information Centre watching a film and enjoying free coffee! We ended up purchasing the film as we enjoyed it so much and it covers so much of what we have seen and some of what we couldn't see because of the dogs, such as **El Questro**. That is an area of extraordinary beauty but dogs are not allowed and you need a four wheel drive vehicle.

I cannot stress enough that if you make the effort to come to this area do not bring dogs and have a four wheel drive. I know I've said it before but we have missed out on so many of the National Parks because there have been no kennels available or because of the condition of the roads. I have certainly changed my mind about what we need if we are to continue our travelling.

I do not wish to make beds up every day, nor tents but if you have a four wheel drive vehicle which is just big enough that you can sleep off the ground and you have storage for kitchen items, clothes and a couple of chairs and table, plus tool storage and room for extra fuel and water cans then you have everything you need – plus a couple of spare tyres! We are still trying to source another tyre and are stuck here without a spare.

The distance between even the smallest of towns is too vast here to take any chances with tyres or mechanics and they often do not cater for the jobs you need doing or have the supplies that you need. For instance, I asked yesterday if there is a chemist here at Roebourne and there isn't and you have to travel to Karratha. This area around Roebourne also includes Point Sampson, Cossack and Wickham but there is not one chemist here.

We really enjoyed wandering around the general store here as they sell such surprising items and too many for me to list here. John contemplated buying a mini electric organ and I bought a board for my swimming exercises as my old one had cracked. We contemplated whether or not to buy a frozen kangaroo tail for the dogs but it looked like it still had the skin and hairs on it so I rapidly changed my mind. We had actually gone in to buy bread and milk! I saw a teapot for $1.99 whereas the same teapot in a supposedly cheap, bargain store in the town of Karratha was $2.99. On the subject of prices, I was reading The International Express the other day and in England they are horrified at the petrol price rises but when I worked it out they are paying a $1 a litre less than we are here in W.A. Roll on Perth where the fuel prices are lower!

We are experiencing rain and it has been so long that we panicked. The awning rattled so we rolled it back up, we put the dogs in the Ute to keep them dry and I even shut the roof hatches. However we left the front door open and John's slippers and the carpet are now wet! It's really rather pleasant as yesterday was hot and muggy. We visited the three other villages yesterday and were disappointed with **Point Samson**, were amazed to find a Woolworths store and large, drive-through bottle shop at **Wickham** and enjoyed seeing the renovation/reconstruction of the old buildings in **Cossack.**

I was struck by the beauty of a woman in a portrait photo on one the wall of one building and read that she had twelve children, seven girls and five boys and as I looked I wondered 'How?' She did not look strong enough to have more than one child, let alone twelve. Her husband ran the merchant store and I was trying to imagine her life and how hard it must have been for her. There was another family portrait with eight children and I realise that they would have been dressed in their best for the photograph but their best was magnificent. When I looked at the buttons, braids, ribbons, lace, pleats, belts and the cut of the men's suits and the females dresses I pondered on the hours of work involved. With a family that is ever increasing in size, both in numbers and physically, keeping up with the clothes for a family of ten must have been hard work in itself. Then there was the washing, the cooking, cleaning and probably bread-making and vegetable plots. I don't know, but it must have been hard especially as the husband was a shipwright, an undertaker and also built houses and his wife acted as a midwife and helped the sick when a doctor could not get there. How did they find the time to do everything? How hard was it when she was heavily pregnant in such a hot climate and where you have to wait for ships, which sometimes did not turn up, to hear news from home or for goods to arrive. How hard was it when there was the smallpox outbreak and the influenza epidemic? In Roebourne there is a plaque that tells of the first European settlers in the area and I was trying to imagine what it must have been like to be the first and only European woman. I was happy to read that they got along very well with the local Aboriginals and I'm sure she would have relished the Aboriginal women's company. I'm neither into museums, the pioneering history nor even explorers but during this journey I have been confronted by some of the things I have read and seen and I cannot help contemplating their lives and comparing it to our pampered present lifestyle. I wonder if they expected what they found to be their reality on arrival in Australia.

We drove around **Dampier** on the other side of town one afternoon but were glad that we had parked ourselves at Roebourne. The major industries are not near Roebourne but were very obvious at Dampier. Local industries include Dampier Salt, Hamersley Iron and the North West Shelf Gas Project. Between Karratha and Dampier it is very flat and there are salt pans along the roadway. I buy sea salt and it is expensive and I felt like jumping out of the car and collecting some of it, especially as most of it goes to Asia!

I really enjoyed our stay in Roebourne as we felt so relaxed at the park and every time we went into town it was a joy to return to. We managed to get two new tyres and it was discovered that not only were they needed but we now have to source two more from Perth! We received our post at last and John had the inspection on the R.V done so that we can renew our registration. That turned out to be such a complicated procedure and once done, we found out that the department in Queensland had already arranged for us to have an inspection done at the Gold Coast at a designated inspection point on a Sunday! Sometimes I think Government department workers are nuts. Last year we just got an inspection done wherever we wanted to and there's no hope of getting one done anywhere on the Gold Coast on a Sunday! He now has an 'Exemption Certificate' so that we can renew our registration in Western Australia. His stay at Roebourne was not quite so stress free as mine as he was fretting that the post wouldn't turn up in time and all sorts of other imaginary woes would befall us like the tyres not being ready and the motor home not passing inspection.

We left Roebourne knowing that we would be seeking an off-road site on our way to Exmouth and we found a wonderful place at the **Robe River Bridge** and camped right alongside the river. It is a 24 hour site only and we got there quite late. In the morning we packed up and were ready to go when I told John that I was just too exhausted to move, let alone drive a few hundred kilometres so we just moved the motor home into the shade and stayed for another night. We spent hours talking to some fellow travellers and enjoyed sitting by the river with them having a few drinks and hope that we bump into them further along the way. We all enjoyed swimming in the river and the dogs were in their element. We did not go to **Onslow** which is a small town on the coast. Onslow was also bombed during the war. We had thought that we would visit every town and hamlet but this northern area of W.A is already getting so hot that we just want to keep moving south as soon as possible.

Chapter 19

EXMOUTH

We will have stayed here for four nights by the time we leave and it hasn't turned out quite as well as we had hoped because of the receptionist here at the park who is unkind and aggressive. It's a shame because another male employee has been so helpful and kind and people seem to be leaving in droves and there are so many empty sites. Another couple who we had met before in Darwin have decided to leave and they are going to stay further down the coast at **Coral Bay** but unfortunately they do not have a site big enough for our van. They did offer us two sites at a cost of nearly $60 per night or more but we have declined! However, we will go there and swim in the ocean because the coral is within swimming distance of the shore and it is apparently stunningly beautiful. The coral is part of the **Ningaloo Reef** and we will be seeing it tomorrow as well because we are going out on a tour that starts at 7.30am and returns anywhere between 6pm to 7.30pm at night. We are so looking forward to it because we will be in a four wheel drive vehicle in the morning, then on the river and on the sea in the afternoon. All our meals will be provided and snorkelling equipment and we will be two of a fairly small group of people. So much of the area is again National Park and the dogs will just have to put up with the kennels again for a day as we are missing seeing too many places. Like the Horizontal Waterfalls, the Ningaloo Reef was on my personal 'must see' list. I think they were the only two things that I mentioned to John before we left! Kings Canyon was an unexpected bonus.

Exmouth is on a peninsula so we have endless beach all around us and have enjoyed a swim with the dogs. There is a huge amount of upmarket development taking place with a new marina, canal estates and blocks of land being sold for very high prices in the same area. It seems a shame because it will end up being like so many other places and will lose its uniqueness. The town itself is very small with a little mall area and a couple of minor supermarkets plus a few other shops and eateries. I went into most of the stores but either got ignored or received curt responses to my questions and was frustrated by the lack of visible pricing labels on the food in cafes, the origin of packaged fish in both food stores, and the fact that the staff would stand around talking in clothes shops and you felt like you were disturbing them if you asked a question. The worst was a woman busy cutting material in a craft shop. I was fascinated by her cutter and would have spent whatever the cost to have purchased one, plus the board she was using but she couldn't be bothered to help me and hardly looked up when I tried to ask her about them. I ended up in walking out and the only place I purchased anything was in the food store and for a sausage roll from a café being a rare occurrence for me but I just felt like buying something trashy to eat! Even that was double the price I would pay at the Gold Coast but I enjoyed sitting outside at their table in the shade and watching the world go by whilst I waited for John who was in the camping shop. A young girl told me that she needed to go to Carnarvon for tests as her doctor thinks she has an ulcer but she cannot afford to go so far and they have no facilities here to test her. She also told me that her friend is about to have a baby but has never had a scan because she too cannot afford to go all the way to Carnarvon. I wonder how the town will cope when the Marina fills up and all the swish houses are completed on their canal estates by the ocean. The only happy person we have met is a girl from Ireland who runs a café out of a van by the ocean and she is enthralled because she can see the whales migrating and she was pointing out one which was leaping out of the water. She returned to Ireland and came back here and she believes she is in paradise. Not a bad place to work with a view like that every day and not too many customers. When we arrived she was sitting talking to a friend and only two other customers had turned up by the time we left.

We have noticed a mark difference in the temperature after sundown and were delighted to feel slightly chilly the first night! During the day it is still very hot though and my back got slightly sunburnt quickly our first day here. It is also windy and we particularly notice it in the evenings and have had to put all the exterior awnings up for fear of them tearing or losing them altogether.

John admitted the other day that he couldn't do this travelling full time despite the fact that he is such a restless soul. He didn't actually say it outright but made a passing comment such as 'We've decided we couldn't live like this permanently'. The next day I revisited the subject by repeating what he'd said and asked 'This 'we' that you talk about – do you mean 'you' have decided?'

'Well, you don't want to do you?' he replied.

'I didn't ask you that. The thought came out of your head, not mine, so I'm asking if you feel that you couldn't?'

It is so hard for John to admit these sought of things so he always speaks as though it was my decision and I'm wising up to this.

'No, I couldn't but I have no idea what I'm going to do with myself because I'm so restless'

'That's your problem, not mine'.

'Well, could you live like this?' he asked me.

I hesitated. 'I'm pretty adaptable and I can adapt to my environment but it's not my dream. My dream is to still own land as land is very important to me and I really want to grow my own vegetables'.

I am careful washing broccoli and so forth because of insecticides and am very conscious of washing grapes well etc but was amazed to read the other day that it is very hard to wash capsicums so that there is no trace of insecticide left. I would have thought that they would have been one of the easiest. Capsicums are one of the very few vegetables that I don't worry about trying to buy that are organically grown. Today I read that we should always buy organic carrots as they mop up pesticides from the soil – like the soils vacuum cleaners!

I'm really glad that we've done this trip but I am not interested in returning to the areas of Western Australia that we've already covered despite the fact that we have missed out on seeing so many of the National Parks. This is not the feeling I had when we went down the New South Wales Coast, up the Queensland Coast and the Southern Highlands of New South Wales. I want to return to many of those places.

The Red Centre has captured my heart but that is more because of the feel of the place than the sights that we saw, albeit that it was awesome on Kings Canyon and fabulous in the Litchfield National Park and Edith Falls. I saw an eleven day trip advertised in the newspaper today and it included the Red Centre flora and fauna and outback towns, Alice Springs, Kings Canyon, Katherine and the thermal springs at Mataranka, Kakadu National Park with a cruise on the Yellow Water Billabong and the cost was $4295 per head and an extra $1005 if you are travelling as a single person. Obviously that means that for John and I it would have been extraordinary expensive for an eleven day holiday and an awful lot of travelling in a very short time which I would find exhausting. Therefore, I am very glad that we have done it our way. So there I would advise making your own arrangements without a set time limit but the mode of transport is arguable. Hiring a motor home is very expensive and hiring a car plus the cost of accommodation and all meals would be very expensive. I also saw advertised today, four wheel drive Utes with tray backs with individually designed slide on accommodation which you could take off once home. This, of course means that there is off the ground sleeping accommodation and the units have pop-top roofs allowing for height of just over 2 metres. There are slide out kitchens and a lot of storage and includes ample water containment.

Water is certainly very a very significant issue. Unless you are in major towns with treated water you have to take care about the water that you drink and in Western Australia in particular, we have noted that the off-road sites rarely have any water available at all, let alone drinking water. It is imperative to carry a large water supply and preferably purchase the large 15 litre containers of spring water for emergencies. Even without big rig we have had to buy water. In many places in the tropical north of Australia you cannot just hop into the river for a quick swim to get rid of the red dust because of the crocodiles, likewise the sea where you can also get attacked by stingers. I picked up the problematic Giardia infection just outside of a major Queensland town at a caravan park and was poorly for months before the reason was found and trips to several hospitals for tests. I had to stop taking the second lot of tablets because it was causing my left kidney so many problems (severe pain which left me breathless). Luckily the first course of treatment does seem to have cured it though. Tank water may not necessarily be clean because you have no idea when the tanks were last cleaned out. Bore water is not necessarily drinkable unless it has been checked and passed annually by the relevant authority. When the dams are low the water quality can be less than perfect, which I believe is what caused my problem. So you need to plan your trips between towns, ask about the water before you go to more remote areas and be prepared to have the storage for plenty.

Another problem in the north of Western Australia is that people arrive with retread tyres which get destroyed on the hot roads and the stony off-road. The tyre company who changed our tyres told us that they had to factor into their costs the replacement of eight tyres a week on their own vehicles in their own area as the stones rip the tyres to shreds. Lesson learnt – always carry two spare tyres and ensure you have good tyres on your car before coming here. We spoke to another couple who were towing a pop-top van and they had had two blow-outs in one day north of here.

Because of climate change it seems that we also either have floods or drought in many places. We met another person who warned us not to fill up with petrol at a Fitzroy Crossing garage because they still had water in their petrol bowsers and were selling it! It caused him a huge problem with his bus and he only found out what was wrong after limping into Darwin. Everything up here is dear too, whether it be for repairs for your vehicle, food or even the newspaper which is $1.30 above the retail price in Perth. We never had this problem in north Queensland as they print an early edition for the northern areas and a late edition for the metropolitan area of Brisbane and we could buy a Saturday or a Sunday paper on a that day in Cairns for the normal price.

None of these problems are insurmountable but I would strongly recommend again that you invest in a satellite phone as there is very little mobile phone reception between towns.

The tour was wonderful and we can highly recommend it and despite the early start at 7.30am we ran late and did not get back until nearly 7pm because we loitered at the headland by the lighthouse watching the sun set over the ocean and reef. Of course, that meant that the return drive was slow as we had to dodge the Kangaroos and Emus that kept running across the road in front the bus!

We started by going through **Shot Hole Canyon** in the **Cape Range National Park** and then the **Charles Knife Gorge.** From the road you would not imagine that the gorges were even there as it just looks like a long sand hill running parallel to the ocean. We went to the top of the range and we had the choice of walking or staying in the vehicle for the descent in four wheel drive mode. John walked for part of it and stayed in the vehicle the second time and it was quite exhilarating. I asked our guide if it was rougher than the Gibb River Road and he said that it was. The views over the **Exmouth Gulf** were stunning with the fringing reef clearly visible under the turquoise waters. Unlike the Great Barrier Reef, this reef comes right up to the coast. The Continental Shelf was also prominently visible as the water changed colour dramatically at that point. It is here that the Continental Shelf is at its closest point to Australia being only 5 kilometres from the shoreline.

The Americans built an aerodrome here during the World War II and along with the British and Australians they conducted a series of operations to Indonesia from here. Exmouth town was built by the Americans to service their military base. We were told the story of some very brave men who managed to sink several Japanese ships in Singapore harbour by using a fishing vessel and by disguising themselves as fishermen. When they tried to do the same thing again two years later they were caught and beheaded.

The American Naval Base was opened in 1967 by the then Prime Minister Harold Holt who was later to disappear when swimming in the ocean. The Americans built the town to service the base and they have a satellite system operational here today which was upgraded a couple of years ago at a cost of several million dollars. We passed by the base where there are no windows and they have 24 hour clocks apparently. Since 9/11 people are not allowed to go along the track we were driven down, right alongside the base and this tourism group is allowed, mainly because they have been operating for over eighteen years. Some people come up onto the track from the beach where they have been four wheel driving as there is no notice at the beach end to say that you can't use it and apparently they will be stopped and given one warning and if they do it again they will be in trouble. Between the American base and town there were hundreds of acres of purple Mulla Mulla wildflowers.

The Australian government and the Americans jointly built the primary school and it was the first school to have air-conditioning in Western Australia. The town is serviced by bore water and there is plenty of it but it is better drunk after filtering.

There is no wet season here so they get very little rain and although the temperatures can be very high in summer, there is no humidity so people don't feel like they are sweating at all. We are lucky to be here at this time of the year as the breezes keep the temperatures manageable even for me. The whales are also migrating back down south and the emus are hatching their chicks and we saw an Emu with its baby as we were driving along. Also, there aren't too many kangaroos around the town at the moment but later in the season as the grass dries out hundreds of kangaroos come onto the sports field every evening to munch on the grass.

The range was originally under a shallow sea and is made up of layers of limestone and it was formed when it was pushed up out of the ocean. Because the land was under the sea there are a lot of fossils to discover and we later saw a large Shark's tooth at Shark's Tooth Ridge. I took photos of some of the fossils although I have no idea what creatures they were! There are a lot of caves and although it is very soft and crumbly people ab- sail down the cliffs into the canyon from the top rim and some do 'boulder climbing' as a hobby. There are many walking tracks through this area.

During this part of the day we were shown a lot of the wild flowers such as the Sturt Desert Rose which is apparently the Northern Territory emblem. It is a type of Hibiscus. We were told that when the Spinifex burnt, a glue-like substance is left over if the spinifex is particularly oily and the Aboriginals would use it as glue for the tips of their spears. They also used the spinifex seeds and the plant was also used sometimes for sore throats but of course they used other plants too such as eucalyptus. We were also shown the Pink Feather flower and this is the only place in the world that it grows. We also saw the orange Banksia flower. The botanist Sir Joseph Banks who came here twice with Captain Cook made note of many of these rare and wonderful wild flowers. We saw yellow Poker Grevilleas and yellow and white Mulla Mulla.

We spent a lot of time hopping in and out of the vehicle to take photos of the views or of plants or to have some delicious fruit cake and drinks! I was sitting in the vehicle near the top of the dunes when it started moving forward and the hand brake appeared to be on. Luckily our guide saw it rolling and managed to jump in and yank it one notch tighter with both hands! I wouldn't have had the strength. We set off again to rejoin the road that skirts the ocean to go to the **Milyering Visitors Centre** and then to **Osprey Bay** for lunch and whilst he was preparing it some of us went in for a swim. You can camp down there or park your caravan or motor home by arrangement with CALM (contact the Tourist Information Centre if you do not have the telephone number) and there is an entry fee cost plus $5 per night per person and you need to bring your own water. There is one tap that you would need to drive to where you can replenish stocks at should you get really stuck. We saw a Red Kangaroo on the way there, some wild horses and many, many Osprey nests. The Herons are also hatching chicks and we saw them too.

After lunch we had a cruise up **Yardie Creek** and it was here, whilst waiting for the boat, that I took the photos of the amazing fossils as there were so many of them there to be seen. We went through the **Yardie Creek Gorge** with its sheer red limestone cliffs and at last I saw my first wild rock wallabies and two Heron chicks, one dark and one white in their nest.

Next it was back to the **Ningaloo Marine Park** to **Turquoise Bay** to snorkel with all equipment supplied. The current can be very strong here and we had to walk up the beach before going in, in order that we could get back out before a particular point or else get swept away. By this time I felt exhausted as did another woman. My legs had been very shaky in the morning for some reason and I'm just hoping that it is not due to one of the bites I have. Most of my bites (more than 22 on my upper body alone) are sand fly bites but I have one on my arm that has gone sceptic and you try not to hear the warnings on the radio that they are putting to air at the moment about the dangers of mosquito bites at the moment. Anyway, albeit that this was what I had been waiting to do all day and the main reason for my trip, I started floundering about and sucked in water after only about five minutes in the ocean and just had to come out and sit down. The reef comes right to the beach. I had just heard our guide say 'Come and look at these sharks' and I just did not have the energy to get any further. For the very brief time I was in the water I saw some beautiful coral, many different fish and a sea snake of some sort and it was stunningly beautiful. I don't think there could be anywhere in the world where the reef is so perfect and if I can say this in very small letters …..I hate to admit it but it beats the Great Barrier Reef in Queensland hands down, from the trips and snorkelling I've done there….. This is so hard to admit because from what I've seen so far of the northern part of Western Australia I cannot imagine why anyone would ever want to come back here for a second visit. John feels the same way. You get these little spots that are interesting or pretty or are good for boating or fishing but between these spots there is absolutely nothing. It is such endless barren landscape. Of course, I am not talking from experience because I have not been able to go into all the National Parks because of the dogs and no doubt they are wonderful and we have missed out on places because of not driving a four wheel drive vehicle but for the average tourist or overseas visitor who travels along the highways as we do then it leaves you numb with the monotony.

We asked a local person in Exmouth what they thought about the new upmarket development and the answer we received was 'White elephant'. I suggested that people who could afford such places would expect more medical services and mentioned the girl who needed tests for ulcers and about her pregnant friend and was told that if you are pregnant then you get shipped down to Carnarvon three weeks before you are due to have your baby and put in a unit (flat) to await the birth! I find this unbelievable.

How come we hear so much about the Great Barrier Reef (I even heard about it in my geography lessons at school in England so many years ago) but not so much about the Ningaloo Reef? We left Exmouth the following day and went to **Coral Bay**, just under 150ks further down the coast, and what an oasis that is! There are two caravan parks, both expensive and one takes dogs. However, we did not stay because they wanted to double the site fee for our bus. The excuse used when John queried why we couldn't park on one of the larger sites was that they are being regressed. I walked past them and they weren't. We seem to be encountering a lot of this apparent greediness in W.A. When we left the park at Exmouth we were hailed by a couple who we had met at Katherine. They had apparently met up with some other people they knew as they were arriving in Exmouth the previous day and when that couple heard where they were staying they said that they would return with them to the park and that they had been staying there anyway and had just booked out. When they all turned up, the couple that we knew asked for a CMCA discount (we are members of this motor home club) and got the discount. We are members of the tourist park so we had received that particular tourist park discount but apparently we would have done better to have asked for the CMCA discount which was more! Anyway, the couple who had booked out had never asked for it before but told the receptionist that they too were members of the CMCA and asked for the discount for their new booking. They were told they couldn't have it because they never asked for it when they stayed before! They were apparently very angry and I think they left without booking in!

I'd love to return and if I did, I'd come by coach (so that I could sleep away the boring journey or read a book), try and hitch a lift on a boat (ideal) and I would stay at the Backpackers Hostel there. The place teemed with overseas backpackers who were apparently well cashed up and there was a happy and vibrant atmosphere. The white sands and turquoise bay with reef within walking distance from the shore provided a stunning view. There's a hotel and a couple of groups of shops and cafes and one particular shop where I could have spent a fortune on hand-crafted sterling silver jewellery with coral insets. I liked a pendant with pink coral and the price was $30 so it is quite reasonably priced. Some of the necklaces were reversible and the jewellery was really well made. This is the place to party all night, have a nap, make new friends from all over the world, go for a snorkel (you can hire equipment on the beach), have a nap, have a swim and eat some prawns, have another nap, go for a quad bike ride over the dunes, have a drink and then join the next night party and it sounds real good to me! There were also job vacancies when we were there such as a shop assistant or for a coxswain with sea experience. It could mean that you just float around steering a glass-bottomed boat over the coral for the tourists but the point is that you could get some cash to keep on partying and do more of the activities. The glass bottom boat rides start at $30 and I think there were two companies doing them with the other one possibly $40. The quad bikes can be hired for a two hour ride one way over the dunes with the driver paying $70 and his passenger $40 or a dearer trip lasting three hours which goes to a lake. One of the restaurants on the front was doing a roaring trade in ice creams and coffee and they had a varied menu with evening dinners starting around the $18 mark.

We drove on South and passed a sign saying that we were passing the Tropic of Capricorn. When we looked at the map of Australia we found that we had been virtually on The Tropic of Capricorn when we left our friends at Rockhampton to commence this tour and the other time was when we were at Alice Springs. So we've done the 'top part'! The only other thing that broke up the monotony of the journey were the sheep which scampered off the road at our approach. They've got more sense than other wild life because at least they recognised the danger of passing vehicles. They must have come to the verges to try and find the odd blade of grass and I do not know how they survive. We managed to reach a good off-road site before dark and today have only driven 35ks to a roadhouse so that we can charge up our electrical appliances. It's a bit silly because we cannot use the water here and have to have our own supply, the air-conditioner overloaded the power supply and cut us off so we can't have that on, there is no pool or anything and we had to pay $21 for the night. However, it's a clean, grassy site and there are en-suite cabins so we don't need to use our water to shower, we can plug into their satellite T.V point provided and we have powered up this laptop. We believe the battery must need replacing because our inverter did not like it when we plugged it in last night whilst John was in the middle of doing some accounts and the battery went dead. We are still able to use the inverter for the other appliances so it must be the laptop battery. We have been having a wonderful lazy day as I did not wake up until 10am and we were here in a flash. John has also suggested that he buy our dinner but having seen that most of what they cook is fried, I'm not so sure about that although the idea of not cooking the cauliflower cheese is nice. I had a lovely salad lunch so I'm not fussed but my man must have his 'dinner'!

I made a sensible and sane decision and had sausage and chips with heaps of salt and tomato sauce for dinner.

We are booked into a caravan park at **Carnarvon** for a week starting from tomorrow and I think we only have about 150ks to go to get there. We have also been told not to expect a change in this depressing scenery until we get past Geraldton which is not far from Perth. We enjoyed Kununurra near the Northern Territory border when we were there but I wouldn't go there again for any particular reason and the distance travelled between there and Broome and then down to Carnarvon will have been 2,451 kilometres and there will be another 480 kilometres to get to Geraldton. Add to that the 513 kilometres to get to Kununurra from Katherine and it's a total of 3444 kilometres (over 2,000 miles) without the side trips that we've done in the Ute. That's a lot of kilometres to see very little but the jewel has to have been Coral Bay which beats Broome hands down for beauty and atmosphere with the bonus of the reef.

Why am I saying this? It's because you really have got to want to go all around Australia and do the much dreamed of 'The Big Lap'. So many people say 'I'm going to do that one day'. One of my sons is already saying it. We keep being asked 'Are you doing the Big Lap?' Then you get the people who tell you that it is their second or ninth trip around – yes 'ninth' and sometimes I mention something about some world event and they look at me blankly because they've heard nothing about it. I've had someone say to me that they never read the newspapers nor watch the news and he asked me why I did. 'What do you want to know for?' he asked me. It is nice not to have T.V and John and I have been amazed by how much longer the evenings seem and have realised how much of our time is taken up with watching it or by reading newspapers but I couldn't cut myself off from the rest of the world and just keep going around and around this one continent. I've also tried to explain to people the difference in distances in Europe by way of saying that you can go 5 kilometres and see so much variety in Devon or you can be in Paris in the same time that it takes to travel between certain places here and they look at me blankly. I've even been asked why I'd want to and that 'It's too dear over there'. Even some of my friends here think it's better to go to Asia purely on the grounds that things are cheaper there than in Australia rather than what they can see or experience by going further afield.

I was listening to the ABC radio yesterday and a young man who had been on the Big Brother series was talking about his life on his farm (it was a farming program) and he was saying that he's done 800 interviews since he was on that show and that 'trashy T.V programs such as that' (or words to that effect) can be used to educate people because it is on air for something like seven hours a day and people are still watching at 3am. He said that the interviews he does in shopping centres and clubs gives him further opportunity to educate people on his organic farming practices (he has sheep and grain) because ordinary Australians do not watch programmes on ABC or SBS or listen to ABC programs about farming. He said that all of the contestants and intruders on Big Brother that he met all had the wrong impression about farming practices and their main gripe was tree felling leading to soil depravation and salinity. He had no one to talk to initially about his work but by the end of the series they are all keen to go out to his farm in Queensland. I found this interesting because it hadn't occurred to me that such programs could give people this kind of opportunity to educate the public. I enjoy learning and I enjoy the world news so this kind of life continually touring around Australia is definitely not for me. I'd love to continue to travel though and do the same around New Zealand and tour around Europe.

However, I have learnt a lot on this trip and have been amazed about what I didn't know, such as Australia being bombed in places other than Darwin, floods and cyclones that I hadn't heard about before, Aboriginal customs and superb Aboriginal art, stories of the settlers and the explorers and this is why I so enjoy the trips that we have done in small groups with local people. I asked our tour guide at Exmouth if he had studied botany and he told me that he had grown up with two uncles, one who was a botanist and both had taught him so much and he was still learning. His family settled in the area around the 1960's I believe and he seems to love every nook and cranny of it. The plants and animals, the rocks and fossils have been part of his life since he found his legs and started exploring. The area is his cultural heritage and I can understand that he probably has no need to go further afield – not that I asked him of course – unlike me who has no deep roots other than being born in England and having a deep love of South Wales and the Welsh people where I once lived. I have been back and it has changed of course and I found that sad because it was not for the better.

Chapter 20

CARNARVON

I had pre-booked for a week. Big mistake as there's little to see or do here. The highlight has been today when we visited the OTC DISH – did you see the film called 'The Dish'? Well, this one was established in 1966 and it was involved with the Apollo and Gemini space missions and tracking Haley's Comet although the film called "The Dish" was based on the story of the one in Parkes in New South Wales and its involvement in the Apollo lunar project. That was is still in use and visitors are welcome. This one is now unused but we enjoyed seeing one close up. It's 29.6m in diameter and is lit up at night and we raced up the stairs followed by Jack and Callie. Callie thought it was a great game and went up again on her own! You walk all around it but cannot go inside because they stopped the tours, which is such a shame. We were very disappointed by the fact that there was no information available to read and we were later to meet some people much further down the coast who likewise complained about the lack of presentation. Message to the Council – get your act into gear!

Carnarvon has a small but pretty town centre and a promenade along the beachfront. There is a walkway across to Whitlock Island but there's nothing there, just sand dunes. There is an Information Centre in town and the toilets nearby are comical. To open the door you press a button and press another to close it once inside. Whilst going to the toilet, press the button for the toilet paper and you'll be able to get sufficient ready for your use! Once finished, don't look for how to flush it because it will do so only if you wash your hands! I had trouble with the hand washing as the soap didn't seem to work and then all of a sudden a heap of cold water came gushing out and the toilet started to flush. The floor is pretty wet so take care – it's all that gushing of water everywhere. The dryer is pretty standard, just place your hands under and it blows hot air. Then you're back to the door and the button pushing again! As I walked out a guy saw my face and burst out laughing so I must have been looking bemused.

We've driven around most of the suburb areas because we continually get lost (or rather John does)!! I've noticed that the children seem to be fully integrated and play together and by this I mainly mean the local Aboriginal children and those who are not. It's good to see. We've been down to the fish jetty and found most of the outlets closed because it's out of season apparently. We did manage to find one fish factory which was about to close and he sold me a couple of huge frozen pink snapper fillets but apparently there will probably be no more fish until Friday and get there early because it all gets sent elsewhere. I asked what time 'early' means but he couldn't tell me and I asked if he was sure he was getting fish in but he couldn't tell me that either.

We've been out to Babbage Island to see One Mile Jetty which they are slowly restoring but it still looks very unsafe to me. There's a rail link from the town centre along a tramway to the Heritage Precinct which is a 20 minute trip each way but that was also closed on Sunday. I think the Heritage Precinct is where the jetty is and there is a load of old machinery and engines rotting away around there. There is a museum there but it was shut on Sunday afternoon – probably because it's 'out of season'. There are so many people here in the multitude of caravan parks with absolutely nothing to do! At all the other places we've been to so far along the coast it is the season and they make the most of it because of all the grey nomads touring around.

Our neighbour (and it turns out they are neighbours back home because they live about a kilometre away) said that he and his wife drove the 75ks each way to see the Blow Holes but it wasn't worth it so we're not going to bother as we've seen great ones before. However, we've got some cleaning done and all our washing and bought odds and ends for the motor home and the dogs have had a ball down on the beach near the fish factories. Jack runs around like a puppy and plays with Callie and then returns to the Ute because he's suddenly worn out and we follow his lead as we feel so sorry for him. His mind is so willing but his body so weak.

Bring your Coles petrol discount dockets because they have a gas station here but no Coles shop. However, there is a Woolworths which offers the discount dockets but they have no gas stations here!

At our caravan site they have had bags of tomatoes for $1 and green beans and cucumbers cheap but in the stores they are not cheap. This surprises me because this is the area where nearly 70% of all the tropical and sub tropical fruit and vegetables are grown for the State of Western Australia. There are outlets that you can go and find but with the cost of petrol it hardly seems worth it.

We went to find the Golf course today and it's another scrubby flat course for $5 a game. John will try it out tomorrow morning but he's not that excited. So that's about it really. Felt rather odd yesterday and suggested to John that I might be feeling depressed because I couldn't seem to get interested in anything. I knew I really had a problem when I actually wanted to do some ironing because it is the very job I hate the most. I really shocked myself! Then last night we were watching a couple of guys coming down the Darling River (to eventually join up with the Murray River) in a tinnie on a T.V program and one of them mentioned the word 'melancholy' and I said to John

"That's it. He feels the same way about how disappointed he is in the Darling River on his journey so far, as I feel about what we've seen so far in Western Australia. It has not lived up to my expectations and I feel melancholy.'

John feels the same way but we will be glad that we have done it later on when we look back on it.

I'm over it today of course and looking forward to the next stop but I have had a very deep yearning to be back home and an even deeper yearning to be closer to one of my son's at the moment. Phone calls just do not cut it with me and I want to spend some time with him. We will be seeing Helen in about six weeks time as I have finally been able to work out, over a period of three evenings, that we are likely to be there in six weeks and she requires that time to give notice at work of her intended holiday. I've spent a lot of this trip wishing I was back home except for those times in the Northern Territory when we had such a wonderful time.

We still have a couple of days to fill in so I've started to think about Christmas cards to the U.K. and catching up on printing some photos for our calendar and I still have one more letter of a general nature to do which I'll enclose in the Xmas cards.

DENHAM - 3rd October 2006

We saw some goats on our journey between Carnarvon and Denham. Oh yes, some cars passed us too. That was about it really except that we stopped at the Wooramel Homestead for gas for the bus and then at the Overlander Roadhouse just after the turn off to Denham. We'll go there again when we leave as it was an education on how to run a retail outlet and café. There were three dining areas, two inside and one outside and when we went in one dining area was completely full. There was nobody in the queue but by the time I had studied the menu there were about fifteen people in front of me. I have never known customers to be served so fast and wasn't aware it was happening until I was suddenly at the front. A very friendly Englishman served John when he came in to pay for his gas and I had been served by a woman who took the order and a girl who took the money and at all times, with everybody, they were friendly and smiling and efficient. Whilst we waited for lunch a coach pulled in and customers poured in and were raiding the ice cream freezer and drinks cabinets so much that the doors remained open for about five minutes so it must be hard work to keep things cold. Within a few minutes they had all been served and were back outside. Our lunch had already arrived and we had only waited about five minutes at the most. We spent most of our time there watching the interaction between customers and service and the place throbbed with people. There were also a variety of other goods that could be purchased including postcards and gifts.

Our site is right at the top of the park and we have en suite bathrooms. They are all in a block and are spotless and late yesterday afternoon I looked inside one of them and it hadn't been used that day so there are obviously more than enough facilities here for everyone. As you go back down the hill there are more bathroom and laundry facilities of course but we have a lot of cabins up here. There is a notice that tells us that they use desalinated water in the showers. We are supposed to be drinking town water but I became ill within a day of being here, to the point that I could not eat and was almost bedridden but when I switched to bottled water I immediately improved. I found out later that the town water is desalinated water and although treated it obviously does not agree with my stomach and Jack seems to have been suffering likewise!

We have steep banks of sand dunes beside and behind us and there is a short cut down to the supermarket in town and to the beach right behind our van. The dogs love the sand dunes where they can run freely. We are also on the beachfront at one end of this small but delightful town. There is only the one supermarket and that is small, a butcher, a baker and a shop which comprises the newsagents, chemists and post office all rolled into one! There are a variety of other small shops and the Shark Bay Interpretive Centre which we may yet go into but it is one of the ugliest buildings I have ever seen – modern architecture at its very worst. I had included it in a photo of the seafront and shops and when John saw it being downloaded he immediately said 'Get rid of it, it's so ugly'. There is no vet in town, nor kennels and the doctor visits on Mondays, Wednesdays and Fridays only and if you are ill on one of the other days then bad luck!

We are a member of this park franchise group yet we found that we were being asked to pay more than is printed in our booklet and when I queried it I was told that it is because we have a bus and therefore we use more power. I disagreed that we would use more power and was told that indeed we would as it has been proved! We didn't argue but it has annoyed us so much that we have had the air conditioner on many times and I have been using the microwave more often. Stupid I know and I've stopped doing it because I feel guilty because of environmental concerns but we actually normally use less of the facilities than those with caravans as we are self-contained. For example, I shower and wash my hair in our own bathroom using our gas hot water system and we pay for the gas. Most people we know with caravans use the microwave a lot as many do not bother with ovens. We don't as we have a four ring burner and oven so again, being gas, we pay for the power. Most caravan owners have an air conditioner and as they are smaller they tend to use them more often whereas we have so many windows to open we don't need it so much. We do have two air conditioners on our roof but can only use one at a time, not both at once. A lot of caravan owners use electric frying pans outside to cook their meat in as it saves getting the smell inside their van. I have known some to use theirs practically every night. The only time we use ours is to roast a chicken or joint of meat to keep us going for a few days without having to cook and that is a very rare event and it has only been during this trip as I got fed up with lighting the oven pilot light. I could go on and on and someone else who has a bus agreed with me and said he uses their ensuite facilities here instead of using up his own gas and makes the most of the hot water to cover the extra costs! They are so silly adding this extra charge because it niggles customers.

At the other end of the beachfront is an area where the dogs can run free off-leash and they absolutely love it of course. Today we had a picnic there but hadn't set out to eat there.

We had driven the 25ks to Monkey Mia (pronounced 'Mya') and when we got to the end of the road we saw an entrance to an area where they feed the wild dolphins two or three times each morning. We were asked for $6 per head and turned around and left because we have seen wild dolphins so many times before. If you get on the car ferry and go out to the Moreton Bay Islands of Macleay Island, Lamb Island and Russell Island for example from Redland Bay near Brisbane you can see them dancing about in front of the car ferry. You will enjoy a magical sea trip as well and it will cost you a couple of dollars each if you are just a walk-on passenger. We have done that so many times because we had owned some land on Macleay Island. Helen and I have also swum with the dolphins at Sea World on the Gold Coast for a more personal experience with them.

So, we drive on a few more metres and there is a parking bay and I see some people going off on a camel ride and I get out to take a photo. A young gentleman who obviously worked there approaches as I suggest to John that he parks the car properly in one of the bays and I tell this guy that I need to find the toilet. He wants $6. Stunned by his response I asked him if he would also want $6 if I went into the Information Centre. He told us that there was a charge to enter the area, which is basically just beach and that it was not a Tourist Information Centre but actually had some displays. Big deal – most good information centres have displays and films running. It had a sign over the top with Tourist Information Centre as far as I can recall and when I said that he didn't deny it. So I asked him if just I could go to the toilet and John would stay put but he still wanted $6. We were so disgusted that we left.

The reason is this. When you turn off to go to Denham from that roadhouse I was telling you about, you travel 129 kilometres along a peninsula with the sea and sand on both sides of you. It is a very tantalising sight after a long journey to keep getting glimpses of the beautiful blue ocean between the scrubby bushes in the sand dunes. There are several places you can go down to the beach and particular places to go and see including Shell Beach (no charge) and the Stromatolites (no charge) which I will tell you about when we've been there!

At Denham itself you have so much beachfront and also a netted area, presumably for the stinger season but which the children seem to love. You also have barbecue tables, toilets, cafes and even free doggy bags provided. Admittedly the Information Centre has closed and we have been told that they have gone bankrupt. This confuses us because surely the Western Australia State Government and/or local Council would fund the Information Centre? If they were just trying to make a living out of commissions on booking alone, of course you couldn't have a viable business. It is a service that we thought was provided by the Government. Anyway, there are other outlets that take bookings and have information including the caravan park.

I had nearly booked us into the caravan park at Monkey Mia and today we found out that we would have had to pay to even get to reception and the cost would depend on how many days we were there. What an absolute rip-off. I'm getting to the point that I will be glad to leave this State. It is so rich in mining but the tourist industry so greedy.

The area is managed by CALM and they have developed some camp sites there but we weren't looking for a camp site. They feed 'wild' dolphins daily which is a major tourist attraction but to say that wild female dolphins come in (sometimes with their babies) of their own accord, as I read in one booklet is a bit rich when the Bottle nose dolphins know that they are going to get fed! However, the CALM rangers protect the dolphins from over exposure to humans because they only feed about twenty-two of them and if people learn more about protecting these beautiful creatures then I suppose a few can be sacrificed to becoming almost domesticated! People used to feed all the dolphins and by that I mean both male and female and their babies but CALM now only feeds the females and do not allow the babies to be fed until they are weaned and the babies that are joining the group are from mothers who are already coming in to be fed. Along the south east coast of Australia you can see the dolphins playing in the wild and they will follow your boat and dance around without being fed and that, to me, is far more magical. However, I'd love to see wild dugong. There are up to twenty researchers from all over the world here at any one time studying different species.

This area as a whole is called the Shark Bay Marine Park and I believe the best way to see it would be via a tour and certainly if you want to see the Monkey Mia area then try and find a boat tour to see the beautiful area. You can do a catamaran trip to see dolphins, rays, turtles, sharks and dugongs and I believe you go out from Monkey Mia and they obviously build the $6 into the cost of the trip but at least you will be there to see more than a beachfront. We can't go because we have nowhere to leave the dogs. There is little point in paying $6 a head just to go and have a coffee beside yet another beach and you need to explore further. You'd be better off spending $10 ($8 concession) on visiting the Shark Bay Interpretive Centre in Denham for far more comprehensive information. If you have a four wheel drive then it is a paradise. Francis Peron National Park is only fully accessible by four wheel drive and there is a huge natural spa there. Apparently the sight of the red and white sands set against the beautiful blue ocean is quite breathtaking so take your camera along with your drinking water.

Shark Bay is one of the very few places in the world with a World Heritage Listing and this means the whole area, not just that one spot. It has 'the largest number of different species of marine and wildlife ever recorded in one place' according to our booklet.

Yesterday we went to visit Little Lagoon and that was lovely and it is far from little. We also visited the Country Club which is really the golf course and there was no-one there. It is very forlorn looking but you can play 18 holes for $5, just like the last place John played. He tells me that it is quite fun trying to work out where a green is amongst the scrub and as some of the holes are a par five it is not easy to know where you are supposed to be heading! There is a mound of dirt to tee off from. It does overlook the ocean in the distance though so that is an added bonus.

We got three loads of washing out and then John went off to golf where he played along side some emus and lost a couple of balls amongst the spinifex and having scratched himself he learnt to use his golf club to retrieve them! I decided that I'd have to cut my hair off because of the wind. It is so-o-o windy here and although it is warm/hot out of it (about 25C during the day), the wind has a chill to it that can make you feel quite chilly at times. During our picnic the other day there were a few sprinkles of rain, the wind was cold and it is certainly not swimming weather for us and even the dogs are not so excited about staying in the sea for long. In the evenings we change into warmer clothes. I decided to cut my hair really short because it keeps blowing into my eyes and most of the time looks wild and dry and I have been told that it we will get this wind all down this coast. I'm getting fed up with the wind already so I wasn't happy to hear that. My hair is now so short that I don't recognise myself, hardly need to brush it in the morning and even John noticed that I'd cut it and that speaks volumes!

As soon as he returned from golf I left him with the washing and dogs and went to the newsagents, for a coffee and then to the Interpretive Centre. I was told that my ticket would last 24 hours so I could come back in the morning. It was so good that I left at 5.30pm having been there for about 3 hours and had not finished watching one of the films so we have changed our plans for today and we are both going there this morning and will leave the dogs in the Ute so I can see the things I missed out on. I'll leave John there and bring the dogs back. I didn't realise that it only opened this year so that has been a bonus of us coming to this region a year later than planned! When I came out I found a wealth of information on the area and picked up an excellent town map and we could have done with all this information when we arrived. There is a list of 18 tourism activities to start with, services, seven different emergency numbers, community groups and services, accommodation and other services making a total of 123 with their locations all marked clearly on the map. It costs nothing to walk into the Interpretive Centre to collect information and there is also an art gallery there that you can look around. On the back of this fold-out leaflet there is a vast amount of information on the area including the history, Aboriginal heritage and all the major tourist attractions. We learnt so much at the Interpretive Centre and highly recommend that tourists start their holiday by visiting it and watching all the films before deciding what to see.

There's a double-decker bus here and we've had a look around it and the couple who own it have fitted it out beautifully. However, as their shower area was full of boxes of Cocoa Pops and toilet rolls I asked them where they shopped. John and I are both convinced that they said that it was cheaper to drive to Geraldton than to buy their food here and they obviously buy in bulk as they live here at the moment as he has been working here for many months. We worked out today that Geraldton is 408 kilometres away so double that for a round trip! You would think they could phone an order through and have it delivered for less than that!

So, what makes this area so special? Why did it gain Heritage listing in 1991 and what does that entail? To be listed it must meet four criteria. Basically 'The place must contain outstanding examples representing significant ongoing geological processes, biological evolution and human interaction with the natural environment'. The Marine and National Parks cover about 2.2 million hectares. Shark Bay, which is protected by the two spectacular peninsulas including Dirk Hartog Island to the west, covers about 25,000 square kilometres. The coastline of Shark Bay is 1500 kilometres long which is greater than the distance between London & Rome! There is a large natural harbour, lagoons, islands and is located on the most western point of Australia. The Aboriginal name for Shark Bay is "Gathaagudu" which means 'two bays' and they are the traditional owners of the Shark Bay area.

There is an overlap zone here between the tropical and temperate marine environments with about 323 types of fish, 80 coral species, 28 bivalve species along with 28 species of plant found nowhere else in the world.

STROMATOLITES - To start with there are three kinds of sea water in Shark Bay. First there is the Oceanic water from the depths of the Indian Ocean. Secondly there is Metahaline water which is one and a half times as salty as ocean water and the third kind, Hypersaline, is twice as salty and it is in the latter water that Stomatolites form. We wouldn't be here without these single cell organisms because they brought the first oxygen to this wonderful earth of ours which provided the conditions for further life forms. The ones in Hammelin Pool, although they are less than 2000 years old, they are similar to the earliest forms of life dating back 300 million years. If you tread on them they will leave a footprint for up to one hundred years and as they are so fragile and grow so slowly, there is a walkway provided to view them. It takes about 1000 years for them to grow about 35 centimetres in height and they have long term growth rates of no more than 0.4mm a year. Shark Bay contains, in the one place, the most diverse and abundant examples of them in the world and there is only one other place in the world where living marine Stromatolites exist.

The first oxygen breathing animals that evolved about 650 million years ago ate the Stromatolites. There's gratitude for you. However, the water in Hamelin Pool is so salty that snails, for example, cannot survive in it to eat them! There is particular interest in them for space exploration as there is the possibility of them to live on Mars.

SEAGRASS & DUGONGS - There are many species of seagrass here and they cover an area of about 5,000 square kilometres. In fact Shark Bay has the largest and most specific diverse seagrass meadows in the world. They are like land flowers and are not seaweed and they flower under water (some have been found at a depth of 15 metres) and some bear fruit. They flower at the same time as in the Mediterranean although here we are at the beginning of summer and there it is going into winter but they follow evolutionary history. This area, therefore, provides a safe haven for the Dugongs (about 10% of the world's population which means between 10-12,000 of them) whereas in other parts of the world they are endangered and you can go out and see them along with the dolphins swimming amongst it.

TURTLES - There is also one of the largest Turtle rookeries in Australia being home to over 6,000 marine turtles and a breeding ground for the most endangered turtle in Australia which is the Loggerhead Turtle and the green turtles.

There are also the humpback whales which pass by whilst migrating, sharks, giant rays and the other wild life, birds and wild flowers. Here you can see the fairy wrens, eagles, terns, cormorants, emus, thorny devils, bobtail lizards, goannas and sometimes kangaroo and echidna or go take a camel ride. There is a project being undertaken at the present time to reintroduce native animals such as the mallee fowl, bilbies, echidna, woylie, bungarra and the threatened grasswren birds near Shell Beach. First they had to catch the foxes by baiting them, get rid of the goats and then had to face catching the wild cats which is more difficult as they hunt their prey rather than be attracted to bait.

Chapter 21

TOWN LOOKOUT - FIRST STOP OF THE DAY

SHELL BEACH – Millions of Fragum cockles have been drifting in for 4000 years, extending 120 km along the coastline and it puzzles the scientists. They have compacted to a depth of 10 metres away from the sea but closer to the water they remain whole. The shells create a pure white beach set against the beautiful blue or sometimes green ocean. Solidified shells, naturally formed, were quarried and blocks were used for building some of the houses in Denham and many stations buildings. Our caravan park site is shell based and they get everywhere and it is a constant battle trying to get them out of the carpet and off our mat outside. If you walk in thongs (flip flops) you find that you can feel them like gravel under between your feet and the soles after just a couple of steps. It beats having to water grass and cut lawns for the park owners though and always looks good.

Just as an aside, I was interested to find out that 50,000 years ago the sea level was about 2 metres higher than now but other than that the geographical area has hardly changed at all. It is very much as the early European explorers found it. It was discovered on October 5th 1616 by the Dutch and the captain Dirk Hartog came ashore at what is called Cape Inscription, which is Dirk Hartog Island and an engraved pewter plate was nailed to a wooden post to record this event. He returned in 1697 and then a couple of years later the first English captain to explore the West Australian Coast arrived and named it Dampier after himself, William Dampier. Then the French arrived in 1772. The French scientific exhibition came with two vessels and the two captains and an anthropologist by the name of Francois Peron explored and chartered a wide area of Shark Bay and many landmarks carry French names today. Captain Henry M Denham completed charting the entire Shark Bay coastline in 1858 and the old maps which were originally drawn were so amazingly accurate that they were used up until relatively recently and you can see them in the Interpretive Centre.

Sandalwood has been exported on and off for over 100 years, American whalers visited from as early as 1792 and there is evidence of pearling trade from the mid 1800's, plus there was the pastoral industry. Today the area relies on fishing, salt production at Useless Loop, pearl farming and tourism, including the Monkey Mia Dolphins.

It is not just because of the biodiversity of this region that we are beginning to fall in love with it! The people in town are so friendly whether it is the people who serve you in the shops or the locals who live here. It is a very relaxed place to stay and as John said today 'it grows on you' and I totally agree. I drove out to the fish factory today which turned out to be in an industrial estate and I slowed down to ask a local lady if I had gone too far. She just burst out laughing and said 'Are you frightened of 'stranger danger?' and I replied 'Definitely not' and with that she jumped in and asked me to give her a lift as she had to collect her car from a garage just past the fish factory. With a beaming face like hers I could hardly be frightened. It was far too hot to walk the distance she had to go and she admitted that she had been out of breath with the effort. The guy in the chemist/post office/newsagents has advised me on where to get coffee, who to visit if I want to meet characters and several other bits of information that have been both amusing and informative. A café I was going into was closing for a couple of hours for a siesta break and said they could serve me a takeaway coffee but when I said that I hate plastic cups she immediately said 'Take a seat and I'll serve you one in a cup'. It is the first time we have come across this type of service in Western Australia and it's a good feeling.

On our last day before leaving we covered the area between Denham, back along the road we arrived on and found that we found more places to stop and look at than we had imagined. Starting at the Town Lookout (which is quite a long way from town), we stopped again at **Ocean Park, Eagle Bluff, Fowler's Camp** and **Whalebone Beach** before going to **Shell Beach**. We drove on to **Goulet Bluff** but it wasn't that attractive and then went to look at the **Nanga Bay Holiday Resort** and Caravan Park but didn't stop there. On our return journey we also stopped at a couple of other lookouts. It was a wonderful day and although we met and talked to people at Eagle Bluff and Shell Beach, most of the time we were totally alone and wondered yet again how we are going to cope when we get back to the Gold Coast and the people and traffic!

At Eagle Bluff we watched Stingrays and Sharks passing below as we were on a headland boardwalk. There were stunning views and everybody was pointing out new sightings to each other. We have yet to see a Dugong though.

At Shell Beach I got an amazing close-up photograph of the shells near the shoreline and we started chatting to a young couple from Perth via one of their sons who told me he was a Dolphin! Kids love this area. Anyway, this young couple told us that the scenery will remain deadly boring until the other side of Perth which didn't cheer us up much. They told us that it is the reason that it has taken them many years to return to Kalbarri and we told them that that is our next stop and asked what it is like. 'Full of tourists and the next time we come up this way we will skip it and come directly to Denham'. I then said that we aren't actually staying in the town but 5ks further along at Red Bluff and he then became quite animated and said we'd love it there. When I asked about Geraldton he told us not to stay there and it's just a town. However, when I added that we are again staying out of town near Greenoch he told me that it is good there. So it seems I have chosen well considering I have no idea what these areas are like! They told us that the other side of Perth is much nicer and that we should go to Margaret River whether we are into wines or not and we had already decided to anyway. Also that we would love Busselton and Esperance but when I added that it would probably be school holidays they warned us to book in now. It's so hard to do when you don't know when you are going to get there. I found it interesting that he also mentioned that it is only when you come north of Perth that the price of everything is outrageous and told him about a couple of our experiences and although they live in Perth they agreed with my perception.

So, tomorrow we leave and will visit Hamelin Pool on our way back to the Great Western Highway.

Geraldton & Greenough (also about Kalbarri, Port Gregory, Horrocks, Northampton and The Hutt River Province Principality)

I have too much to tell you so will start by telling you that we visited the 'rellies', have met Royalty and seen a huge pink lake since I last wrote. The 'rellies' were the Stromatolites and as they gave us the opportunity to be here we just had to visit them. However, do not go at midday with two dogs in tow when it's blazing hot as there is no shade anywhere. We did the walk down to see them and back in half the time it takes most people because we were getting burnt. As I'm writing this, I have a jumper, jeans, socks and slippers on just to keep warm and John has his winter clothes on too! The comparison seems almost laughable. Apparently there are five places in the world where living Stromatolites exist and we will see a second place further down the coast.

Anyway, to get back to the travels, we reached Kalbarri rather late as it took longer than we had thought to get there. It wasn't just the time that we took over visiting the Stromatolites, nor the Devonshire tea we enjoyed at the caravan park there but the fact that when we reached the main road and returned to the Roadhouse that I told you about before (the busy one) I went to pay for my petrol and found that I'd lost my Bank Card. I think I stayed calm! Luckily I had the last receipt I had been given in the wallet so having obtained a telephone book I found the number and phoned the chemist back in Denham and yes, they had my Bank Card. Whew! The lovely girl who had answered my call said she would post it to Geraldton Post Office and told me when it would arrive.

The Chemists in Denham also houses the Newsagents and the Post Office so you only have to take a couple of steps to each different counter. I almost became on first name terms with John, the Chemist who sold us our newspaper! First of all he gave us directions and advice and then he ordered my smoking replacement thingummyjigs which came in the next day. I asked him where to buy the best coffee Callie ate something on the beach started vomiting so I rushed in to see him again and he found me the address of a retired vet! There is no resident doctor or vets in town but after several suggestions from other customers he came up trumps again but luckily we didn't need it.

When you turn off the main highway for Kalbarri it seems an endless journey back down to the coast. I couldn't get CDMA reception unless I was at the top of a hill and then as we descended again I would lose it. The road was interesting as it continued to go up and down all the way and there were so many times when we would think 'Surely this is the last hill and we'll see the sea' but on and on it went. I managed to get through to the caravan park we had booked into to warn them we would not be there until after dark and just as the Manager asked 'Where are you now?' the phone cut out again. I phoned again and had a stupid conversation with another man who sounded the same who told me that we hadn't booked in! It turned out that I had phoned the wrong park the second time! After we had booked in our neighbours told us that they had made an advance booking at that second park but when they arrived they were told that they did not have room. They were understandably very upset as it is a member of a major caravan park franchise. I had phoned the same park a few weeks earlier (thus the mix up with numbers in my telephone record book) and when I asked if he had a powered site the response I got was 'Of course not, it's the school holidays' which I had found rather curt and rude. The park we stayed at was at Red Bluff but unfortunately it has been sold to land developers and will be shutting down this week for good.

PINK LAKE - SHOWING COLOUR MORE

Kalbarri is such a pretty town, the scenery is glorious and we had a wonderful time even though we did not get chance to go to the Kalbarri National Park as we were only there for three days and there was nowhere to leave the dogs anyway. However, we did visit many of the coastal cliff lookouts including Eagle Gorge, Island Rock, Mushroom Rock, Shell House Gorge, Grandstand, the Red Bluff lookout, Natural Bridge and Pot Alley Gorge and we loved the latter three the most. The Red Bluff one was obviously near the caravan park and we had already been to the beach and had walked across the beautiful red-coloured rocks and it was just as stunning at the top. Pot Alley Gorge doesn't sound wonderful (well, according to John it doesn't) but we absolutely loved the views there. We saw a couple more wild flowers but this place is supposed to be a sea of colour at this time of the year but the drought has destroyed that delight for us this year.

JOHN WAS INVITED TO SIT IN HIS ROYAL HIGHNESS' CHAIR

We also took the dogs for a walk along the Murchison River at the other end of town, visited most of the beaches in town and went through the dunes between the town and our caravan park for the dogs to play and to sit and watch the sun set after a fish and chip dinner one night. The town has parkland along the beachfront bay and what with the turquoise sea, beautiful sands, the river, trees and the red rocks it adds up to a very special feast for the eyes.

THESE ARE FOR REAL

Chapter 22

When we left Kalbarri we travelled along the coast road and stopped at **Port Gregory** for lunch before continuing on to Horrocks. We wouldn't have wanted to stay at Port Gregory but the lake is enormous and on the way back out it did glow pink to such a degree that I had to stop to take a couple of photos. **Horrocks** (odd name isn't it) turned out to be quite lovely and we were absolutely delighted with it because it was like going back in time with all the old beach shacks and the way they were placed in little streets. We loved it there although it doesn't take long to see the place as it is very small. There are so many covered areas to sit under such as a pergola or the thatched roof covered shelters on the beach or the shade sale on the foreshore parkland. It is unique and unspoilt. Apparently the town is surrounded by reef but we didn't have the time to go in the sea as they next day we were off to visit Royalty. The previous day we had stopped at **Northampton** for fuel as it was only four kilometres out of our way most of the town seemed to consist of all the original buildings. It is a lovely country town and we had enjoyed our visit to the Information Centre. We returned to Northampton and turned north to go up the main highway before we turned off to **The Hutt River Province** Principality, an independent Sovereign State inside Australia. We were welcomed by His Royal Highness Prince Leonard who is the Sovereign. I have never met anyone who talks as fast as he does and I'm sure that his speech does not keep up with his thoughts as I believe he has an intellectual capacity at least five times that of mine. He left school at fourteen years of age and became a clerk and then an accountant and by the age of eighteen he also had his own store. After three years in the RAAF he had an exporting firm, three trucks and three storied warehouse. Between times he also built and acquired several houses and buildings. You get the picture – industrious sort of guy. When we met him the other day I realised that he is now 81 years of age but he appears to have more energy than most people of half that age and a mind that is racing along with a wry sense of humour. The story of how he became an independent state within Australia with his own passports, money, stamps, laws, and of course the Constitution has been recorded on his behalf and we bought the book which His Highness offered to autograph for us. There is a web site apparently and as there is just too much to tell you, I suggest you look it up!

GERALDTON.

We left Horrocks and arrived here, about ten kilometres south of Geraldton on Thursday and we are delighted with the park as it is set against the river and the sea and we can walk to both. A sign near the beach tells us that it is called Cape Burney. There are no restrictions on the dogs on the beach either which is great. The park has a beautiful and very large gazebo with barbecues; a games room with table tennis and pool tables as well as a television set and the camper's kitchen has a full range of electrical appliances including two upright cookers. Crockery and cutlery is provided and large table. Some of the people in the caravans have been popping down there to roast a joint of meat and about eighteen of us invited ourselves to someone's lamb roast the other day! The lady carrying the roast told me she had bought some herbs that day and when we arrived at the kitchen the same herbs were there growing outside the door for people to pick! There are a lot of trees in this park and the wild birds are obviously going to build their nests in them judging by their amorous activities all over the park, including in the middle of the road and they take no notice of you as you walk or drive by. So we are surrounded by the trilling, chirping and warbling noises of the birds and sometimes it can be quite comical to listen to as there are so many varieties of birds.

We are here for two weeks and I certainly need the break as I find the sight-seeing exhausting at times. As I told John, I tend to see things through the eye of a camera lens and am just as likely to spot a beautiful piece of bark, an insect or a wild flower when we are stopping to look at an ocean scene. Rocks and cliffs hold an endless fascination for me because of the colours and textures and a sea shore with shells can keep me occupied for hours. So, by the end of what is supposed to have been a quick trip out I come back with my head full of nature's wonders, and a collection of shells or stones plus a camera full of photographs, the total of which can keep my mind busy for another 4-5 hours. John probably just goes and looks at the view and comes back with two or three 'scenes' in his head and he's ready for the next trip or can read the newspaper whilst I am still 'back there' in my head. I am having some lovely dreams though!

We arrived with the need to buy some food and get some washing done and that is what occupied our first day and we didn't see much of Geraldton whilst shopping. We also needed to catch up on odds and ends which we did yesterday. It's Sunday today and the market was on right next to our park. I should amend that and say that it is almost inside the park because there was a little train for the children to ride which came around the park and even under the washing lines. I had got up early expecting to get all my vegetables and some eggs but there was only one outlet which had minimal produce and I ended up with silver beet (a bit like spinach), honey (having done some taste-testing first), a home-made steak and mushroom pie and a home-made carrot cake. I wasn't able to cross anything off my shopping list despite the size of the market but came home delighted with my purchases.

When the train started careering around the park we thought it time to leave and we went to The Greenough Pioneer Museum and it was absolutely wonderful. The first owners moved into the four room cottage in 1862 and the house was extensively extended over time. Elizabeth and John (our namesakes) had 9 boys and 5 girls and Granny Maley to look after, with the help of maids and farm workers of course. John was a prominent colonist born in 1839 and he married Elizabeth when he was 23. He was a very industrious man and had involvement or ownership of various businesses. He died just after Christmas in 1910. What fascinated me so much were his diaries and I really could have stayed there reading and researching all the information for about three months. There are so many fully furnished rooms to look at and the included the children's toys and school books and clothes and all the utensils in the kitchen, the crockery and ornaments in the dining room, the drawers full of different types of lace, the musical instruments in another room – I could go on and on – plus there were all the photographs of the family. Outside there was more to see including the old duel toilet where I suppose you could sit alongside your husband and have a chat! It is an extraordinary collection and is beautifully presented. We had planned to go to Greenoch Historical Village but when we got there we realised that we had to pay another entry fee and there was so much to look at again that we changed our minds, had a coffee, gave the dogs a run and came home. We had seen so much historical stuff already and John felt the same way as me in that we didn't think we could take in more than what we had already learnt in one day. We will go another day when the dogs have had a good run first.

Monday was virtually taken up by a hospital visit for me for tests in the afternoon. I hadn't woken up until 10am! Today we set forth along the highway to Greenoch again and turned off to visit the Ellendale Pool, stopping to marvel at the height of the windmills along the way. I was so busy taking photos of the wild flowers that I hadn't noticed that we were all covered in flies! It was truly awful and it is the first time that either of us has ever experienced that amount of flies since we emigrated so many years ago. Ellendale Pool turned out to be a bit of a disappointment and there were flies there too and it seems that I am going to have to get my hat and net which have remained unused since I bought the net at a shop near Kings Canyon in the Northern Territory. It seems strange because this area is so-o-o windy and the tree trunks grow upwards and then bend over until the branches are lying horizontally on the ground as it is always so windy along this coast. The wind nearly knocks me over at times so why the flies like to hang about puzzles me.

We found the village of **Walkaway** fascinating but were sad to see a large house and the Wesley Church boarded up. It saddened me because I chose to be Christened and Confirmed as a Methodist in the Wesley Church in Maidenhead (England) when I was a teenager. In Australia today there is the United Church which I believe is a combination of the Baptist Church and Methodist and having attended both churches whilst growing up I had preferred the Methodist and found the churches quite different in so many ways.

We went to the Hampton Arms Inn to view the books, the Bric-a`-Brac Shop and the building itself rather than for an alcoholic drink. It was wonderful! There are thousands of books, some rare and on every subject imaginable. I purchased Sophia, Living and Loving (Her Own Story) plus a novel by Jennifer Bacia (actually two bestsellers in one volume) and John purchased The Unruly Life of Woody Allen. As we are both still trying to plough through Bill Clinton's book we will not be short of something to read for the rest of this trip. I also picked up a free book the other day in the laundry buy an author unknown to me so I am well pleased. I've read about a third of Sophia Loren's book whilst sitting on a stool at the pub! We only left because we felt sorry for the dogs stuck in the back of the Ute! There's a website if you're interested www.westnet. com.au/hamptonarms you might find that book for which you've been searching. Told our new neighbours who were only here for a couple days and they went the next day, had a ball and came back with books.

We took the dogs to the beach before coming home and they both went ballistic – even Jack pranced about which was so gratifying as he is so deaf now and looks at us so blankly at times with his eyes slightly hazy. We are going to look for a Vet tomorrow to see what we can do to help him as we wonder sometimes if he is in pain.

I've just got the washing in and put a lamb roast in the camp oven kitchen – for John. I'm not allowed meat for three days and then have to return to the hospital. I think my dinner is a boiled egg! I had to cook the lamb because it's been defrosting in the fridge for two days now but the smell is going to drive me insane so I'll know how it feels to be the dogs when we have a roast.

Annual Optician check – told just inside limit for passing my driving sight test for long distance (shock). Booked car in for service, ordered a new battery at last for CDMA phone and managed to get one pack of my mini toothbrushes and ordered more. Couldn't manage either of the latter two anywhere in Northern Territory or Western Australia thus far (feeling of accomplishment). Thought there would be a K Mart as I have a problem with my vacuum cleaner I bought there but seems I'll have to wait until Perth and the carpets are getting worse by the day!

Vet at animal hospital poked Jack so hard in one ear that he complained, so they sedated the poor thing and we had to leave him there for hours and it turned out that there was nothing wrong with the ear (frustrated, especially with the bill and the fact that they didn't check his eyes as requested). Jack didn't seem to recognise us at all when we picked him up and he is totally ignoring me. It doesn't matter how much I stroke him, he refuses to look at me! I've tried waving my hand in front of his face and he will look the other way and in front of him but will not turn around or acknowledge me in any way at all. He must be very angry with me for holding him still at the Vets today and for leaving him there. Two can play at that game – I've given up. I'll see what he's like tomorrow because it's amazing what a treat can do and I have a packet of doggy biscuits!

Went to Geraldton Cathedral which looks impressive on the outside but felt very disappointed once inside. The stained glass windows were lovely but the grey and orange striped walls may have had something to do with the fact that John and I both vocalised the fact that the place felt hollow with no atmosphere at all. Callie had a pee on the lawn outside so she was happy.

Went to the HMAS Sydney Memorial (very impressed). 645 men died in during a battle with a German Raider on 19th November 1941, more casualties of World War 2 that we'd not heard about. Both vessels went down and neither has been found since. It is a very moving tribute and the area provides extensive views of Geraldton.

Drove around the harbour and Callie had a quick swim at the beach at the northern end of town prior to picking Jack up. The beach goes on endlessly into the distance. We have seen most of the town centre now and both of the major shopping centres (spent too much on food and John not happy with his budgets as they no longer seem quite right!)

I had blood tests yesterday and French pathology nurse couldn't get my blood to flow and asked me if I drink anything! She'd managed to bend the needle but was delighted to find blood coming out of the vein in the other arm (amusing). We are not the only couple in this park trying to get all these 'business' things out of the way before arriving in Perth. The parks in Perth are expensive so we do not want to waste any time doing anything except sightseeing when we get there.

Helen tells us that a large parcel of post has been returned to her marked 'uncollected' and we have no idea where we were supposed to have collected them from! (She didn't have the parcel with her at work and couldn't remember either).

Really getting fed up with the wind and we were told yesterday by some happy campers that (a) 'You get used to it' (they live in W.A.) and (b) 'You'll get it all the way around the coast and won't get away from it until you leave Western Australia.' Another 'unhappy camper' told us that he had his awning up in Exmouth and the wind bent the metal frame so badly that it needs major repairs or replacement.

Invited to a free dinner provided by the park owners tomorrow night. We'll have the choice of fish, steak or chops with salads and all the trimmings and 'Just bring your drink'.

So, tomorrow is a work day. We are going to clean out our two air conditioners and clean the extractor fan in the bathroom and do laundry. I really ought to wash the dogs too but if they are going to in the sea again it seems a bit pointless (big decision). After tomorrow we will still have five days left before leaving and I'm sure we'll find plenty to do. Everywhere we go we see signs indicating a turn off the main roads to see recommended 'tourist drives'. We have yet to walk along the river here, we want to go and visit the Western Australian Museum Geraldton (can't remember why but I did read something that I want to experience there) and we still haven't been back to explore the Greenough Historic Hamlet and Visitor Interpretation Centre. We passed Greenough Woodworks the other day but it was closed and apparently that is worth a visit too as there are some wonderful pieces of furniture made out of weathered raw timbers. En route I also want to get a photo of a horizontal tree that I saw, just to remind me of the wind here! We have this huge fold-out pamphlet with maps listing so many places to see and the pamphlet was provided in a bag of tourist information leaflets when we arrived at the park so we haven't had to visit the Information Centre at all.

We have two sets of clothes every day along this Western Australian coastline because in the morning we put jumpers on and as soon as the sun disappears, as it has just done as the clouds have appeared again, the wind is really cold so we have to get changed again. On the weather forecast the other day it said that Geraldton had been 35C – rubbish! I had had a jumper on all day. Whoever obtained that temperature must have been in the only sheltered spot in Geraldton waiting for the midday sun to reach its peak temperature. The whole of this area should be producing its electrical power via windmills. Our van rocks around at times here and it is pretty heavy when parked with full tanks of water and both fuels.

I read in a magazine that if you have stubborn marks on your car windows then dab with milk wait a few moments and wipe off. Not sure if it works as I rarely clean my windows but thought you might like to know that.

Well John did the Central Greenoch Historic Settlement but I couldn't go because as soon as the hospital said that all my tests were clear I went down with gastroenteritis that very night! Drinking only bottled water now and I have improved considerably. Having seen the photos I'm not too worried that I missed going there. We went to the old gaol in Geraldton yesterday which houses crafts for sale and an elderly gentleman was making peacocks and kangaroos and all sorts of other animals out of strips of spray can containers. We were very impressed. We then went on to the museum and watched a film of the Batavia shipwreck and the subsequent massacre by some of the crew of most of the survivors, many of whom were women and children. Amazing story albeit horrific because people still did survive and the main perpetrators were hung. There are several books about it if you are interested. One lady suffered horrific hardship and when she did eventually reach the East Indies to join her husband she found that he had died a week earlier! She returned to Holland. We also learnt a lot about local shipwrecks including the battle of HMAS Sydney. The museum houses many items from the wrecks that have been recovered including the original Batavia stone portico.

Spent the last couple of nights and mornings sorting through copious information to find suitable caravan parks to cover the school holiday period which includes Christmas and New Year. We kept getting warned that we should have booked already. I use my free hour of phone calls in the morning but keep running out of time, so I will be back on the phone again tomorrow morning. Christmas through to past New Year is sorted and we will certainly still be in Western Australia. I look up the name of a place and think that we'll only stop one night and move on and then find that we have to visit 'The Valley of the Giants' or 'Treetop Walk' and all sorts of other things I've only seen in travel shows. So, I'm now working backwards from when we'll leave W.A to the stop that we hope to make after the park I've already booked in at when we leave here. I am so fed up with it all but it has to be done in advance.

I realise it is complicated by having the dogs and the big vehicle but mainly it is because of the holidays. John wouldn't really discuss it or take it seriously until he heard me say from the lounge couch at 1am that I could not find my passport. 'Why do you need your passport?'

'To fly home for Christmas because I'm damned sure I'm not going to be stuck on the side of the road for Christmas and New Year'.

'You don't need a passport to fly domestically' he replied.

Rather stunned as that was not the response I was expecting I retorted 'Well, I think you do with all the new security in place'.

'Where are you going to go?'

It wasn't until the next morning that he told me that he hadn't been able to sleep for a while afterwards and that he did understand where I was coming from.

I really meant it too. I also contemplated getting Helen to go to the Real Estate office to get them to accompany her to our unit to find my passport so that she could bring it with me. The other thing I thought about is booking myself into a first class hotel for about three weeks, including all meals and pondered about whether I'd let John come and visit me or not. He was lying in bed thinking about what trailer to buy so that he could tow the car!

So having had a temper tantrum, I found out today that all my photo files had rearranged themselves and I couldn't find anything in order, which is retribution of the highest order. Luckily I have numbered all our travel photos in the order that we have travelled and as we are into our second big trip, I'm already into the one hundred and thirty something. John has taken the car into town for its service and will have a lovely cup of coffee and melt-in-your-mouth cake of his choice at the bakery we went to yesterday (after visiting the museum) and I have spent the whole afternoon sorting out the photos. As I now have RSI in my right wrist I'm signing off. Ta-ta for now.

Before we move on I ought to tell you that there are 122 islands covering 155 kilometres along the coastline here at Geraldton. They are called the Abrolhos Islands. They are quite a way from the mainland which means that we would have to first fly and then go on a boat to see some of them or charter a boat. They lie on the edge of the continental shelf and it is these islands and their coral reefs that have caused at least nineteen shipwrecks. Aptly named, Abrolhos means 'Open Your Eyes'. It is a superb area to scuba dive, snorkel, to surf, for wind surfing, fishing or twitching or if you want to see dolphins. For whale sightings come here between May and October. The islands are isolated, pristine and teeming with marine and bird life – an ecological heaven.

We have met a lovely couple who we will probably keep in contact with. We started talking because they have also bought an American rig from the same company that we bought ours from so many notes were swapped and we looked at each others vans. Kerry and I have also had some similar experiences which made conversation very easy. However, on our last morning she and her husband were rather incensed at hearing on the radio, a 'baby-boomer' travelling around with her caravan saying that there is a wide gap between the people with motor homes and those with caravans and that those with caravans are very friendly. Well, Kerry was fuming as she and her husband honk their horn and wave to everyone who is travelling and she reckons it is the people who have caravans who discriminate and I have to agree. Kerry also told me that the best friends she's made so far whilst travelling have been those with caravans but we are still in touch with people who travel with tents, caravans and motor homes but have experienced discrimination and it can be quite nasty at times with us being pointedly ignored because we have a motor home. We usually approach those people because we are interested in buying a smaller set-up when we get home and I usually say that our 'van' is pretty old being built in '1988' and 'far too big' and their attitude changes. But Kerry is right because it is usually us who has to make the approach in the first instance although I do not think that the men are as bad as the women. Some people seem to think that because we have a 'big rig' we are therefore snobby and rich. If only! People with old buses are usually very interested in ours and are twice as likely to stop for a chat. I've said to John before that if we get something smaller it will be quite nice to just 'slot in' to whichever place we find ourselves instead of not knowing if people are going to be nasty or nice!

Chapter 23

DONGARA 'The Lobster Capital' (apparently).

And that's another thing. Don't be as stupid as us and go around Australia without being able to fish and having the gear. We are at Dongara and an elderly guy just sauntered off to the barbecue under the giant pergola with two fillets from a Taylor he'd caught last night and he has more in the freezer. Yesterday I spent $12 on a piece of fish in Woolworths in Geraldton. I must learn to fish but what should seem like something so simple because it must be a basic instinct to catch food and eat it, seems impossibly complicated to me. I've watched the fishing programs with interest for a couple of years but every time they pull a fish in I have no idea what it is until I'm told. So the other day, I'm in the Post Office and they have these huge laminated posters on various subjects and one of them was of fish. There are so many different fish! How on earth would I know what I'd caught and that's only the start of it. There are all these different rods and lures and different bait for different fish. I just want to walk out into the sea with a net and catch one that I recognise and know that I like to eat.

We are here for three nights and everyone is very friendly but we arrived late as we were saying our farewells to several people and John wanted to flush our water and waste tanks out. It was a little complicated finding our way down to the harbour where the park is and the dog beach is fully covered with seaweed which is a bit smelly. There have been so many gale force winds lately, the seas have been rough and East of Geraldton last night they apparently had a hail storm which was severe enough to pulp the crops. The farmers are suffering so badly with the drought and now this. I listen to a lot of farming programs on the ABC channel whilst we travel and the federal government is offering subsidies so that the farmers can reseed next year. A lot of sheep have been slaughtered in the last few months and some farmers in Australia have committed suicide. Some farmers in Western Australia are being offered lessons to get their truck licences to give them a second career until, hopefully, the drought ends and the mines have said that farmers have skills that they need (mainly with machinery) and have suggested employment on a fly-in/fly-out basis because they are so short of workers too. In the meantime the interest rates are about to climb for the third time this year and vegetable and fruit prices are increasing rapidly. Everything is costing more except that petrol, in some places, has dropped down a little. I heard on T.V that in Karratha you can rent a four bedroom home with no games room or pool for $900 per week!!!

That's truly outrageous and reflects the lack of rental homes available. I had thought that the Gold Coast was expensive but it's half the price there.

The guy who had the beautiful fish (it must be beautiful because it's actually fresh unlike the fish that I buy) told me that years ago he was buying gas for a few cents a litre (can't recall the figure but under 20c) and then it was decided to export the gas to Japan which was delivered there for 8c per litre and on the Friday he had filled up at the normal price and on the Monday it had gone up to 50c per litre! It is about that in Perth I believe and double up that in the north of W.A. Why do we export all our gas when we need it here and why should we pay more than the cost of delivery to Japan – it's all beyond me. I was watching three economists on T.V a few years ago and they were talking about many different budgets in several different countries over the last fifty years or so and none of the economic decisions had been successful long term. It was fascinating seeing these highly skilled economists debating and arguing their cases but all had to agree that there is no perfect system.

Most of the coastline has high sand dunes and we are tucked behind dunes now. However, I was told that everything rusts quickly here whether it is a car, gutters, your refrigerators in your homes – anything that can rust will do so. There are so many times, for so many reasons that I long to be back over the border in Queensland, although you get rust there too if you live too near to the sea.

Dongara and Port Denison are linked via the road and Dongara is the main town area (which is more like a village) with Port Denison being the beaches and harbour although there are some shops there. Dongara is famous for the Moreton Bay Fig trees which line its main street (Moreton Terrace) and they can be seen in many other areas in the vicinity and this year, 2006, marks the centenary of their planting. The celebrations will be included in their annual festival in November when the Blessing of the 'Blessing of the Fleet' also takes place. Port Denison is famous for its multi-million dollar crayfish (western rock lobster) industry and you will see a giant one on entering via the main highway, made by a local artist.

We've been here for three nights and I am 'Dongo'd out' as we have been up, around and through the area many times. The dogs have had lots of swims, I have taken too many photographs, we have enjoyed the scenery, the Port Denison Marina, the Irwin River, the old buildings and heritage trails and the best blueberry muffin that I have ever tasted in the coffee shop in Dongara. We enjoyed the Blue Ocean Gallery (found via Golf Course Road) and the eighteen hole golf course looked so good (it actually has grass on it) that John has nipped off for a game now (3pm) which gives me a chance to catch up on this. We went to visit The Priory Lodge, built in 1881 and it is a beautiful building which was once used by the Dominican Sisters. I skipped breakfast because the leaflet we had been given in the Information Centre told us that they serve Devonshire Teas and we arrived there about midday and I was starving. There were no cars outside and an elderly man inside mumbled that he hadn't even got any cream so couldn't help us!

When we leave here tomorrow to head for Leeman we will be leaving the section of coast, being between Kalbarri and Dongara-Denison, called the Batavia Coast In hindsight, I'm glad that we went to the Museum in Geraldton and learnt more about the Batavia, not just because of its unusual historical story but because even here there have been shipwrecks and it makes you realise just how treacherous and how unique this coastline is.

LIZARDS AT LEEMAN

LEEMAN & GREEN HEAD

We enjoyed our few days in Leeman mainly due to the fact that the owners of the park were so laid back and helpful. There was another lovely gazebo to sit under, we could choose our own site and were able to wash the dogs with the main water supply although the owner offered to change his sprinkler system so that I could use the bore water as he reckons that the water is so good that you can drink it. So I asked 'You've had it tested then?'

'Tested! What do they test for?' he replied so I explained why it was necessary if you were going to drink it!

I was a little surprised that they charged for using the barbecue as in most parks they are free and the washing machines were a little dear at $4 a time but we were all very relaxed and happy there.

I didn't go to the nearest beach and John said he was going to avoid it as it was completely covered in seaweed and looked really bad. However, on the last day he took the dogs there and he said that it was metres thick and dry and Callie loved it and he and she were bouncing up and down on it like a trampoline but Jack fell over and he had to help him keep upright!

We also met a really nice couple there who were moving down to Jurien Bay because there are more shops and they suggested that we follow them and that they would look after our dogs if we wished to go and see the Pinnacles.

So we moved on the next day stopping at Green Head to have a coffee and look around. I found craft items that I had been seeking since leaving Rockhampton at the caravan park shop there! I have been to the biggest of craft shops and they have never stocked them. The owner there told us that the locals don't much like having a caravan park in Green Head as it spoils their peace and quiet. We were surprised to see a lot of large modern homes there and it had a very different atmosphere than we had expected. There was one spot on the beachfront where I could have taken a beautiful photo of the beach but as there were no other photos that I wished to take of the place I decided to forget it.

JURIEN BAY

We arrive at the caravan park to be given the choice of two sites, one of which would only fit a caravan so there really was no choice. We set up, trying to get as near to the fence line as is possible without hitting a huge tree and then I realise that we are on a double site which means that where we open our door, the adjoining site line is almost on top of us. We put up the awning and park the vehicle on the site beyond so no-one else can put their van there as there is so little room. Then I read the site rules which state that you must not park on any spare site. The wind is so bad (the news warn of gale force winds) that we are forced to take the awning back down despite all the guy ropes in place and awning flap grips as it feels like the van is about to take off like an aeroplane and we go out in the Ute for a look around the area to get our bearings. We return to find a bus parked outside our door, so close that there is no hope of putting the awning up anyway and the men who live in the bus have tried to park as far away from us as possible whilst keeping inside their line limit. I go to sit outside and it is like sitting in a train corridor and when I give up and go inside I can watch their T.V as it is so close! We decide that we'll leave as soon as our three nights are up and not stay an extra day as we were contemplating. The reason we are annoyed is that there are so many vacant sites, huge open spaces with not a van in site. The men left the next day and they were totally bemused as to why they had been told to only go onto that site. It's a good way to lose customers.

Likewise our new friends, who have a lovely site, suddenly find themselves with people parked on their space with a small motor home and both couples are confused because again there are so many spare sites around them. The new couple also left the next morning! So I went to the office and I think I spoke to the park owner and I told him that we would not be staying on an extra night as we had mentioned and I told him why. He looked perplexed and said that he would have had no complaints if that bus had stopped on any other site I responded that we are all going to the sites we are told to go to believing that the others are pre-booked. After we had left the park our friends told us that they had five lots of tents and vans parked on their small area and that he hadn't even been able to get his car out at one time, yet there is no-one parked at all in the huge area where we were! He made me laugh because he was listing all the rules and ended up by saying 'Rule 154. Though shall not laugh.'

This morning I went out to stock up on food but it was so expensive that a few items cost nearly $90 and our new friends tell me that they went to buy two items, bought a few other things and the bill was $50 and they are not impressed either. I return to find a tent parked on our other side, right near our windows, yet again there is about two acres of empty sites! They are worried that their children will disturb us and that they would try to keep them quiet. I told them that kids are not kids long enough nowadays as it is so let them make as much noise as they want because after all, they are supposed to be on holiday and hopefully excited. I also told them that I'd try and keep my 'kids' quiet as Jack has now found his bark again. They cannot understand why they have been made to come to their site but they won't move as this is their first camping experience and judging by the confusion of putting up their new tent and unpacking all their new camping equipment I don't think he could bear it. He reckons he's only been used to hotels in upmarket hotels and units so I told him to keep reciting to himself 'This is fun. This is fun'. He said he looked at our van and said 'That's camping'. I told her she only needed to sweep out her tent with a broom and I need a vacuum cleaner and she shuddered!

There are some fairly nice sandy beaches but there's really nothing to rave about here. It's o.k. Our new friends have both got a stomach bug and are feeling a bit weak and wobbly and are visiting the doctors tomorrow morning so I'm not sure if they'll be looking after the dogs tomorrow and we are leaving the following day for Cervantes. I took a bottle of brandy to them and told them to try the bush remedy of a 'hot toddy' and he said it worked for him!

There's a 'scrappy' golf course according to John, not nearly as nice as Dongara-Denison. We are hoping we enjoy Cervantes more and I am also hoping that when we go inland to Gingin we'll get away from the wind for a while as it really is becoming so tiring. I tried to go outside and read a book but it's impossible as even the chair blows over. We are also in love with our fly swat as the flies are driving us nuts.

Sophia Loren was my first 'idol' and other than believing that I would marry Elvis Presley when he found me, remains to this day a person I admire and who I would wish to emulate. I have just finished reading her book Living and Loving, Her Own Story by A.E. Hotchner and I was struck by the following words which is the embodiment of why I drive in a separate vehicle and what I have meant by needing 'space'.

'True happiness is impossible without solitude. I devoutly believe that. I need solitude in my life as I need food and drink and the laughter of little children. Extravagant though it may sound, solitude is the filter of my soul. It nourishes me, and rejuvenates me. Left alone, I discovered that

I keep myself good company......In solitude, I read and experience what I read. And in solitude, I deal honestly with my feelings, and with myself. I test new ideas. I redress any missteps I have taken; solitude for me is a house of undistorted mirrors.'

Now why couldn't I have put it like that! I do not like to feel lonely. I find that a rather frightening experience but I do need solitude to be able to be in a relationship. I sometimes refer to it as head space or tell John that my computer (head) is full up so please don't talk for a while. He understands thank goodness. When I went shopping without the dogs and John the other day I stopped the car at the park by the sea and just stood there and breathed and I could feel a physical change in my body. I only stayed about five minutes but it tasted like the sweetest nectar to be totally alone for those moments.

It was so good to read those words and when she says that she experiences what she reads I felt elated because I always feel that I am an actual character in a book and I 'feel' their experiences. It is the same with films which is why I cannot watch horror films, science fiction or indeed anything at all that will scare me. Even with a current program I watch nightly, I have to put the mute button on sometimes and look away and that is a program that kids watch! If someone is being chased it is me being chased. If someone is sad I feel sad. I love good comedy! To know that someone else feels like I do is a revelation to me!

Chapter 24

CERVANTES

The night before we left Jurien we went out for dinner with our friends and I ordered one glass of red, house wine. I had started drinking a whiskey and lemonade prior to leaving but hadn't drunk much. Despite eating a roast beef dinner whilst drinking my wine, our friends had to accompany me back to our van because all the vans looked the same to me, whilst John drove home as he had taken the Ute with the dogs in the back so that they would know where we were. When John arrived home I told him he simply had to listen to one of our outdoor chairs as it was 'alive'.

'Listen, you can hear things moving about inside the seat.'

John put his ear to the chair and calmly told me it was raining! I hadn't noticed and it was the sound of the raindrops I had heard splattering onto the vinyl covered seat. It is so long since we've had rain that we panicked again with John asking me 'What do we usually do with the dogs?'

Our friends called by in the morning and told us that they were also going to Cervantes to have a look and that they would see us there. They passed us on the road as we were travelling there and we were travelling back! I phoned them this morning and they had seen the same scenery that we had seen yesterday afternoon, that being the shops, the beaches and the lookout.

We travelled slowly to Cervantes because the wind was rocking the van about and John wasn't that happy about the trip. We had booked into the park for four nights but when we arrived the girl told us that they did not give refunds and suggested that we book on a daily basis! I commented to John that I wandered what she knew that we didn't know! Why would we wish to leave? We booked in for only two nights.

They have a unique lounge area inside the office/shop where you can sit and read and there are some bookshelves with 'swap' books and I'm sure I've got something to swap, plus some more shelves where the books belong to the owner and you can borrow them for a $20 deposit and I duly paid my $20 and am now reading 'Bill Wyman. Stone Alone' written by Bill Wyman with Ray Coleman and I've learnt about the childhoods of all the Stones but am only up to page 155.

There are 642 pages plus appendixes so I don't think I will have the time to finish it unless I stay up all night tonight as we are going to leave tomorrow!

We went to the Information Centre but the lady there had a job to answer any questions let alone lift her head up from whatever she was doing and I felt we should have apologised for disturbing her! I spent an inordinate amount of time looking around the Information Centre and the shop (which annoyed me as many things had no price on them) just for something to do.

When we were on the beach in the afternoon the wind was so strong that it bowled Jack over, nearly bowled me over, I had trouble shutting the car door and I had sand in my hair, eyes, ears and nostrils. John had constant trouble with his eyes, whether at the caravan park or the beach, as the sand got behind his contact lenses. We climbed up the steps to a lookout and I immediately went back down as I couldn't cope with the wind. First item up on Channel Seven news was the fact that there was a huge storm coming, covering the area from Jurien to Perth with very large hail and would everyone get themselves and their vehicles under cover.

I tried to eat the dinner I'd cooked but gave up half way through as I was so tense. Our front windscreens were facing the direction of the gale and there are trees all around us. It was too late and getting too dark to dismantle and pack everything away to turn the bus around to save the windscreens. John moved the car closer to the van and put the dogs into it and shut them in much to Jacks disgust but in doing so he had placed the Ute under a huge tree. Then we waited. We saw small branches go flying and heard people with cabins hammering timber over windows but we couldn't do anything but wait. We waited until we were too tired and went to bed and nothing actually happened in our area, nor in Jurien. I have no idea what has happened elsewhere as we only have two channels working on our radio here and one is a Christian station and doesn't seems to have news and we have not heard a news report on the other. Last night the latter had non-stop music without interruptions (which we actually wanted as we wanted weather updates) and this morning it is the music 'countdowns' and we're now at number eighteen in the charts and still no news. Every time I turn the T.V on it is sports on three channels but I did enjoy an interview with Andrew Denton on the only other channel about his newly published book called 'God on my side' (I believe). Apparently he was more candid during this interview than he is in the book.

John has gone off to see the Pinnacles and I am dog sitting and battling the flies. Like the sea lions at Jurien which we didn't see because the sea was so rough, the Pinnacles are a main tourist attraction here. It costs $10 per car to drive into the National Park but it is so hot today and the thought of putting the dogs into 'cages' whilst I go off to enjoy myself wandering around a pile of limestone deposits (up to three metres high) made me feel just too guilty. Jack is not too good today and John thinks he's in pain. He said that he cocked his leg to have a 'wee' but then carried on peeing whilst walking as though he couldn't hold his leg up long enough to finish. Yesterday he was like a puppy on the beach and he is suffering for it today. Only just over a week and he'll see Helen again but sometimes I look to see if he's breathing despite his apparently strong heart.

JOHN AT PINNACLES

The Pinnacles (John)

'The track through the Pinnacles was clearly marked by small rocks through a brilliantly orange-yellow desert country with a distant backdrop of turquoise sea. I had great fun driving along the path between a great variety of the Pinnacles, some several metres in height some joined together in weird shapes, stopping occasionally for a photograph or to climb observation platforms and hillocks. The track was several kilometres long and I wondered at times if I had gone the wrong way, a fascinating experience. On the way back I stopped at an idyllic bay with a blindingly white beach with brilliant blue/green water, strangely called Hangover Bay, spoilt only by swarms of flies which forced my rapid retreat back to the car. A bus load of tourists had just stopped for afternoon tea and I wondered how the tour operator would handle the flies and his guests at the same time.'

There are other things to look at here and if it wasn't so windy the beaches would be beautiful. There is Lake Thetis for example which is only three metres deep but the level rises and falls with the tide from no obvious source. There are circular mounds up to a metre round which is apparently 'calcareous algae' from the Stromatolites. That does not tell me if they are living now or does it? Anyway, they are flatter looking than the ones we saw before. John went to see them and took some photos for me.

STROMATOLITES - FASCINATING LITTLE CRITTERS

Stromatolites (John)

'The Stomatolites seen on the way to the Pinnacles were a disappointment as they were limited in number, size and variety as compared with those we saw near Denham.'

These damned Stromatolites are beginning to give me a headache! I got around to reading an old article from The West Australian newspaper which lists '501 things you should know' and it was in the fourth week of the 501 articles. The article is on new research of a 10km section of rocks in East Pilbara called Strelley Pool Chert and critics argue that the Pilbara ones could have been formed by chemistry or physics, not only biology because apparently the fossils are too varied. So, if I've given you any wrong information it is the result of the wrong information so far recorded and in print!

As we leave Cervantes we leave behind the stretch of coast called the Indian Ocean Drive which stretches from here to Exmouth. We then enter the stretch of coastline called Sunset Coast.

GINGIN

We turned up at the Gingin Caravan Park and bought a couple of meat pies which we had to eat in the van because of the flies. We were trying to decide whether to stay at that park or another about twenty kilometres away. Neither is actually in Gingin. We drove down to the village and had a quick look around and I felt quite unsettled because we honestly did not know what to do! We ended up booking in for one night. I felt very ratty so I decided I needed to be alone and drove back to the village and took some photos, purchased a few items including a fly net for John to wear over his face as he was longing for one like mine and then I sat by the old Anglican Church and tried to relax. I wanted to go in but it was locked. There is a lovely parkland area, a stream with a little wooden bridge over it and a paddle wheel in action. The gentle green scenery enveloped me and calmed me down and I realised that I do not like uncertainty and seem incapable of making decisions in a hurry. I need to know where I am going, why I am going there and know in advance that I want to be there, which is a bit difficult on a trip like this. John couldn't seem to make a decision either! By walking around the village and trying to soak up the atmosphere I was trying to feel familiar with the place and therefore, hopefully, more comfortable.

After our first night we booked in for a further two nights and have got the washing done. John has gone to visit the Gravity Discovery Centre. One of my sons is having a holiday on the Sunshine Coast in a beachside luxury unit and millions of people have been attending Melbourne Cup parties and have spent about $130M on betting, in Australia alone, with first and second places both going to Japanese horses! So the cup goes off to the Land of the Rising Sun whilst the jockey who won the cup tries to stop crying tears of joy. My entertainment for the afternoon was trying to tune in the T.V manually because the automatic tuning was so abysmal and preparing a cauliflower cheese dinner!

Gravity Discovery Centre (John)

'I went to look at the Gravity Discovery Centre which was some 20 kilometres down the road from our Gingin Caravan Park. This is the sight of a Gravity Wave Interferometer, which is part of an international joint venture with sights in USA, Europe, South America and Asia to measure gravity waves from the far reaches of his universe, investigating black holes, the size of the universe etc. I saw many gravity related demonstration mechanisms which only a science graduate would understand, but fantastic for any budding schoolboy scientific genius. I was fascinated with an Ion Drive Lifter which has been used to drive a deep space probe. It is an all-electric rocket with no moving parts. This is the way to go and I reckon that the fiery rockets we use to blast off from earth are wasteful and will seem old fashioned in a few years. There were also videos on astronomy, covering the Solar System, the Milky Way and other star systems. There was also an amusing obituary to Pluto which has now been downgraded from a planet to an asteroid by the world astronomy authoritarian scientific eggheads.'

We were talking to a guy who has been working here in this park for the last six weeks, along with his wife and he was saying that they sold up sixteen years ago and have been travelling around and working all over the country ever since and they love it. That is a 'way of life' but it is not for me or John. My friend in Tasmania phoned tonight and she said 'I want to go for holidays, not marathons' and that just about sums up my feelings. No wonder we have got along so well together since we were at High School! I love friends like that who can tell you what you think, or rather what they think but know that you do too if you know what I mean! With other people, if I dare to say that I will not be doing this again I get an immediate response of 'Oh, well, we'll go back because it's beautiful and we love it. Didn't you like ....? Of course you didn't go to .....National Park or you would want to go back.'

And I think 'Good, excellent, glad you love it but why do I now feel guilty for having expressed my feelings?'

Even worse is when someone retorts 'Oh, it's my sixteenth time' because I look at them with my mouth wide open (dangerous around here with the flies). I think the guy we were talking to this morning said it was their sixteenth time.

The greatest sin is if you mention anywhere outside of Australia to those who have never left this Continent. I might say 'I'd like to spend any money we have left on going to Europe' and the responses have varied from 'Why?' 'What for when we have so much to see here in Australia?' to 'Oh, I couldn't stand that'.

It leaves me absolutely baffled. These kind of people do not even ask what Europe is like to find out why we want to go and if they did at least I could just say 'To see my family'. They have no interest at all in anything except their own back yard.

John returned from his outing to the Gravity Discovery Centre to tell me that he had found the other caravan park that we could have gone to and that it is in a more rural setting with grass and that I would like it. Because the bore water is so salty here we cannot connect our hose to their tap and had, in desperation, connected our hose to the water tank twice to fill up our water tank but took only enough to keep us going. We did not want to contaminate out tank water and used all of what we had left first. We used a bucket of hot water from the laundry to wash up in, I used their spotless showers and toilets constantly (which I never normally do) so that we were using the bore water and we did everything we could do to conserve the drinking water that we did obtain from their fresh water tank. However, we received a remark 'Hope you are not using up all the tank water' and felt embarrassed despite the park fees not reflecting the water difficulty, nor has it got a pool or concrete slabs or grass for the vans. So we moved to this new park. We had forgotten to ask about the water!

When we arrived we were told that we could drink the bore water but it has a lot of iron in it. The first thing we did was to give the dogs some water and as John was filling our tank I noticed a brown scum on the top of the dogs water and a heap of brown sludge in the bottom of the bucket and yelled to John to turn the tap off quickly. I skimmed the water off the top of the dogs bucket and prayed they could stomach it! By this time we would have had some of this rotten water in our tank but at least it would have been diluted by the fresh tank water that we arrived with. We used up the water that we had in a five litre container and John went in search of the park owner and asked if he drank tank water. John got our bottle filled up! We stayed two nights before we paid them cash for those two nights so we are paying them by the day, in arrears. The owner only wanted cash and we didn't have enough so the owner had to wait until we could find a bank. John goes there to get the bottle filled up and pays them for the night at the same time so we continue to get the fresh water to drink, for cooking vegetables and for making gravy. Other than that we are using up what is in our tank and using their shower and toilets instead of our own. The washing facilities are excellent as they have the toilet, shower, sink together in each cubicle along with pump-action soap and freshly laundered hand towels daily.

John thoroughly enjoyed the Gravity Centre learning more about black holes, the art of curved space, anti-gravity and magnetic levitation, magnetic force, gravity waves, Einstein's equations of space and gravity and endless other stuff. He said that there was a lot of 'hands-on' stuff and for kids and students it is a marvellous place to take them.

Last night they offered a 'bring your own everything' barbecue under their huge verandah but it was so cold that we huddled inside the van with the fire on. Another reason that we didn't go is that friends had turned up. They had seen our van from the road as they had driven via the coastal route and were heading towards Gingin. They decided to come and stay for the night but they left this morning as they did not like the water situation. As they were arriving, we were setting off for the coast to have a look at, what we had read and expected to be, the fishing villages of Seabird and Ledge Point, stopping first at Guilderton and ending up in Lancelin.

Guilderton was quite nice and our friends had stayed at the caravan park there but there was a notice up saying that no dogs were allowed in or anywhere near the caravan park, park or river! There was also only one shop which surprised us. We drove around and the rest of it was mainly a residential housing area. **Seabird** and **Ledge Point** were major disappointments. They are not 'fishing villages' but real estate marketing suburbs with new houses, new land releases and new townhouse developments. We should have given them both a miss completely. **Lancelin** was a little better, especially at the southern end where the windsurfing lessons were taking place and we chatted for quite a long time to the owner of the business about the changes to the beaches and environment that had taken place over the last twenty years. What used to be a huge beach is now a small beach. Man has interfered with the currents to the detriment of the environment yet again. She also told us about similar events in Germany and we told her about the Gold Coast.

I needed potatoes so we visited a supermarket and were happy to find some reasonable prices and excellent service. Likewise the service in the chemist and the café was excellent; the latter where we ordered hot roast beef and gravy in rolls, which were grilled so that they were beautifully crispy on the outside. We were happy to return home though and I drove as I had seen so many flowers that I wanted to photograph on the way to the coast and wanted to drive slow enough to be able to stop at a moment's notice. John told me that I could have told him to stop but I worried that if I called 'Stop' as he was travelling at 100kph he might have reacted instantly and the dogs would have flown through the windows.

I'm sitting here stunned by the news that Belinda Emmet has died as she was a favourite media personality of mine. I first noticed her beauty on Home and Away (one of our daily T.V programs) and was sad when she left and even sadder when I heard that she had breast cancer, particularly as she was so very young. I then recognised her acting ability and she returned to her acting profession only to find later that the cancer had spread to her bones. She married her very well known T.V personality partner and continued to appear on T.V for a variety of reasons, always looking frail but determined and always presented to the public her beautiful smiling face. Somehow, although everyone knew how ill she was, she seemed invincible because she kept appearing on our screens. What with Steve Irwin (crocodile hunter), followed by Peter Brock (a well known racing driver here) and now Belinda, I cannot help wandering how young people are coping because when I was young I really had no idea about death. My father refused to have a T.V in the house until I was in my teens and when an older friend of mine was killed in a train crash, I recall my mother not wanting me to attend the funeral as she thought I was too young to cope and I would have been about sixteen or seventeen at the time! Now young people see it on the news all the time and even very young children have been mourning very deeply for Steve. Death is part of life and I think it was only my generation who were relatively protected as we were not alive in Britain during any war years and I left Britain before the Falkland war so I have been particularly lucky. I have the luxury of pondering this question. I have heard people say that they feel like they 'know' someone in the even though they have never met them. I met Steve Irwin but feel even more deeply about Belinda, perhaps because I tried to follow her progress with always so much hope in my heart that she would finally win through.

Now for something completely different! We are finding the road rules in W.A so confusing because there are double white lines across so many turnings. For example, if you want to go into a shopping centre car park there may well be double white lines which mean that you cannot cross them but everyone else is doing so. Another example was when we were coming down the main highway and wanted to turn off for the Indian Ocean Drive, because we were going to Leeman and Jurien and there again were the continuous double white lines! We have no idea how we are supposed to get to the road we want other than drive over them as neither our bus nor Ute can fly yet have no idea if we are breaking the law!

We have not visited the West Coast Honey company up the road between Gingin and this park and I believe that you can taste-test the honey and buy honey ice cream and other delicious honey products. However, we are off to see Two Rocks and Yanchep tomorrow and John has gone to the **Southern Cross Cosmos Centre** tonight so we are taking nearly full advantage of what the area has to offer. I was expecting him to be back within minutes because it is cloudy and has been raining. Perhaps he's watching the lightening through the twenty five inch one which is the largest telescope available to the public in Western Australia. This telescope is called Obsession. I actually contemplated going but as I'm not obsessed by the cosmos I thought that I would probably look at Saturn and be awed by all its rings and a couple of other constellations and would then think 'Right, seen that, let's go' whereas John would be wanting to chat to other people about things of which I have absolutely no understanding and I would get bored and fidgety and ruin the evening for him so I'm dog-sitting once again. Tomorrow morning we are invited to a free Devonshire tea/coffee at the park so I'll skip breakfast and meet some of the other visitors. Tomorrow will be our last day before leaving for Perth where we will actually stay put for two weeks.

Well John enjoyed his evening but added that there were only two other couples there and a load of kids who naturally wanted to see through the telescopes first. He asked them if they were going to be astronauts and one young lad answered 'Not me. I'm going to keep my feet firmly planted on the ground' which rather amused him. He didn't see the universe through the giant Obsession because the guy running the place said it would take too long to set up but he did see through a 12 inch one. He also loved the computers where you could ask to see a planet and the guy would program it with a hand-held handset and the screen would zoom towards the planet. He saw twin stars, one of which was blue and the other red but apparently people see them in different colours. The earlier clouds had cleared the atmosphere and the roof rolled back and they had the chance to see the cosmos in all its glory.

'Which water container do I use for a cup of coffee?' John asked, adding 'I'm so damned confused with all this'.

So was I. We had completely run out of water in our holding tank which we had been using to wash our hands after patting the dogs or for flushing the toilet during the night. The water from the taps outside was getting even browner but we had dug out the dogs emergency rations stored under the van and were using their other water container for them when we went out. We had the container that we were getting refilled but we now had a bucket of water from some other source that John had found for washing up with. The 'good water' was being used for drinks, gravy and cooking vegetables but sometimes we would forget and wash our hands in the bucket water forgetting that that was also for cleaning down worktops etc. Somehow or other a jug had come in useful and now we were getting muddled up as to which water was in the jug! It's difficult to describe but we would use the jug to get bucket water for rinsing the sink or for the toilet but would also use it to transfer water from the good water container to fill the kettle. We became so fed up and irritable that we started to get irritable with each other. John noticed that the park owner had at least two huge tanks of rain water that were overflowing and that added to his annoyance. When we went to get water off the owner he would take us to this kitchen where he would carefully transfer his water from a big container to our smaller one using a jug and being very careful not to spill a drop. They did not drink the water that he had been telling us was quite harmless. We just wanted to get away from there and get to Perth but as the bus had an appointment for new tyres to be fitted at 1 o'clock on the Monday we couldn't move earlier as we were to get that done on the way to our park.

We decided to take ourselves out for the last day there to visit two other 'towns' on the coast to the south of where we were staying. We had been told that there was nothing there but we enjoyed that day out more than we had when we visited the northern beach towns. There was far more to see at **Two Rocks** including a harbour, a huge statue of King Neptune which Alan Bond had had built when he had planned to build a theme park of some sort years ago. It was an area of sand dunes with wire fencing in disrepair but a shopping village had been built and he had apparently planned to base himself there if he had won the America Cup for a second time. Nobody has done anything with the area since he pulled out of the venture and a shop owner reckons that he sold it to some Japanese company and that some bits of the area have been sold off since. I bought an item of pottery and we then headed off for the second place on our itinerary which was **Yanchep.** That was a surprise because it was just a huge residential area and the local shops were back at Two Rocks. Anyway, we managed to find a cup of coffee and the dogs had enjoyed their swim at Two Rocks and we came home happy.

TWO ROCKS - KING NEPTUNE

Chapter 25

PERTH

We got hopelessly lost and it was nerve racking because I was following John. We were driving through a very busy area in peak traffic when John suddenly pulls up in a spare place at the side of the road where there was nowhere for me to park and we were so frightened of losing each other. We kept asking directions and were told to take the third right into a particular road only to find that the road did not exist and I was winding down my window and getting taxi drivers to do the same and our two-way radio was buzzing. We got to the tyre place about ten minutes late having left ourselves an extra hour to find it! We saw most of Perth's roadways but little else. Then we waited and waited with two very hot and eventually very hungry dogs as they did not finish until after 5 o'clock. There was a water dispenser and plastic cups and I must have drunk eight or nine of them whilst I was there but was dehydrated as it was going straight through and the temperature hovered around 35C. The previous night we had been so cold that we had all the windows shut, the fan heater on and I was wearing jeans and two jumpers. We had only come a hundred kilometres further south!

The caravan park reception closed at 5pm! I had been phoning of course and warning them of what was going on and a gentle, smiling lady greeted us when we finally arrived absolutely exhausted at around 6pm. We have a very long, solid site built from bricks and are situated right next to the toilets, showers and laundry which was excellent as I knew that I needed to do three machine loads plus hand washing and some bleaching. I became ecstatic with joy at finding that inside the shower block there was a separate room with a bath in it. I was also overjoyed at knowing that there is a very large swimming pool here because we haven't seen one for some time. Dogs fed, a shower and hair wash in my own shower with lovely fresh water, a scrambled egg tea and a cup of coffee, along with a good book and I was in heaven. Also the T.V works properly at long last so we were actually able to see the last of Andrew Denton's shows for the season later in the evening. I must have been exhausted because John had trouble waking me up at 9.30am! So today I have been doing all the laundry and am catching up on this and John has set off to find the shops and other utilities that we are going to need. Tomorrow Helen arrives in the afternoon and I will do a big shop in the morning. The people here are so very friendly and one guy has expressed interest in buying a bus like ours so perhaps we'll find a buyer in advance but he'll have to wait until May unless he has a van the size we want in which case we can swap!

SWAN RIVER PERTH IS SO HUGE

17th November 2006

Tuesday was a mad day because we went shopping, returned for lunch but when I opened the fridge to put the shopping away I saw that a new bottle of milk had spilt all over everything inside the fridge and was beginning to drip onto the carpet and into the vegetable and salad bins. In the meantime John was piling $200 worth of shopping around my feet, all over every available work space and in the doorway! I kept telling him to leave it where it was whilst I cleaned up. I had stuff everywhere and we were tripping over it. Some of our purchases were to be stored under the rear bed and under the seat where he wished to sit to eat lunch. Then I remembered a bit of hand washing still in a bucket in the shower. By the time I had cleaned the fridge, got most of the shopping away, put the hand washing outside to drip dry, it was time to leave for the airport. Our park brochure says it is a ten minute drive to the domestic airport and we had forty-five minutes, leaving ourselves plenty of time. We turned left onto a highway at my insistence but John felt we had gone the wrong way so we went off and came back on and went the other way. As it turned out, we were both wrong and were on the wrong highway! By the time we were entering the airport car park Helen was waiting outside with a huge suitcase. I had a text message ready stating 'Just entering airport car park' and sent it just as she was trying to ring me and she got cut off. I tried to phone her but we think she was phoning me at the same time and I got cut off! Eventually she phoned again and by this time she was wandering around the car park and I was at the entrance to the airport because John had dropped me off with instructions 'Don't move'. I had nipped inside whilst he parked the car and couldn't find her anywhere. We met in the middle of the road! By the time we got back to our van I was literally shaking because I had not had the time for breakfast nor lunch and was stressed out. Relaxing being on holidays isn't it? We had emptied out so many items from the back of the car to fit her into it and they were on the bus floor inside and when I saw her large case I wondered where on earth she would put it. We're sort of sorted out now with Helen using the front passenger seat for her suitcase! She reckons that she had to bring a large case because of our mail which we need to sort.

The next day she wanted to meet her friend in Perth. This friend works for a highly regarded watch company and had many stores to visit and training to conduct and is flying around the country and across to New Zealand fairly constantly. Because of the paperwork involved she told Helen that she wouldn't be able to stay with her at the hotel after all but would meet us in town. We had a call from her whilst we were trying to find somewhere to park and she told us that she had tried six multi-story car parks and all were full and directed us where to go. We found a place but had a fairly brisk, lengthy walk to find the Mall where we had arranged to meet for coffee. We thoroughly enjoyed catching up with her again and did see a little of the City and afterwards drove beside the Swan River and looked at the harbour, picking up many leaflets on sight-seeing trips along the way. Everywhere you stop there are parking fees though so even if you just want to nip into a tourist information shop there is a minimum charge of $2.50 per hour for example. John stayed with the car whilst we dashed around as the parking fees were mounting by the hour. At least now we have more idea about what we want to see and do.

Perth is a very beautiful city with malls, markets, endless cafes and restaurants with outdoor dining, trees, parkland and some very fine old buildings. The Swan River is so wide in places and so beautiful. However, whoever told me that Perth is easy to get around, they must have been joking because every time we go out we get lost despite having purchased a new street map! The Council must be altering the roads all the time because invariably there are turns that aren't on the map or connection roads that have been re-routed. The traffic is whizzing along and before you have had time to read the road sign you find yourself on the wrong highway. Yesterday a sign directed us to head straight on to find the highway we wanted and then we hit a T-junction and there was no sign at all to say whether you were supposed to go right or left so we went straight on and ended up in a housing estate!

Jack's been poorly today and we had to find a vet to get him more tablets. He hasn't eaten his breakfast for the last two mornings and I think Helen was disappointed that he didn't make more of a fuss when she arrived but I told her he has a bit of dementia and can't help it. I'm not sure of this but I could see she was hurt. We've got him more tablets today but he was sick on the way home and he hadn't realised that he had was peeing in the back of the Ute and that is the sign that someone told me to look for when he really is nearing his time to go. This afternoon he has perked up and he has yet to have one of his tablets so I'm hoping he improves again. We had to go to yet another shopping centre to get our vacuum cleaner replaced and got lost again! This shopping centre was so huge that it wasn't pleasant and although Helen and I both walked separately down to the other end of the centre, neither of us actually found Woolworths and both of us ended up shopping in Coles. Tomorrow, if Jack is alright, we're off to Fremantle or Freo as the locals call it. On Sunday, Perth is hosting the finals of the Red Bull Air Race and every pilot has over twenty-five years of flying experience. John and Helen are going whilst I dog-sit again and I'm so hoping it will be on T.V.

FREMANTLE

Loved it and I think that the longer you spent there the more you would discover and I'd like to return and stay in a backpackers and really explore. As it was the weekend there were the two main markets running which seem to start on Fridays and go through to Sunday. The arts festival is also on but we did not see any example of street performers which I had expected. Perhaps it only comes alive at night! However the cappuccino strip was packed out and I heard a local say that the locals have deserted it so it was probably full of tourists like us. Apparently the locals go to other back streets to meet now. Helen and I went into a clothes shop and Helen immediately saw a green summer dress. Helen had picked up three skirts that she wanted to try on but ended up only wanting the green dress, so I bought it for her for her Christmas present. She looks so good in it and the colour brings out the colour of her green eyes and shows her very fair hair off beautifully. We walked around a fair bit admiring the buildings, the trees, the malls and ended up in The Round House which is the oldest permanent building in W.A and was a prison. We had a beautiful view of the harbour from there as it is on a hill.

We later drove out of town and headed further down the coast and found a beach for the dogs to have a quick dip as they had been so good and Jack was so hot and tired with all the walking he had done. We chucked lumps of seaweed for Callie who prefers that to a ball because she plays a game of 'killing' it! She shakes the seaweed with ferocity until it is all in tiny pieces. Her hunting instincts are obviously intact! We returned along the endless freeways with endless traffic which drives me nuts, we did see a fair bit of the suburban area between Perth and Fremantle and the residential roads were a treat for the eyes, mainly because of the mass plantings of the Jacaranda trees which were all in bloom. A sea of purple blooms greeted us wherever we drove and I noted that even more are being planted.

The Red Bull Air Race

As John and Helen arrived home the T.V coverage of the race started at long last! I had been flashing around the different channels since 10am and had seen car racing, the Australian Open Golf Championship, motor bike racing and several other programs. John watched it all over again. The race was apparently first held in 2003 and the eleven finalists came from all over the world. Prior races had been held in many other countries such as Budapest, Spain, San Francisco and Istanbul. In Istanbul 1.5 million people had watched and Spain attracted an audience of one million people. In Perth over 300,000 people attended and that just about epitomises the difference in population per square kilometre in Australia and the distance Perth is from other major capital cities! In Britain they only held the time trials as the race was cancelled because of the weather!

They flew over the Swan River through pylons twelves metres apart, conducting compulsory aerobatic manoeuvres and they could lose points for flying too low or high through the pylons. Either mistake would mean a time penalty of five seconds but if they hit one the penalty would have been ten seconds. The G-force can cause the pilots to suddenly see in black and white only, lose their peripheral vision and then they could black out completely so they had to flex their muscles backwards to get more blood back to their hearts to provide more oxygen. 10g's is like ten times your own body weight being pressed down on top of you and during this race one pilot went over 11g's. Watching the best pilots in the world compete in this way was exhilarating.

ROCKINGHAM, POINT PERON & MANDURAH

The trip to Rockingham south of Perth was boring and uninteresting. We stopped at Rockingham and had a look around and I took a photo of John and Helen on the pier standing under a lamp post which had two lamp arms, on top of which were perched two pelicans. We enjoyed Point Peron which was very scenic and arrived at Mandurah after lunch. Initially we thought it was a lovely place because we stopped at the seafront and went into the shops there and the town looked pretty but when we drove further along we realised that it is predominantly a vast housing estate. They are very nice houses, many very large but we didn't come here to see what we can see at the Gold Coast! We have decided that we won't bother staying at Mandurah for three days as planned and have extended our stay at this caravan park. Not one of our best days considering the amount of traffic and roadway that we had to cover.

JUST BECAUSE THE ROCK FASCINATED ME

SWAN VALLEY

On this trip we first headed for **Guildford** which is a very lovely small town dominated by the Grammar School which is housed in beautiful buildings with vines hanging off the walls and a beautiful Church beside it. The streets are tree lined and we spent quite some time there as there were historical buildings to view and information aplenty on the town history.

We then covered the suggested tourist drive which is called the Swan Valley Food and Wine Trail and stopped at The Chocolate Company for some free chocolate tasting which of course led to us all purchasing a treat each. The journey was easy and we stopped at a fruit stalls but they mainly wanted to sell us trays of peaches and when we offered to purchase about six peaches we were turned away! Eventually we did find one place that sold a variety of fruits and vegetables and stocked up. We then set off on another tourist route as we were planning to visit the Goat cheese factory but it has been sold! We ended up stopping at F.R. Berry Reserve to have our afternoon coffee break and to give the dogs a much needed break and a swim in the creek. It was really nice there and there was one couple camped there with their caravan. We wore the dogs out before returning home. It had been a pleasant day out but the highlight was really Guildford and we saw only a few white and a couple of yellow wild flowers throughout the whole trip so we were a little disappointed. Of course, if you are into wineries then you would find more to do than us!

PERTH – KING'S PARK & CITY

We dropped the dogs off at the kennels at drove into King's Park which is huge and contains the Botanic Gardens which were beautiful. The views of the City and the Swan River were stunning from up there and we spent most of the morning exploring the area. The State War Memorial was particularly moving. We then managed to find undercover parking on the other side of the railway line & bus station which had a set fee for the day and we set off to explore the many city malls and to find **London Court**. With arches at either end, London Court is built as a Tudor street and it is stunning. I went into a shop that only sold teas and another that sold all foods from the U.K. and it is here that you can find those sweets that are not sold in Australia and Bisto gravy or the stuffing mix that your mother used to use! There is a replica Big Ben clock that chimes every quarter of an hour at one end.

We enjoyed a coffee in one of the malls and people-watched for a while and then I cost John a fortune with just two transactions! I bought some new training shoes which were diabolically expensive and reminded him that I was nearly out of Channel No 5 and as Christmas was coming it might be an idea to buy some for me and 'Please do not buy the Eau de Toilet as it doesn't last and make sure it is the perfume'! We also visited some second hand book stores and I found one that I wanted which Helen has bought me for Christmas. I now have some money put away to get something for John but he's as useless as toothache when you ask him for ideas! Helen gave up on him which is why I now have this money, from her, tucked away.

We picked the dogs up and Jack was panting so badly and didn't ease up until late in the evening. I was worried about him but we had already booked them into the kennels the following day so that we could go on a boat trip along the Swan River to Fremantle. We decided that we would not hang about either end of the river trip and get back to them as quickly as possible and hose them down when we got them back home.

The river trip was relaxing and we knew that we could ask for a free coffee or tea although they did not offer it to the passengers and I don't think most of the passengers knew about it. We nearly missed the trip altogether as we were waiting at the pier which was identified on the leaflet but began to worry five minutes before departure time only to find that the leaflet was wrong!

The first explorers here were Dutch and the river was originally called the Black Swan River because of the black swans, some of which we were lucky enough to see. The river is 3.2ks wide at its widest point which I think was at the area called Melville Water, along the stretch where the Canning River meets the Swan River. We were told that the river is 240ks long. We stayed on the ferry for the return trip and were rather stunned when we were told that one home had cost 62.5M just to build!

When we arrived back at Perth we decided to try one of the free CAT buses to get back to our car. There are three routes, colour coded and the buses are very regular which is good because the first bus that arrived wouldn't let anyone on! When we got on the next one it became crammed full of people and it was getting worse at every stop and when I called to Helen around someone's thigh 'Do you want to get off at the next stop?' I heard a faint and breathless response of 'Oh, yes please'. As Helen said afterwards, we could have walked back to the car quicker and we wouldn't have had to experience such terror. I remember thinking that I wouldn't be able to get off as there was a particularly large woman blocking the aisle so I hissed upwards towards her right ear 'Are you getting off?' and she replied that she was so I followed her rolling rear end, which was all I could see, praying that Helen had somehow made it off. From 3pm onwards the roads are horrendous with traffic so we had a long, tedious journey back. We picked the dogs up and the owner said they'd had three or four walks which rather amazed me as it was at least 35C and she added that she 'worried' about Jack. She did not expand on this odd statement but he now seems to be rather addled in the head and we're wondering if he had a small stroke because of the heat. He sometimes has no idea where he is and it rather shocked Helen who was the first to notice the next day when we were in a park. He had run across the grass with Callie and was standing with another group of people and Helen followed and found him very agitated and looking at the man as if to say 'It's supposed to be John but it doesn't smell like him'. I saw her bend down and stroke him as if to calm him down and wondered what was going on. Later that day I saw the same confusion.

COTTESLOE AND SCARBOROUGH BEACHES.

Having been disappointed with what we had seen south of Perth along the coastline, we answered Helen's wish to visit Cottesloe Beach as it is a name we all knew of. We found that rather disappointing too so drove up to Scarborough Beach which certainly met our needs more as there was a choice of outdoor dining and Helen was shouting us dinner! The 'Fremantle Doctor' had arrived so we chose a table outside but well shielded from the strong wind. Apparently it is called that because in the summer it arrives every afternoon and as people cool down they become sane again – something like that anyway. As we are absolutely sick of the wind on this coast, we have another name for it! It is always a topic of conversation, even amongst the locals. A middle-aged lady was taking a brisk walk along the seafront and said to me 'Isn't it beautiful?' She was referring to the coastline. I had asked Helen at Cottesloe and at Scarborough what she thought of the beach and she just looked bemused and said 'It's just a beach' which just about sums it up. It's not particularly beautiful, it's just a beach. There's no particular scenic spot and for the first time we returned home without having taken a single photograph. I can usually find a rock, a tree or some lovely parkland if the beach is a bit boring or perhaps a harbour but there was simply nothing worth photographing.

However, our meal was superb. We went to the smaller of two seafood cafes and I am glad that we did as the bigger one which had tables partly in an arcade of sorts, became jam packed full, probably because it was cheaper. We all had fish and chips and salad but the portion of fish was large, the salad came with olives (not that I like them), feta cheese and a large amount of other salad vegetables and the portion of chips was small. The sort of meal that we like rather than a plate of chips adorned with fish! We also enjoyed beautiful coffees which I put down to the fact that the Italian owner had made them and they sure do know how to make a good coffee. John had an expresso and I told him he'd need double the amount of sugar. Not the sort of thing to drink in the evening but I used to down them as a teenager before work in Switzerland when I had had a particularly late night out clubbing the night before. You could stand the spoon up in the coffee and sugar but it was the quickest wake up call for my brain.

Helen left that night, as the plane was taking off a gale was blowing up and we had to get the dogs in the back of the Ute and pack everything up quickly. In the morning we couldn't find the dog leads or John's shoes initially as they had slid away under our van. The gale hadn't affected Helen's flight which surprised me as she had had a particularly bad flight between Melbourne and Perth coming out to us. Her return route did not require a stop in Melbourne and was direct to Brisbane but she apparently could not tilt her chair as the exit door was behind her and she only got one hour's sleep. Her Dad met her at the airport in her car and she drove him back to Regents Park and then had to drive back down to the Gold Coast where she at last fell into bed. That night she had booked to go to a comedy club show and somehow made it.

KALAMUNDA

The day after Helen left we discovered one of the prettiest villages that we have seen in W.A and it is only about five kilometres up the road! We had seen so much that was boring with her on our suburban trips out of Perth and here was one right on our doorstep and I felt frustrated that she hadn't stayed just one day longer.

The town centre is adorned with Jacaranda trees in bloom at the moment and garden beds of roses and there are walkways, pavement cafes, arcades and a beautiful park. We enjoyed a very good coffee there, visited the butchers, browsed around a train carriage that stocked locally made crafts and the dogs had a walk in the park before we realised that dogs were not allowed in it! We admired the water fountain and the many sculptures dotted around the town, bought the Saturday paper, ordered a mini-expresso pot from the café and then set off for the Zig Zag Road which came out at the bottom two kilometres from our park. We could have visited the Mundaring Weir and Mundaring itself but were happy to return home with a camera full of photos.

Kalamunda hosts the Spring Flower Show, Arts, Community Arts and Harvest Festivals, Agricultural and Wine Shows, Arts and Crafts Exhibition and the Darlington Arts Festival and along with its second-hand book shops and Town Theatre it is exactly the type of town that John and I are looking for to purchase our retirement home. John wants to move it to Queensland!

Helen arrived home to a heap of post for us and two items required our attention and it was fortuitous that we had stayed on in Perth for the extra days. I had to make two visits to the local Centrelink office (Social Security) as they required copious information to renew my Health Care Card which means I can get discounts on prescriptions if needed. That is the only income I get, the benefit of a Health Care Card. My taxation return showed a two thousand dollar deficit this last financial year so we need to do something about that. I could have earned about $8000 and still not have paid any tax. Should have done some fruit picking!

Our last day in Perth and neither of us will be sad to leave but are glad that we have seen the attractive city. We went to Kalamunda again today and we are more in love than ever with this delightful town and it will be a highlight of our visit for me.

We had some neighbours arrive the other day and I watched as the wife stood under a tree (it was very hot) whilst her husband ran around connecting everything up and then he came and gave her a hug and smiled so beautifully and she then ventured into their van. I thought 'How sweet. What a lovely man' because he was dripping with sweat. This is in stark contrast to what happens when we set up because I am as busy as John and he is usually yelling out 'Is the power on?' (a light appears if the connection is good on our power board inside) or 'The water is now on you can run the taps and check for air bubbles.' I am inside dashing around as he usually asks 'Is the kettle on yet?' I was rather in awe of this woman who had her man so much under her control that the air conditioning was going before she entered their van! I really must get John sorted!

The tow truck driver was just as busy as her husband had been earlier because they had been towed to the site. I was rather confused as I watched a vehicle on a truck towing a caravan until I realised it was a breakdown service. Anyway, it turns out that they had been going up a steep hill and he had lost all power to his vehicle with a heavy caravan on the back. Imagine that. How terrifying but he was lucky enough to coast into a space beside the road. What bemused me was that he told me that they were returning home and that his wife had now missed her hair appointment! Really important in the scheme of things don't you think!

BUNBURY (AUSTRALIND)

We love where we are in Australind as it is next to the wide river inlet which is tidal and there are homes on quarter acre blocks around and it's away from the main road into Bunbury. Australind has its own town centre which is sufficient in itself but if you need the large shops then it's only ten minutes to Bunbury. All we have to watch out for around here are the kangaroos and the possums rather than traffic.

There are two parks here and we picked the less advertised one which is further along the inlet and we have already extended our visit by three nights as everyone is so friendly here. There is one couple who are here while they build their new home on the hill behind, another young couple who work 'fly in/fly out' at the mines (she works in the stores), another couple who have sold their bus to their neighbour here and have bought a house around here. We thought how lovely Kalamunda was but now we love this place too!

I had to make a card yesterday for my friend who taught me how to make the cards in the first place so I had to find a different pattern to use. I sat out under the pergola as it was so hot and a lady came up and said 'What are you doing?' with a strong emphasis on the word 'are' so she must have been puzzled for some time. I explained and she asked if she could buy some off me and then she showed other people and now I've sold seven of them. Because I have been using them myself for Birthday cards, I now find myself with a severe shortage of them so today will be a card-making day again. I felt chuffed that anyone would want them! I couldn't stop giggling and proudly showed John the cash I'd received but I have never told him how much I have spent on the craft stuff I've bought because he'd have a fit!

It's nice to be amongst nice people again who are relaxed because we were in Perth for over two weeks and no-one was particularly friendly and I had some odd encounters. I went to the butchers in Kalamunda and I asked for some veal steaks and added that I wanted them thick. The guy serving me said 'No you don't'. I looked at him astonished and replied 'Yes, I do'.

'You'd be better off buying that then' he said pointing to some steak.

'No thanks'.

So he cut two veal steaks and I told him that I would accept them but could he please cut the next two twice as thick.

'No. You'd be far better off buying that' he again said pointing to some steak.

By this time I'm getting pretty bemused so said very loudly 'Who is eating this veal, you or me?' The other guys serving turned around as did the customers and I believe it was the owner who looked astonished. I got my two thick steaks.

Then I asked for some lamb steaks cut the same way and he lived up to his name by butchering the meat. I bought it because I could not be bothered to argue but it was a scraggy bit of meat so I cooked it slowly that night and the meat was tender. I asked if they had any rump steak and off he goes again!

'You don't want rump steak, you want this sirloin.' I'm beginning to realise he's trying to get shot of this steak that is sitting on the shelf!

'No, I don't. My husband prefers rump and doesn't like sirloin'.

They didn't have any rump steak of course and I blessed John for not being in the shop because he would have piped up that he likes all steak and is not the least bit fussy!

I came out with four very small lamb portions and four small veal steaks albeit that two of them were thick but the cost nearly blew me out of the door. I went to Coles and bought the rest of my meat including rump steak, pork chops and chicken sausages. No-one argues with you in a supermarket.

Staying on an extra three days at the caravan park cost us more than the first week I think. We didn't get our twenty dollar discount for being a park member and they had realised we had two dogs. I had told them when booking but apparently we had to pay $5 extra for a second dog per night. Some people opposite us were awaiting the arrival of relatives from England who were going to stay in their van with them. I told them that there had been no extra charge for Helen, only the dog! They told us that they had their own shower and toilet but that when they went to reception they were told that they had to pay more money per night for the extra two people to stay in their own van than if they rented a tent site! So, they rented an extra site and put a tent on it and put the beds in there – how daft is that! The rules and costs seemed to vary whoever you met at the reception desk. When we arrived it was the owner but when we extended it was someone else.

So, back to where we are now. We drove into Bunbury and around and up and down (two lookouts). We took heaps of photos and gasped in astonishment at the development in the Marlston area of town. There are so many brand new huge homes and they are all on top of one another. I tried to visually gauge the distance between two of the homes and there couldn't have been more than two inches between them. What happened to boundary lines here? We took a photo of two homes from the Marlston Lookout because one crosses over in front of the other which means that the windows to one side of one house overlook the sloping roof of the other and it must block any light from coming in the windows let alone the awful view! There has been massive development on the hill with all homes vying for a sea or harbour views and it continues down the bottom with a new shopping area and roads. It's all very spic and span. On the way home we spotted a shipping terminal and another Alcoa Aluminium plant – how lovely!

Chapter 26

Oh, I forgot to tell you about our journey from Perth and should have mentioned the fact that we stopped at Armadale on the way here. That's a lovely town but it was so busy that by the time we had found a parking place we were so relieved that we just bought some coffees and left! A lady on an adjoining table said it is the Christmas rush and I was thinking 'Well it is the thirtieth of November and perhaps people here do things in an orderly manner unlike us Queenslanders who tend to leave everything until the last two days and then shop for enough food to last a month even though the shops are usually only shut for one or two days!

Anyway, because I didn't tell you about our journey you won't know what I mean by that last sentence where I mentioned the Alcoa plant. A couple of years ago I had marked on a map an area in W.A that I wanted to avoid if I was ever to go there on a trip. When we knew we were coming here I marked this fifty kilometre radius on the map we were to use. When we left Perth the road we were to take goes directly through these small towns. Since we have been in W.A there have been copious articles on Alcoa and on the problems caused by their industrial operations on the local communities in these towns. We have read about illnesses, rashes, nose bleeds and although there have been many heartbreaking stories not all locals seem to be affected or worried. A few years back Alcoa bought properties off locals who wished to sell them and now they have made the same offer again. However, Alcoa sold some of those homes and the people who bought them in good faith, feeling that they were buying into an idyllic country lifestyle and who wish to now sell their homes because they have discovered the local problems or have become sick are not subject to the Alcoa offer of buy-back. There have been people on television who desperately want to sell and get away and get well again. What amazes me having been in the Real Estate business, is why purchasers were not told about the problems some people have had. When I sold real estate we had to tell people if there was anything that might be detrimental to the property and I would have thought that there was a risk to all people who buy property in the area and that there is a 'duty of care' legally to provide information. We have read that the clouds above the area have chemicals in them. On the day we were driving through it was raining so I put my internal air conditioner on and hoped that John would get a move on. He suddenly talks to me through the two-way radio asking if I wanted to stop and we were right outside an Alcoa plant. I kept saying no and he kept saying it was lunchtime and why not and I ended up in screaming through the two-way 'No, no, no, no, no'.

The penny dropped. 'Oh, is this the area that you don't want to stop?'

'Yes'. We go another twenty kilometres and he pulls off the road for lunch. We are still within the area that I didn't want to be but I gave up. He had been driving with the windows open which did not impress me much, particularly because it was raining so the clouds were releasing whatever toxins might be in them and we had only been there about ten minutes when his nose started pouring with blood. I couldn't help but laugh and told him it's a good job we don't live in the area because he can't even stop for lunch! I noticed a stark difference in the clouds as we came out of the area. Instead of heavy, grey and thick, they were white fluffy clouds with patches of blue sky between.

The Government has given approval for Alcoa to increase its operations despite the recorded health issues which appear to be relative to these plants.

I'm not sure whether the plant down in Bunbury said 'smelter' or 'refinery' but I wasn't that happy to see it there.

We're back with water problems. When we arrived we asked if the water was drinkable and were told it was fine. I then added that I had been visiting hospitals around Australia and had to know it was good water and asked if it was bore water. 'Oh, if you want water to drink there is a tank over there'! Oddly enough we do need water to drink and to cook with and we are very thankful that we did not attach our hose to the tap because the bore water has that gaseous odour about it yet again. The tank (rain) water is not that clean with bits of black floating around in it but there is also a smell of chlorine in it and I'm not sure if they have bought the water from elsewhere but at least it should be safe.

Having spent yesterday trying to make some cards but getting caught up in conversations with the local park residents instead, we got out of the park today and went inland to explore. First stop for a coffee break by the river was at **Donnybrook**. We had already made our first purchases of the day when we stopped at a Fruit Barn. John added his purchase to my basket of salad vegetables and local garlic. It was a bottle of onions pickled in honey and garlic. Won't we smell nice! We liked Donnybrook probably because it is such a pretty town.

Next stop was **Balingup** where we tasted several samples of cheese and came away with some Caraway Cheddar and then we learnt a little more about Alpaca wool at the adjacent Alpaca shop. There was nothing that I wanted to buy but I was struck by the fact that the stock was being sold for half the price than that being sold in the southern highlands of New South Wales two years ago! We were shown the finest of the Alpaca wool, the very softest and it is absolutely beautiful and was comparatively so cheap. We set off to find the Old Cheese Factory Craft Centre and it is huge. Apparently it is the biggest in W.A and had every kind of craft imaginable for sale including a lot of furniture. We purchased a new wooden chopping board made out of a beautiful piece of Jarrah.

Our last intended stop was **Bridgetown** where we first stopped by the river for the dogs to have their second swim of the day. The bridge is fascinating when seen from underneath because it is all made out of timber. In town I bought some embroidery threads for my card-making and some stickers from another local shop and we felt that we had supported the local communities. However, on our return journey we also stopped at a farm and came away laden with beautiful Pink Lady apples, the sweetest of plumbs, mushrooms, cauliflower and a bag of lovely tomatoes.

We made a quick detour to **Greenbushes** on our return journey where it seems that all the shops are closed down but John wanted to see the old ore mine. He climbed the walkway and took a photo and said that he couldn't see the bottom.

The last few days we have been socialising more than we ever have anywhere else on our trips and last night people emerged out of the vans at such a pace that we ended up virtually having a party. We are opposite the large pergola and barbecue area which is, in itself, next to the toilets and shower blocks so we are seeing people continuously and they stop to talk. I'm not getting a thing done but I've laughed a lot and that's what this is trip is supposed to have been about.

Last night I was reading in the paper that you can train your memory to assist the brain patterns with the hope of averting dementia. I couldn't even understand the questions, let alone the answers. My memory for names is abysmal and I strongly advise you to do a few memory exercises before leaving home so that you do not stumble as often as I have done. There are three ladies here who are all called Jan but I get them muddled with Loraine and …. Oh I can't remember her name! Then there are all the partner's names to remember. I had a name yesterday but didn't know where the lady lived and I had a message for her and her name was Jan. I kept going around asking 'Did you ask me to…' but I couldn't find the lady. I ended up trying to knock on van doors, which is really difficult when they have full annexes up and they are all zipped up! I found the right lady eventually and passed on the message.

For the whole time that we have been travelling along this W.A coast all we hear about is mining, shortage of skilled workers and what people are earning. Everywhere we go we see new housing developments and in most cases the houses being built on them are huge. The abundance of mining, new housing and money is almost obscene and John and I wonder just how happy the workers are with their super, huge new homes, especially as the housing interest rates keep rising. We met a lovely young couple in the caravan park who have just sold their bus and have bought a low-maintenance home on an acre of land and they were laughing as they told us that they won't know what to do with all the room they will have in the home. The home is on an acre of land and has three bedrooms and an en suite, plus 'another room but we don't know what it's for'. I told them that is their rumpus room or family room or if they want to be really upmarket 'media room'. They reckon they are going to put socks on and slide around on all the empty floorboards for fun. They are earning $80 per hour between them at the Argyle Diamond Mine and they fly in for two weeks work with the third week off. They seem to have their heads screwed on right unlike many young people who expect their first home to have four to five bedrooms plus a study, three bathrooms, family and media room.

It was this beautiful young lady who asked me if I'd seen the 'red spiders with black bums' around and said she had even seen one down at the beach! I didn't go back to the beach after that!

When we left the park we had many people standing around to farewell us and I warned them that they would have me in tears if they didn't go away! We left late as usual but did not have far to go to get to Busselton and with John following me this time, I took the opportunity of driving through the town centre and on down to the beachfront where we stopped for a coffee and for the dogs to have a swim. The latter was probably a silly idea as I had bathed them both the previous day which is a back-breaking job and Jack looked so fluffy and beautiful. **Busselton** was really bustling and we were quite excited to see such a happy holiday scene. We could see the two kilometre jetty and decided that it would be our first place on our itinerary the following day. We had to drive on through town towards Dunsborough and our park is actually closer to Dunsborough than it is to Busselton despite its postal address.

Today we wore ourselves out by starting at Busselton and then everywhere between that and Cape Naturaliste including Dunsborough. At **Dunsborough** we visited Gelato Buonissimo because of their authentic Italian gelataria. The ice cream was sublime. I also wanted to visit Fig Tree Lane and we both wanted to go to the jetty which was actually a bit disappointing. The train isn't running because it needs repair and we couldn't leave the dogs in the back of the Ute for too long. We have been unable to find a kennels here. We returned to our park for lunch and then set off for Dunsborough. We found the original bakery and John was lost because there was too much to choise, but I quickly decided on a blueberry pie. We also found a recommended second hand book shop. Dunsborough is absolutely wonderful because it is pretty with so many areas of lawn with many flower beds and trees. There has been huge commercial development there as well but the architecture is so varied and the only way I can describe it is that it is 'quirky', artistic and very, very pretty. We purchased a beautiful glass plate made out of recycled glass, which will not only be a beautiful piece to display, it will also be used fairly regularly for fruit and for biscuits or whatever.

We explored the coastline as far as **Castle Rock** and then returned to town to get on the Naturaliste Terrace turning off to visit **Meelup Beach** and on to **Eagle Bay.** There are signs everywhere around that area to say that no dogs are allowed and there are more signs on every beach. Well, we couldn't offload the dogs so they had to come with us but we didn't allow them out of the car which meant that they spent a miserable afternoon. We returned to Naturaliste Terrace and set off for Bunkers Bay, Cape Naturaliste to see the lighthouse and then down to see Sugarloaf Rock before returning home. We enjoyed the area because it is free of mines! We also enjoyed the road trip because of the stunning views. We stopped by the roadside overlooking the most exquisite bay with white sand, rocks, green foliage covered dunes and a sea of the brightest turquoise we have ever seen. The sun was shining and the water sparkled. We stayed awhile and enjoyed our beautiful pastries whilst sitting in silent awe.

However, there were signs of new housing developments even in tiny Eagle Bay. By the time we arrived home we were exhausted with all the sight-seeing and so were the dogs. We were supposed to have already visited Yallingup and Canal Rocks but we must leave that for tomorrow despite the fact that tomorrow had been reserved for the Margaret River area. The following day we leave for Augusta on the other side of Margaret River but we could return there from Augusta if we don't have enough time to see everything. We should have allowed more time for this area but it is so hard to know in advance. John grabbed a leaflet from the Busselton Tourist Information Centre today so I know he wants to visit The Margaret River Chocolate Company! I want to visit Margaret River Nuts and Cereals where they also sell jams and pickles, onions, honey and chilli sauces but I particularly noted the chocolate and yoghurt coated nuts! Who needs wine when you can sample chocolate?

I've just had a shower, not in our van but in the shower block because we again have the problem of not being able to connect to drinking water here. We filled up the tank with town water from the laundry block before we settled onto our site but now John is stringent with his wish to make sure the water lasts in the tank. He has a bucket for me to pour down the toilet, a container with drinking water that he keeps refilling from the town water tap at the laundry block for the kettle and another bucket for washing our hands. I'm so confused that I'm spinning and he's already worrying about the next caravan park! I'm wondering why we bothered filling the tank and we'll probably leave here with our tank nearly full anyway because of all the buckets. Actually it won't be because when he's not looking I use the tap!

In Australia the hot tap is usually on the left and the cold tap on the right. However, in the last park they were reversed in the laundry and as I was hand washing clothes most days I was getting very frustrated because I automatically used the wrong tap. I also had to wash my hair in the laundry because I had an ear infection and couldn't get any water in my ear and I nearly washed it in cold and gave it the final rinse in scorching hot water. Anyway, I get to the showers here and they have one tap above the other and without my glasses on I cannot tell which is hot and cold so I stand at some distance and guess! As the temperature has the uncanny ability to alter after the first couple of minutes, I invariably grab the hot tap and turn it up and have to leap out of the way as I scald myself. We're paying for this and there's no pool here and the games room is the most miserable empty room I've seen for a long time. John said he saw three teenage girls sitting there last night looking most disconsolate.

Chapter 27

We have been in a lot of parks with no pools on this coast and it has been really hot. At the last park there was no pool and we had temperatures in the thirties (centigrade) most of the time we were there. Here it is much cooler, particularly at night and yet we have only moved about 60ks further down the coast.

You need to do a trip like this when you are younger unless you have a wonderful memory, not only because of the names of people but also because people ask you what caravan park you stayed at in a particular town and I can hardly recall any of them, let alone the town they are talking about! The girl on the check-out in a supermarket the other day said that she and her husband are selling their house to do what we're doing and she looked as though she is in her twenties. I have also met mothers who are doing it with young children and mothers who have done it in the past. Those who have done it do not recommend it whereas those doing it now say that it's great and home schooling is just a matter of discipline and that it is really quite easy. The only benefit that I can see in travelling like this when the children are young is that Dad is obviously going to be with the kids as much as Mum is and vice versa.

Young children will forget the trip after a while. For older children, who would benefit from touring and who would learn a lot that would be of value, although it would be difficult not to be able to mix with their friends. If it were just for a year then perhaps it would be beneficial but if it were for longer I think that the kids would miss a lot of benefits that they would gain from attending a school. I've heard some parents on T.V say that they are protecting their children from being influenced by their peers, to such things as drugs and sex and that their children learn more and are more advanced in their school work when home schooled but I believe that you have to grow up and become an adult sometime and that is part of the senior school education.

Learning to mix with their peers, making life-long friends, learning to work as part of a team, competing in sports events, discussing the issues that are important to their age group with friends as well as with their parents, learning to get along with teachers and classmates that they perhaps do not like, learning that other people live very different lives to themselves and have very different backgrounds or religions and that is acceptable in society – all those kinds of things are learned during teenage years and there are hundreds of other examples.

I heard an educator on the ABC radio the other day say that most kids are employable when they leave junior school if they can read and write, are honest, have initiative and are willing to learn because that is exactly the kind of person that ninety per cent of employers are seeking. I silently commended him as I listened but kids have to learn life skills which cannot be learnt from books, lectures or from the internet and they are certainly not going to learn them if they spend the majority of their time with their parents and siblings travelling around Australia. That's just living in 'a pack' where each member knows their place and it never alters. Life isn't orderly like that unfortunately when it comes to relationships outside of the family and in the work force.

This travelling is great but it is not a life with any depth to it in my experience. Now if I were cycling around the country raising money for charity there might be a point to it other than pure self indulgence.

For example, if you don't like a place you can leave which is not a very good example for a future working life now is it? If the temperature is too hot or too cold you can move. If you don't like the view you can move! I find it utterly ridiculous when I put it like this but it's a fact. I do hope we are going to be able to settle down when we get home!

Well we did make it to **Margaret River** despite the fact that we got off to a late start from Australind, via Busselton, because I slipped down the van steps and cracked my head and ended up in a heap on the grass with hot coffee all over me! I was also crying but didn't know why. The same thing had occurred a couple of years ago when I did the same thing at Eumundi at the Sunshine Coast and hit the same spot on my head. My doctor wanted me to have dye put through my brain and have it checked out properly but I declined her kind offer as I'm addled enough as it is. I was in tears yesterday morning too, so I seem to be making a habit of it. My ex-husband has been very ill in hospital and it's amazing to me that having been divorced for twenty-three years and separated for even longer, it matters not a twat when it is the father of your children. I found myself just as worried as if I had still been married to him and frustrated that we are three and a half thousand kilometres away. I guess that over the years you try desperately to forget all that was bad in the marriage and concentrate on those moments you treasured like the birth of your children, as much as for their sake as your own sanity. To remember too much can sometimes be cruel. So today, having unravelled myself, I phoned him as he had returned home from hospital last night but I had to explain that I'd have to call him back tomorrow as I wasn't really too bright myself but wanted him to know that I cared!

We nearly didn't go out but with pain tablets under my belt I slowly got what we needed into the car except for any lunch for myself as I couldn't imagine being able to eat ever again! Naturally I was starving by 11.30 but our tour today included a visit to The Margaret River Chocolate Company, The Margaret River Cheese Factory and Margaret River Nuts and Cereals where I had breakfast because I taste tested their different breakfast mixes. I had several milk and dark chocolates and tried all four of the cheeses on offer. I didn't like any of the cheese but did buy some blackcurrant yoghurt which was very cheap.

We started our trip by heading for Yallingup but called in at **Smiths Beach** first for the dogs to have a frolic because we knew that we were heading into National Park area yet again and that they would have to stay in the car. There were a couple of reasonably older buildings but a mass of new units are being developed there. There were no signs banning dogs here so we all enjoyed ourselves, especially Callie who attacked the seaweed again, picking it up and tossing it about and then shaking the life out of it!

Yallingup has a pretty coastal scene and the houses that are there are well established and are dotted around the hill. Yallingup is an Aboriginal word meaning 'Place of Love'. After Yallingup we went to **Canal Rocks** beach which was fascinating with the waves crashing between the rocks. There were a few fishing boats in the harbour and nets were out.

Next it was time to head inland which was when we did all our taste testing en route to **Cowaramup** where John had his picnic and the dogs and I ate his crusts! By this time it was well after lunchtime but I was determined to get to Margaret River and it didn't take long to get there at all because the road is good and we saw hardly any traffic. There I made a beeline for the bead shop, despite being waylaid on the way by the clothes in the Hemp Shop. A book shop called me in and so did a Book Exchange shop. By this time John was so tired he wanted to just sit in the car so we decided to return home. We are very glad that we went because we know exactly where we can stop with the van on our way to Augusta tomorrow. We'll take a break by the park there at Margaret River for the dogs and for our morning coffee.

We passed so many wineries today and I cannot imagine how long you would have to stay in this region if you were interested in wine tasting. Some neighbours beside us at the moment are going tomorrow and the first thing I asked is 'Who is driving?' Not all of the wineries are marked on the maps that we have and I can't even count the ones that are marked as there are so many of them.

A neighbour said this morning that this area is the jewel of W.A and we agree with him. However, do not rely on the maps you acquire as things move! The cheese factory has moved down the road. Also a turning which showed on one map as being in a town and on another being on the other side of the same town was in fact before the town and took us by surprise and we nearly drove past it because we weren't yet looking for it. We have found this to be the case so often in W.A. and when you are a stranger to the area it confuses you even more. Let's face it, what man believes his wife when she is map reading anyway and is he honestly going to believe you, without looking at the map himself, when you find that a factory has walked down the road or a road has jumped to the other side of the river and its bridge? No, we didn't have a row today but we have done in the past!

This area is by far the nicest area that we have visited here in W.A and we are hoping that we enjoy the remainder of W.A just as much. Although I have mentioned places that we have liked before, there have sometimes been isolated or the surrounding areas have not been so nice or there has been too much traffic or endless roads of nothing. This area I am talking about now encompasses a large area of ever changing scenery and tourist attractions. Children are well catered for and there are sporting venues, golf courses, endless fishing and diving opportunities, magnificent caves to explore, endless hiking paths, outdoor cinema, historical attractions, every kind of arts and artisans to watch as they work and everything for those who like gastronomy. Package these attractions with calm water bays, rugged cliff scenery and crashing waves and plenty of surfing beaches, rivers and wetlands and the whole is a sheer delight for the holiday maker.

We returned to Dunsborough this morning as we left the dogs' leads somewhere yesterday and also because I put the fire on last night and smelt burning and it wasn't coming from the fire but from the power board which has a surge protector! I actually saw sparks flying out of it and my first instinct was to turn the individual switch off on the board but luckily I stopped myself and turned it off at the wall. Then we didn't know what to do with the power board as it was so hot that we thought if we threw it out of the van we might start a grass fire so we put it on the metal cover of the cooker hob to cool.

In Victoria at the moment they are battling huge fires and fire fighters from New Zealand have flown in to help. The fires were started by dry lightning strikes. That's weird isn't it? I didn't even realise you could get them. My friend from Victoria has just told me that they had temperatures of 41C today and she lives on the coast whereas the fires are way inland where it gets much hotter. So many towns are under threat and people are packed and ready to evacuate at a moment's notice but the fire has been jumping twenty kilometres and starting afresh because of the strong winds so how on earth can they get it under control? I'm sitting here with a jumper and jeans on and have shut all the windows and it will not be long before we have the fire on again. This is Australia and I shouldn't need to be reminded by now about how vast it is and how varied the climate can be. Time to download all the photos I have taken again today before we move on tomorrow.

FLINDERS BAY NEAR AUGUSTA

We had a lovely journey here today because we didn't have to go into a town at all until we arrived at Margaret River. We pulled up to be told that I couldn't park where I was because Father Christmas was arriving! The Rotary Club were having their Christmas party in the Rotary Club Park but I think our dogs caused a bigger sensation than Santa did later in the day because the children were delighted with them and the dogs were delighted with the fuss they attracted.

The day got even better when we arrived at this caravan park at Flinders Bay because the site they had booked for us is huge and absolutely lovely as we are surrounded by bushes which attract the birds. It is a lovely park and is a few steps to the ocean. We were told that we could pay them tomorrow or whenever and have a look around first in case we would prefer a different site. It is a very dog-friendly park too and they provide doggy bags at reception. When John returned to the office to pay, the female owner, Lorraine, offered John a large bag of complimentary organic lettuce from her organic garden. I was stunned because yesterday we had been running all around the region trying to find some organic lettuce and had failed to find any! John assured her that

I would be delighted. Andrew then turned up at our van with a giant T.V aerial and booster so that we have the best reception we have had so far in W.A. He fitted it and secured it for us and ensured it was tuned in properly. We also received a $3 per day discount because John is a 'senior' because 'We reckon you've earned it.' We had a lovely walk along the beach and returned across parkland and the road. Tomorrow we'll go exploring.

11ᵗʰ December 2006

I started the day sitting outside watching what I believe was a fairy wren hopping around our site but try as I might, I could not get a photograph of it. It was so blue and so beautiful. Then it was the washing and I realised that it was seventeen days since I'd washed the sheets! Whilst I was hanging them up another lady told me that she had just done hers and I told her how long it was since I'd washed them. She told me that she had the same problem as the days go so fast and the weekly change of sheets seems to get forgotten but how lovely clean sheets are. I told her that if I was really rich I would have someone to wash my floors, have clean sheets on my bed every day and have a massage every morning. John had just turned up and she said 'Is he too old to train?' and as I didn't answer her and just looked blank she added 'I guess so'.

We set off to explore Augusta which is a very small town and then on to the Lookout and the Golf Course as we had been told that it is very hilly and picturesque. You pay on an honours system and put ten dollars in an envelope and place it in a box. We returned for a coffee and lunch and then explored the coastline visiting the Old Waterwheel (the water was used to mix the mortar for the lighthouse) and the Cape Leeuwin Lighthouse. It is at the most south-westerly point of Australia and is where the Indian Ocean meets the Southern Ocean. When I returned to the Ute there was a very good looking young coach driver petting Jack. I laughed and said that now that I'm older and no longer pretty I am beginning to wish I was a dog because I used to get lots of attention years ago and now Jack gets it all!

The dogs were so exhausted when we went out after lunch that they didn't want to get into the Ute. It's the first time that has happened and we believe that they are exhausting themselves with their beach walks or are just fed up with being in the Ute travelling these endless roads. I hope they sleep well tonight because we are off exploring again tomorrow to see Hamelin Bay as we leave again the next day. Pity, because I am guaranteed an endless supply of organic lettuce! Lorraine told me this morning that she has no idea why she offered John a free bag of it yesterday and I told her how I had been looking for some throughout the previous days touring without success and she immediately offered me more. We have only eaten half of what she gave us yesterday so I declined but will probably take advantage of her offer before we leave.

So, we set off to **Hamelin Bay** with excited anticipation as we were wandering why we had heard the name mentioned so often. What a shock when we got there to find that it is National Park and that dogs are obviously not allowed and all that was there was a caravan park. The roads were being done and development is taking place of course but all we could do was have a quick look at the beach and go! It reminded me of Eighty Mile Beach where we found that a caravan park had virtually taken over the area of access to the beach for two wheel drive vehicles. It was just as stunningly beautiful too and we would have liked to have stopped longer.

We then headed for a Lookout which you can access from Caves Road. Don't bother unless you have a four wheel drive because the road starts off fairly good and then turns to sand. John decided to walk and I stayed with the dogs because by this time they were getting too hot and still couldn't get out of the car because we were again in National Park. John never found the Lookout and we returned to Caves Road and set off for Prevelly Park which is only about 5ks from the Margaret River town. We had a map indicating where a dog beach was but by the time we had climbed up and over the dunes we were all so hot that we could hardly be bothered. We ensured that the dogs got thoroughly soaked and cool but Jack was puffing again by the time he reached the Ute with the effort of climbing steps and dunes. Then it was out turn because we still hadn't had our picnic lunch and it was around two o'clock. We searched for a park or some shade and finally found one tree that appeared to be on public land at the end of a cul-de-sac opposite the only shop in **Prevelly Park**. John walked over to the caravan park opposite to use their toilet and Jack couldn't even be bothered to try and follow him. We were all so relieved to find some shade that we stayed there quite a while. If you want to see this area and if you have a dog, do yourself a favour and put it or them in a kennel for the day!

We had seen all the coastline around the area and it was so pretty but everywhere there were signs stating dogs were not allowed so we would just stop, take photos and leave.

We ended up covering Caves Road from one end to the other during our sightseeing trips and it is aptly named as there are over 360 limestone caves between Cape Naturaliste and Cape Leeuwin and the public can visit some of them, mainly along Caves Road. Names such as Mammoth Cave, Lake Cave and Jewel Cave entice the traveller but it was too hot to leave the dogs and we have seen enough in past travels.

We decided to head to Margaret River and stock up with bread and milk and to fill our water container with some town water. We are retaining our two, fifteen litres containers that we've bought for while we are off road over the next few days as we have very little water left in our tank.

Tonight we feel lucky as we hear on the news that Kalamunda, that beautiful small town near our caravan park in Perth which we wanted to move to Queensland, is threatened by fire. One house has been lost and the smoke is so dense people are being affected by it. At Scamander in Tasmania, another favourite place of ours, several homes have been lost to ferocious fires and in Victoria the fires are still burning.

Tomorrow we leave the Margaret River area which encompasses Busselton, Dunsborough, Yallingup, Augusta and Margaret River itself. We now head down the South coast at long last and on to the East Coast which is more familiar to us.

I had a lovely start to the day because John had packed our chairs and outdoor table away so I went over to the barbecue table near our van and I could hear the sound the hundreds of birds' wings flapping. There were so many of them in the trees surrounding me and they are such tiny birds that it seems like butterflies are dancing about. Then I saw the little blue bird again. I've only seen the one blue one and it danced around the grass in front of me and this time I did not move as I didn't want to frighten it away. Then Callie came over and I sat on the ground with her on my lap and listened and watched the birds whilst giving her a cuddle. It amazes me that the park is almost empty. The owners decided that they wouldn't have permanent people living in it but the fact that I could only see one other van in the distance behind more trees was an absolute bonus. The grass is green, the hundreds of trees healthy, the beach is only a few steps away, the facilities are spotless and the owners are exceptionally eager to please. The owner told me that he doesn't like putting up lots of notices like some parks; they prefer their guests to feel relaxed and not governed by a list of rules. He also told John that they had tried putting people who own dogs together in the park but that hadn't worked. At last a park owner with some sense! Owners of dogs hate it and dogs hate it and the male dogs end up peeing on everything just to stake their claim and it really does become very frustrating and horrible. Then you have those dogs that yap every time you walk past them with yours. Some owners of parks just don't use their brains or perhaps they like barking dogs and pee everywhere!

This park is truly a lovely park and it is so beautifully situated. I heard a man in an information centre tell a customer that the main beach for Augusta is the one which runs all along the edge of the park here at Flinders Bay, but the public area is at the other end so the beach near the park is virtually private. The weather has been perfect because it is cooler at Flinders Bay than, for example, Esperance by about eight degrees at the moment and because we are on the eastern side of the Cape, it is sheltered from the winds.

So we set off wishing that we had allowed more time to relax in this lovely park and it was not long before we were surrounded by trees. We headed towards **Nannup** and then turned off for Pemberton and it was a beautiful journey although it was a slow journey because the road was very windy and hilly. We travelled through Karri Valley and the woody smell wafting through our open windows made the journey even more beautiful. The Karri trees stand so tall and straight and form a canopy over the road allowing just enough dappled sunlight to filter through to provide a beautiful scenic drive. It is a little difficult if you have a dog that needs a pee because it is nearly all National Park and there are baits around for the foxes.

PEMBERTON - GLOUCESTER TREE - SEE CLIMBING BARS

I turned the radio on and the first thing I heard was that feral pigs are spreading in the south of Western Australia. Not the nice home-grown kind of pigs that make great pets (and also taste good) but the nasty, big and dangerous pigs. Some that have been caught have weighed in at 90-100 kilograms! I needed to know that today as we are spending the next two nights off-road by forests! The next thing I heard was that the locusts are heading to Albany and should arrive within the next two weeks. How lovely, they'll be there to greet us when we arrive. They can stuff up vehicle engines so we'll have to get some fly wire and fix it over the radiator grills.

Do you know what a bar fly is? I didn't but then I've already told you that I'm still learning the Australian language. It is the person who is always sitting in the pub at the same place day after day, year after year. You needed to know that as it's a really important piece of information.

TREE TOP WALK - JOHN ENJOYING HIMSELF

We reached **Pemberton** and John jumped into the Ute and after a quick stop at a very pretty Information Centre we set off to find a tree. Not just any tree though but one that we could climb called **The Gloucester Tree** in the Gloucester National Park, about three kilometres out of town. The Gloucester Tree is around 60 metres tall. If you have the time, which we didn't, to travel about fifteen minutes out of town you could climb either the Dave Evans Bicentennial Tree (which is the tallest at 75m with 130 metal spikes) or The Diamond Tree. These trees sway around by the way so it must be a delight to reach the platforms at the top. In the Big Brook Forest there is 300 year old giant Karri tree which is reached via a boardwalk.

Anyway, to see the Gloucester Tree we could leave the dogs in an area with shade and walk to the tree, a distance of about three kilometres. It saved us park entry fees for the Ute, we saw a beautiful deep red Lorikeet (I think it was a Lorikeet – it looked like one but we had not seen one that colour before) and the walk was very easy and pretty and we needed the exercise anyway. It was also good to know that we were walking on a very little bit of the Bibbulmun Track which runs from Perth to Albany! I can now say 'Yes, I've walked the Bibbulmun Track' without explaining that I did all of six kilometres of the 963 kilometre track!

Two things stopped me from climbing the tree and I will always regret not having done so as I love challenges like that. Firstly it was because of Jack as he has had a very bad stomach for the last two days and the walk had not been the one kilometre as we had been told so we had taken longer than expected to reach the tree and we still had to return to the car. The main reason was that a Japanese girl who had just descended was waving her hands around. I asked her with hand signals if her hands were sore and she nodded that they were. The spikes provided (really for fire lookouts) are very easy to climb, even for someone with short legs like me and I had come here with the sole purpose of ascending them but the spikes have ridges on them to stop your shoes from slipping and it was these that had caused the poor girl sore hands. I felt thwarted and confused. I kept thinking of Jack and worrying about him and trying to imagine how my having very sore hands would affect the next few days and wishing to goodness that someone or some guide book had suggested wearing good gloves! I would have willingly bought a pair of gloves on the spot so there is an opening for an enterprising person! We took the decision to return to the car (it was a beautiful walk incidentally) and just as we arrived back it started to spit with rain. We got Jack out and his back was burning and we poured water over him and got him to lie down in the shade. To get him to leave the vehicle and lie under the tree required me to sit under it and I was quite happy to do so for Jack's sake until John told me that he could see giant ants all around me and that they could be climbing up my jeans. We left! (I was later to find out that an ant had indeed crawled up the inside of my jeans and I have another travel wound to take home with me. I am covered in different kinds of itchy bites at the moment with the worst one being on a finger but I also have one on either side of my forehead. Some bites are large and round, some tiny and itchy and others hard bumps!

We all ended up with 'travellers' tummy' over a forty-eight hour period and Jack and John were the first to get it with Callie and I promptly coming out in sympathy by the following day. It lasted several days so it obviously has to be the water we are drinking as we are not partial to their dog food. I am still regretting not having climbed that tree but you can understand my sympathy for Jack! I want to go back and at least try to climb it but we can't because of being booked into van parks during the school holidays.

We returned to town and took a few photos of it and I took several of one tree outside the information centre because we both loved it so much and then, at the advice of the man on the counter, we retraced our steps by exiting the town the way we had come and going to Walpole via Northcliffe because the journey is beautiful and at least we would get a thirty kilometre nearly straight stretch of road which would be better with our bus. We had missed lunch and it was now about 2.15pm and the rain was getting heavier but the journey was beautiful as we travelled along part of the Great Forrest Trees Drive. There are so any ferns growing, not only under the trees but also lining the roads so they must get a fair bit of rain here. Pemberton is surrounded by three National Parks so it is a particularly lovely area, particularly if you like walking. There is a timber industry in Pemberton so on the one hand you've got logging and on the other tourism because of the same trees which is a paradox. If you are outside the Information when the deep red roses are in bloom, take the time to stop and smell them.

We also stopped at **Northcliffe** because I had heard a loud noise about eleven kilometres back along the road but there had been nowhere to stop safely. My right head light and bracket had come loose and a lady immediately stopped and asked if we needed help. That wouldn't happen very often on the Gold Coast or in Brisbane. A nice rural town but neither of the petrol stations sold gas which was what John was looking for. They had diesel, unleaded and pulp for sale but no gas. What on earth is 'pulp'? (John told me later that it means Premium Unleaded Petrol.) There's a Northcliffe Pioneer Museum, the Northcliffe Federation track if you feel like a walk and apparently a caravan park nearby. It's a pretty little town with flower boxes lining one road and quite a large Northcliffe Hotel. We also saw a sign indicating a steam train. We still had about 98ks to go to get to Walpole and we were rarely going over 70kph.

I put the radio on again but soon had no reception because of the trees. I had heard enough of the water shortage problems in Australia anyway. Some elderly gent phoned in to a talkback radio show and he thinks he has the answer and that two canals should be built, one down the W.A coast and the other in Queensland. He suggested we did this instead of laying pipes. I have never heard anything so idiotic! Many thousands of kilometres of canals! Think how much water would be lost with evaporation in the same way that pools and dams lose their water. In one town in Queensland there was a vote on whether to use recycled sewerage. It was daft really to give the townsfolk a vote because of course they said they didn't want it. However, a guy on the radio was saying that we drink it if we go to London and have been doing so for years. That was new to me! Does our Queen know she is drinking recycled sewerage and what about Charles organic vegetables? Didn't be grow some at Buck Palace?

Chapter 28

Anyway, we are now parked off road about sixteen kilometres before Walpole and it is very relaxing. We have a table and two bench seats right outside our van door, the awning up, it has stopped raining and the sun is shining and John has just made me a coffee so tatty-byes.

I didn't wake up until 10am! It was so peaceful and quiet where we had parked and it was the first time that we had been totally alone off road at night. I had thought it would be a bit eerie but the silence was wonderful as was the complete darkness. When I did manage to pull myself together I rushed around the bus like a whirlwind packing everything up because I knew that we had a lot to see that day. First stop was **Walpole** where we parked the bus near the Information Centre and dropped in to see them and to collect a map. We were told that dogs were not very welcome in the area and we couldn't stay in town that night so our thoughts of staying off road near the community centre which was listed in our off-roads book went out of the window. However we left the bus there all day and were told that we could fill up with fresh town water and there was a garage selling gas. Actually there were two but we purchased the gas at the dearer one, much to John's annoyance when he later found out, because the other one did not advertise his prices so we hadn't realised.

Our first destination was the **Nornalup Inlet (The Knoll)** not far from town so that the dogs could get nice and wet and cool before we had to leave them in the car whilst we went to the Tree Top Walk. It was beautiful there and well worth the visit.

The Treetop Walk is in a **Tingle Forest** and we were able to drive up to the entrance and leave the dogs in the car park well protected by trees. This walk was something I had been looking forward to for a long time but I was actually a bit disappointed with it as I felt I had seen better elsewhere. Just as we started along the walkway we met a young English tourist who was being helped back to the ground as she was suffering from her fear of heights and the swaying of the walkway didn't help. She was very upset with herself as she really wanted to do the walk and I felt so sorry for her. However, she could do the ground walkway which we did afterwards and it impressed us much more and it was a very pleasant and easy walk. John managed to delight some Japanese tourists because he found what looked like a man's watch on the Treetop Walk and asked some Japanese tourists if they had lost one. As they did not speak English it was an interesting conversation because they got the idea of the watch but thought he wanted to know the correct time. Suddenly one of the women beamed and indicated that it belonged to their family and she called her little son who was some distance away and he came running up looking both shocked at his empty wrist and delighted that John had been so good as to find it for him and he thanked John in perfect English. I will remember his beaming smile forever.

For those that are interested, Tingle trees are known to live up to 400 years and they are of the Eucalyptus family. The Red Tingle starts flowering during summer after 30 years and has small, white flowers and the tree produces a bumper crop every four years. These trees can reach up to 75 metres and they have huge trunks at the bottom which can be up to about 20 metres in circumference. The bark is rough and stringy and is a grey to brown colour. They are only found in the Walpole-Nornalup National Park and surrounding areas with high rainfall.

The Yellow Tingle grows to approximately 35 metres and flowers after about seven years with white flowers and cup-shaped fruits. These trees have a yellow timber with a straight grain.

The Karri trees which are also found around here are also of the Eucalyptus family and can grow up to ninety metres being the world's third tallest hardwood tree. It has pale, smooth bark which turns a salmon pink in the autumn when it sheds its bark.

We drove around the remainder of the Valley of the Giants Road which loops back to the South Coast Road. En route we stopped for another red tingle and karri forest walk to see the **Giant Tingle Tree** which is 24 metres high and is the largest, living, girthed eucalypt known in the world.

The Karri Sheoak grows to about fifteen metres and is rather like a pine tree. The bark is thick and corky. It needs the heat of the summer sun or a fire to release its tiny winged seeds which are inside woody cones.

It was time for more water so we set off for **Peaceful Bay**, Lilford Rock and **Point Irwin**. You can stay at Peaceful Bay Caravan Park with dogs and pay at the village shop. We had toasted sandwiches there for our lunch and they were lovely. It was beautiful down there along the coast. We attempted to go down the tract to **Conspicuous Cliff** but the road was corrugated and very, very rough and we could see that it would be a long arduous journey to get to our destination so we turned around. My car has collected as many travel wounds as I have and needs body repairs. The fact that our mobile did not work if we did have problems also convinced us not to go on but it would be fine in a four wheel drive.

When we got back to Walpole we decided to have a look around the town and stopped at the Walpole Inlet which is another beautiful area and you could walk there from the main street. By the time we did get back to the main street the shops were all shutting so John fed the dogs, filled the van up with gas and then fresh water from the tap by the information centre and we went to a café, which also sold bakery items and ordered fish and chips and bought two large iced fruit buns for 70c each as a treat for the following day. However, despite a beautifully presented meal with about four pieces of fish and heaps of fish, lemon, salad and sauces we subsequently could not get rid of the taste of the oil and I ended up with a very bad stomach which lasted twenty-four hours. I guess the deep fat fryer oil had been over used and it totally spoilt the meal for us. I wish I'd purchased more of their fruit buns though!

So, it was about eight o'clock at night when we finally arrived at our second off-road site for the night and it was not so good as there were so many large blow flies around (some people here call them biting flies and others march flies). There was another van further along but it was not such a nice place to stay. We had been told back at Walpole that we could have stayed at Rest Point Holiday Village but we had tried to phone them during our free phone time between nine and ten o'clock one day and there had been no answer and not even an answering machine and it was so late that we just wanted to drive off road and sleep.

This caravan park business with dogs is rather odd over here because the leaflet for the Rest Point Holiday Village does not indicate that dogs are allowed and we heard today that there had been another park in Perth, not far from ours with a Big Four sign outside plus a "No dogs' sign and not only was it not a Big Four park (they never allow dogs) but our new neighbours stayed there with their dog! Never trust neither leaflets, nor information in books if you have a dog and always phone because you may be surprised. There are far more parks that allow dogs than are advertised.

Today was an easy fifty kilometre run to **Denmark** and we are staying at the River mouth with our site overlooking the bay and it is absolutely stunning with a continual vista of pelicans, sea gulls and egrets flying around, congregating en masse or gracefully floating by. We are literally about ten steps to the water which delights the dogs and by the park entrance is the river inlet.

I saw my first snake today. It was not a very big snake and it was slithering across the road between Walpole and Denmark. I've now seen three in the twenty-six years that I've lived here, discounting those in wildlife parks.

I went to explore Denmark this afternoon and wore myself out. It is wonderful and so surprising because when you drive through you see just a few shops along a main street but when you start to walk around you find several small timber floored shopping precincts with plants and seating surrounded by all sorts of shops such as a gallery, organic or 'real food' store, clothes shops, newsagents, jewellers and cafes. It's really interesting and unexpected.

Also many of the shops are multi-functional so that the IGA food store connects with the hardware store but it is also a drapery store and sells footwear. Jassi Leather Works not only sells Ugg boots but is also a library and herbarium. The Spot News sells newspapers and stationery along with souvenirs, toys, ice cream and yoghurt and you can also use the internet there. I liked the name Crafti Gelati Café because they do sell authentic Italian ice cream and it is also a craft gallery. And so it goes on and I am now so confused about what is where because nothing is as it seems! Some of the shops have the oddest of combination products on display. I think I picked up some free tourist leaflets from a natural health or organic product shop yet the information centre is just across the road. Add this to the fact that there are two IGA stores, which is like having two Woolworths or K Marts within metres of each other in a relatively small town. Having questioned several people about this the only answer I received is that they have different special promotional products each week, are owned by different people but run by the same company! I love places like this that are barmy! The shops saying it sold Real Food had a lot of organic products but also sold wonderful Italian pasta products and I was convinced by the saleswoman that I had to try some of her free Italian Christmas cake as it is a speciality. Along the same road I came across an Organic shop. Then I found the Health Food shop with lots of natural products such as shampoos. A lot of the shops also seem to do book exchange services or sell second hand books but you wouldn't know that unless you went inside the shop so every shops needs to be explored. There's also a candy shop which I did not go into but it looks very inviting with all the Christmas treats on show. Anyway, I only went into some of the shops in one street and was absolutely exhausted so I returned to the van without having got a map from the Tourist Information Centre which is also right there in the middle of everything and I did not get time to go into a delightful looking small church that beckoned. I'll just have to go back and try again! I love this town, it is delightful. John was not so impressed with the shops when he went to town the following day (he hates shops but even he went into some of them) as he was impressed with all the parkland and river views.

My greatest joy at the shops was finding some of the Margaret River Dairy Company blueberry yoghurt. It is sublime. We have a fridge full of fruit at the moment including sultanas from a farm, plums, kiwi fruit, dates from a health food store, a huge bag of Pink Lady apples from another farm shop, far too many very sweet oranges and yet with stomachs that are churning with travellers tummy we just can't face any of it but we can always eat that yoghurt despite the rich blueberry content and I have just noticed that there is a blueberry farm here so guess where we are going tomorrow! I'll just have to cook some apples and blueberries and freeze it until we feel a bit better.

We are only here for three nights and I want to stay three months, especially as we are staying at a park which is so stunningly situated and with a van site with such incredible views. We also have a lot of places to explore, washing to do and a camera that's totally full up with over 100 photos to download! It's nearly 11.15pm, John's gently snoring on the settee and I guess it's time for bed.

I've found out what my little blue bird is and I've purchased a post card of it. I will quote off the back of the postcard because it has a web site where you can view it and see for yourself how beautiful it is. So with thanks to Nu-color-Vue, Australian National Postcard Company here it is. 'Male Splendid Fairy-Wren. Out of the breeding season, you may notice male splendid wrens, but in their courting plumage they are among the most striking birds of the forest. With their iridescent cobalt blue feathers, these little birds certainly are splendid. Visit: www.naturebase.net

I actually asked someone in an information centre about them and was told that they are surrounded by many hens. No joke! This one seemed to have hundreds of them in his harem which probably explains why he was dancing around with joy! Apparently his colours will start to fade as the courting season ends and he will lose all the blue except for a tip on the end of his tail. They are apparently difficult to spot because they stay so close to the ground and are territorial which explains why the one we saw stayed around our site. When we left I said to John that it would be glad to see the back of us because we were so obviously on its patch of ground.

We got two loads of washing on the line and I got stuck into some vacuuming, last week's ironing and catching up on this diary as it was all out of sequence. I did manage to sit outside a couple of times for a few moments to watch the pelicans glide by and the beautiful white egret wade around in the shallow water in front of me but how is it that one job can lead to another so very quickly. I cannot recall how it happened but I think it was when John said that the fridge smelt. I found that some milk that had leaked from a bottle and found that it had congealed into cheese and it became a mammoth task as there are clips holding the shelves in and they were glued into place by the mess. I ended up having to empty the fridge (it's full size) and I had stuff everywhere and every time I picked up a bag of, for example, cauliflower or whatever it dripped more milk everywhere else. John had been bringing the washing in and I had a rotting lettuce in a bag in the bathroom sink, every worktop covered and was cursing as I used a screwdriver and pliers to try and get the clips out so that I could release the shelves. Then I had to find my cleaning brushes so more things came flying out of a large cupboard because I needed to scrub the grooves that I could not reach with a cloth. Actually a cloth didn't work anyway and I had to use strong cleaning products and a scrubbing brush to get the 'cheese' off the fridge surfaces. The computer was still on, the ironing board out and I should have been cooking dinner so some lamb chops were sitting on the bench top drying out! I still had a hundred or so photos to download. Absolute chaos and the day had passed me by when all was back in order. Photos are downloaded, all the ironing finished, everything put away, we've had dinner and I've finished this so I'm off. It's time to relax with the Saturday paper.

Day out touring

Started the day with overdue phone calls because I panicked last night when I suddenly realised that Christmas is a week on Monday! I needed to know if the people we met previously on the road were going to be with us on Christmas Day because of what food I need to buy. I was going to make my own mince pies, made out of shortbread pastry. Should I bother or go and buy some? Do I buy prawns for lunch and if so how many? I will need to find a bakers and order croissants and Danish pastries as we always spoil ourselves for breakfast on Christmas Day. We usually have a simple lunch of fresh seafood because it's usually so hot but would I buy a turkey – hardly seems worth it if there are just two of us. My head was spinning last night. If I buy a leg of ham I could freeze it just as I could the turkey and that would provide us with so much meat already cooked and so useful when travelling. Should I make a sherry trifle? It turns out that they are way behind us and they hope to catch up with us by New Year. Judging by what we have covered over the last couple of weeks they have no hope!

Take Denmark alone – there is so much to see. There is a Dinosaur World and Parrot Jungle World and Reptile Park which we won't be going to, a toffee factory, the Thurlby Herb Farm, café and gift shop, a Western Australian Wildflower outlet, the Maze. A leather works and coffee shop, a Sandalwood factory, the Denmark Museum, the Pentland Alpaca Stud, Animal Farm and Wildlife Park, Djarilmari Timber Products, a Bartholomew's Meadery which sells honey wine and honey ice cream. There's the cheese outlet that sells wine and fudge along with home-made chutneys, relish and grape jellies! There are over thirty galleries and craft shops in and around Denmark, many talented artists, about fifteen wineries, berry farms, orchards, river cruising, horse-riding, rock climbing, whale watching, bird watching, wild flowers to find and bush walks plus lots of beaches and the Bibbulmun Track. There are the Mount Lindesay and Harewood State Forest walks. In one of the leaflets it says that Denmark's year is filled with festivals, exhibitions, competitions, concerts, pantomimes, market days, live shows and movie nights. I think we'd better stay on for a year! It is also an environmentally aware community with a 'Clean and Green' image. At the moment they are building the world's largest water barometer at the Information Centre and that will be finished in 2007.

Our first stop today was at one of the two bakeries in town because they have won three gold medals this year for their meat pies. I asked which ones they won the medals for and apparently it was for the steak pies, the salmon pies and a potato pie (not sure if it was a combination of potato and something else) and we came away with pies for dinner. Our first beach scenic stop was **Ocean Beach** which was very beautiful with its sand bar and bay inlet but the dogs couldn't go on the beach there so after going down to look at **Wilson Head** we went on to **Lights Beach** where dogs are allowed and they had a wonderful time although Jack got bowled over by the waves. Next it was our turn to have fun because we went to Greens Pool and had to clamber over the huge rock face which I loved, to get to Elephant Rocks. It was wonderful there and I had a ball. It's very wild and natural. All the coastline had been and we were very impressed because we didn't see any development!

Then it was back to the highway to turn off onto McLeod Road to find the Cheese outlet where we sampled a few cheeses, John tried some chutneys and pickles and we both sampled some red wine and bought some lovely Camembert. We continued along Scottsdale Road to do a loop back to Denmark and stopped at the Alpaca outlet but the goods for sale were very expensive. They had some beautiful teddy bears at over $200! Jumpers were a similar price.

We had our picnic lunch in Harwood Forest at a barbecue table provided and returned to Denmark. We passed so many places that we could have stopped at such as Tinglewood Wines and Puzzle Shop - after a few wines I would think a puzzle would be rather difficult so I find that an amusing combination. Another outlet sells chocolates, mushrooms and champagne!

We finished off our day by taking a few photos of the town centre and John showed me the river and bridge and parkland in town and the bridge over the river by our park which is part of the Bibbulmun Track. It was a lovely day and unfortunately it is now time to start packing up again but at least we will be able to stop for a ten day break over Christmas and we do not have far to go to get there. We never made it to the Blueberry outlet today because we realised that we would be passing nearby it on our way to Albany tomorrow.

Chapter 29

ALBANY - 22nd December 2006

We never made it at all because I had a gastric stomach yet again having only been back on the park-provided water for two days. I'm back on bottled water and recovered quickly. Thus it was that the first day after our arrival I did absolutely nothing except sleep. Our first stop in any new place seems to be the town and so we found ourselves exploring the shops and arcades the next day returning with two month's supply of dog food and groceries, but we did enjoy an authentic expresso at an Italian restaurant in the main street and found the ABC shop which always seems to yank us inside its doors by an invisible force. We also found the Tourist Information Centre after first getting lost and seeing some lovely parts of the older suburbs and parkland. The Bibbulmun Track from Kalamunda is right by the Visitors Centre. The main street leads down a hill to the waterfront so we took the dogs along there for a walk which they appreciated. I was relieved that I had at least accomplished the purchase of a leg of ham for Christmas and a fresh turkey that is small enough for me to be able to cook in our van oven.

Albany was settled in 1826 which was two years before Perth was settled, so they want you to know that fact here. That's your history lesson over and done with for Albany.

The next day we found a good vet and had a chat with him and ordered tablets and John is there now with Jack so it gives me a bit of time on my own to catch up with this. Then we went up to the Mt. Clarence lookout where the War Memorial is and what wonderful views the area provides. Albany was the embarkation point for Australian troops in the First World War. We spent quite a while wandering around the area and taking photographs despite the fact that it was only 19C, very cloudy and dull. This is summer and a high of 19C is almost like winter for us at the Gold Coast so we had jumpers on! As I write this the sun has appeared for the first time since we arrived.

We then headed for the coastal road stopping at the beginning of Middleton Beach at a lookout area, on Middleton Beach itself further along where the dogs were allowed and then on to Emu Point. What a lovely area it is with Middleton Beach being such a huge bay with such white sand and sea of various hues of blue. Although it is now the school holidays the whole area that we drove around was quiet, had beautiful views and lovely, old-fashioned residential areas.

We talked to a guy fishing at Emu Point and he showed us what he'd caught on his way home from work for his dinner. He had quickly caught a couple of good fish and was about to go home. I was praying that John was listening and might yet be converted to giving fishing a go so that I wouldn't have to pay the crazy prices in the shops. John seems to think I could learn! We went to a seafood café we'd read about but one look inside and another at the prices saw us back out the door and heading for the headland where we had talked to that guy, where there is a Japanese Restaurant and a café with excellent coffee overlooking parkland and ocean with islands in the distance. It was delightful as were the service and prices.

We spoke to a very elderly lady there who had just converted her four door hatchback car and that day had bought herself a very comfortable camp bed which she showed us. She gleefully told us 'I can do what you are doing now. It's going to be such fun'. She was so proud of her new vehicle and her new bed and the modifications that she had had done to the vehicle and she was a joy to talk to.

I cannot recall what we did yesterday except that all I seem to have done since we got here is to visit shops. I was trying to find a CD for John, a particular book that he wanted and something else that I can't mention because he reads this but that I was also unable to get. I changed tack and decided to try and get him an electronic synthesiser that would be small enough for him to have on his lap, along with ear phones so I wouldn't have to listen to it! He used to have one many years ago until it packed in and I knew that he wanted another one.

So I set off this morning to the shops yet again and was gone for four hours spending almost all of that time on a fruitless search. I did have one break at my favourite brand coffee outlet which only opened in Albany the day before yesterday and had a lovely chat with an elderly couple on who were sitting at an adjacent table who are staying in a hotel in town. They offered to take my mail and post it for me as they were on foot and I had been trawling up and down the high street trying to find a parking spot without luck and by this time I was in an undercover shopping mall with them still clutched in my hand (the letters that is, not the elderly couple!)

Anyway, I had to start again with what to buy John, the man who has everything he needs, or so he tells me. I still had money from Helen in a separate wallet to buy the CD with, which I can't get, so I had to worry about her present to him too. Eventually I found a note about something that I had thought of buying John some months ago and I managed to get the last one available anywhere in Albany – a popular present it seems. He now has two presents from me that I hope he likes and I've sent him off with the money from Helen to buy his own present from her! As he reads this diary I have to be careful I don't mention what I bought!

I also had to find a fresh seafood outlet that I had been told about to organise some king prawns for Christmas lunch (the turkey being for dinner because hopefully it will be too hot to eat turkey at midday). Although I took the wrong road to start with, I did find the seafood factory fairly easily but the return journey was something else altogether as I had to keep turning the car around and trying other streets. I ended up back in the town centre yet again which absolutely delighted me of course having spent four hours there already that morning!

Helen has a new job which she is very excited about because it will give her even wider experience in the fitness field and the money is better. It's near Brisbane where we first lived when we came to Australia and where she went to junior school. However, as her Dad lives fairly close she is thinking of keeping her base at the Gold Coast and staying with her Dad a few nights a week which, if it turns out alright, will be really nice for both of them as they get little chance to see each other at the moment with the hours she works. This week she is working fifty hours.

Colin also phoned to say that he had stopped work now for the Christmas holidays and he really needs the rest and he wanted to send us a thousand dollars. Isn't that nice? He might owe it to us but that's beside the point because you are always grateful if your children remember that they owe you money and offer to pay you back!

I heard two teenage boys in town the other day and one asked the other 'Did you get any money off Mum?'

'Yes, I got two dollars'.

'I didn't!'

'Oh no, it wasn't Mum. I went to Dad afterwards and got it off him'.

I was delighted with this conversation because they were delighted that they had two dollars and because they looked around fifteen years old and I had just been reading in the paper that kids as young as seven upwards are now a large target for the advertisers and are called Tweens because they have so much disposable income given to them by their parents.

The kids that I overheard are certainly learning the value of the dollar unlike the 'Tweens'.

24th Christmas Eve 2006

Yesterday was a rather lousy day although we did go out to try and cheer ourselves up! We had been saying how lucky we are to be able to say 'Let's have another coffee and another chocolate biscuit' when so many people cannot and reflecting on what it must be like for the many people for whom even water is so hard to get. With this in mind I took the 'white' washing to the laundry which is very close to our van and put that on, returning to do some hand washing. I first washed a pink jumper of mine and a couple of John's best casual shirts before tackling the remaining bits and pieces. Some of it I was going to spin out in my spinner in the van but decided it would be prudent to drip dry John's two shirts so that I could avoid having to get the iron out! I went and hung them up (about 12 paces from our van) and returned to spin out the rest. So within 5-10 minutes at the most I returned to the line to find that one of John's shirts had been taken along with the clothes pegs!

I was so angry and upset. I later said to John 'Why am I so upset over a shirt? It's just a shirt after all albeit that it was a favourite shirt for both of us.' It was the fact that there were only three people around. One was an elderly lady who was doing a pile of washing in the laundry and she had her chair there and was using the dryer too and I kept finding her asleep in the chair. Whilst I was hanging them up an English couple beside us returned in their car. I didn't want to suspect any of them but I did! I told this English couple what had happened and told them how sad and angry I felt but I could not shake off the horrible feeling of having something stolen and how quick the person had been who had stolen it. John reported the fact to the office and they said that the same thing had happened the previous Christmas and again it had been a man's shirt. I would rather have given the person the money to buy a new one because the one they took was two years old and had been a Christmas present to John. As we haven't met many friendly people here we were already wishing that we were elsewhere and now we did not feel 'safe'.

The fact that it has happened two years running, points to the culprit being a resident or someone who works here such as a cleaner. You can tell from this diary just how it affected me and I put up some notices in the ladies, gents and laundry asking the person who had taken the shirt off the line whilst it was still dripping to leave it in a bag at the office or leave it in the laundry, obviously (The notice disappeared from the men's toilet on Christmas morning so perhaps some guy realised that his gift of shirts for the past two years may well have been stolen! I hope he confronted whoever gave them to him so that no-one else suffers the same frustration at Christmas in future)

So, we took ourselves off to the Mt Melville Lookout in town. We reached the water tower and thought it a bit disappointing before realising we could drive higher up to a tower that we could climb and it was well worth it because we had such wonderful views from there. Like Mount Clarence we had three hundred and sixty degree views of the town, the Southern Ocean, mountain ranges and the waterways. We let the dogs out and they had a ball and we clambered up and down rocks and paths before climbing up the stairs of the tower, exiting at each door for more extensive views. We caused Jack complete and utter confusion. When the dogs had got to some exterior steps which led to the tower they did not want to climb them and we can only put it down to the yellow stripe across each step. Callie got over her fear of those steps and followed us and Jack found an alternative route to the tower door. However, when Callie heard our footsteps echoing up the metal stairs she dashed back down the few stairs she had climbed and Jack ran away from the tower. So every time we came out of the tower on a new level we would have to call to them and although that is a complete waste of time with Jack because he doesn't hear us, Callie commutes our messages to him. Each time we came out onto the platforms we would see them heading off back to the car and would have to call them back! It was a bit too much for Jack because he went around in circles on the spot a couple of times, poor thing. However, at least they had their freedom because the rest of the afternoon was going to be totally boring for them as we were heading into National Park and they wouldn't be able to get out of the Ute.

We set off for **Frenchman's Bay** which is surrounded by the **Torndirrup National Park** and that was just what we needed as it was wild scenery and a windy day and we did a lot of clambering over rocks which got rid of our 'cobwebs'. The scenery reminded me of parts of Wales or Cornwall. The sky was grey and the waves pounded ferociously again the cliffs and rocks and I took copious photos trying to catch the spume which was shooting into the air. We saw The Gap (from the viewing cage as it is a sheer chasm with the surf being 30 metres below) and the Natural Bridge (a huge piece of eroded granite forming an arch) and Cable Beach (stunningly beautiful) and John went to look at The Blowhole which was an 800m walk each way plus a lot of steps and although he could hear the 'blows' he couldn't see a thing so it was a complete waste of time.

I had stayed at the car because there was a big sign which stopped us which read 'If you have a dog in your car turn around' or some such words. So there we were stuck on the road by the sign which was so dangerous instead of in the car park!! Anyway, by the time John returned it was five o'clock and we returned home without seeing the Frenchman Bay town or the Salmon Holes and still with the Vancouver Peninsular to explore so we'll have to go back again another day.

Today we finished off our shopping which was relaxing and pleasant because nobody seemed to be rushing around and many people were just having coffees with friends or wandering around window shopping, quite unlike earlier in the week and there were plenty of places to park. We also went looking for the times of church services and although I thought I was going to go to the Uniting Church, we have now decided on midnight mass at the St Johns Church, an Anglican church built in 1848. It is a beautiful church and there will be communion (for me) and it was the first Anglican Church consecrated in Western Australia which makes it rather special. Well I think so anyway and I feel the need to be somewhere special this Christmas. I am so looking forward to being back in a church, particularly as communion is included. It's time to stop worrying about such trifles as a stolen shirt and get things into perspective, particularly with so many people suffering around the world.

Boxing Day evening

A particular conflict whilst travelling in a motor home or caravan is when one wishes to catch up on one's diary and ones husband is watching a program on the war with the Zulus and Queen Victoria's involvement and as you can tell, 'one' has listened to our present Queen's Christmas message. It amuses us here that we hear it before you do in the United Kingdom because you are all in bed asleep (unless you have children who have got you out of bed just after you've drifted off to sleep to tell you Father Christmas has arrived). I do recall one Christmas whilst staying with relatives when their children got us all out of bed about 3am. It happened to be the Christmas that the parents had bought their son a set of drums and their daughter some other musical instrument. So that we wouldn't be left out we also had musical pipes as gifts. The house was in an uproar and I thought it was hilarious and promptly fell pregnant with Colin who arrived nine months later. Never discuss having a baby during Easter holidays as I did because your child will not thank you for having a Birthday at Christmas. Now how am I going to concentrate on where and what we did today. Perhaps I won't.

On Christmas Day we greeted many other people who greeted us in return before retreating back into their vans. We have found the people here unusually distant. So it was a very odd day and John came in at one point and said 'I give up' meaning with our co-holiday visitors. It was also extremely quiet in the park except for one young boy who had a tricycle and who went around us all day shouting out 'toot toot'. That changed to 'flat tyre, flat tyre' and I asked him if he had removed the valve on purpose and he happily agreed that he had so that he could have a flat tyre. He told me that he had pumped it up and although he was so proud of his mechanical abilities, it was practically flat A kindly gentleman did the pumping whilst I tried to get through to this young lad that he must not do this in future and that he could ruin his tyre and he listened attentively. I got some gold chocolate coins out and sent him back to his Mum with one for each of them and peace returned for a while.

We followed our usual practice of having a croissant for breakfast and a Danish pastry (although John had cereal first and double everything). It took me two days to finish my Danish pastry which was wonderful and full of walnuts. Despite the fact that I heated the croissants in the microwave instead of battling our oven, they were surprisingly lovely and were nearly as good as those I used to eat in Geneva for breakfast. Of course the chocolate mints had to be opened and the crystallised ginger – we do grow such beautiful ginger here in Australia. Lunchtime was again standard – King prawns, seafood sauce, rolls and a plain lettuce and cucumber salad. As we didn't have the family I didn't need to worry about pasta and potato salads, coleslaw, beetroot and make the rest of the salads that we usually have to do nor the fruit platter. I certainly did not feel as though I had overeaten but things went wrong when I had my first glass of advocaat. I only ever buy it at Christmas and I do love it so and along with a mince pie I was suddenly quite certain that I would not be cooking a turkey for dinner! I was having trouble keeping awake too because the previous evening, before we went to church, I was so sleepy that I had a coffee at around nine o'clock and after we arrived home at 1am I was wide awake and couldn't get to sleep until about 3am. I think I'll skip the midnight service in future because I was just so out of it on Christmas day.

We had ham and tomatoes and rolls for dinner instead, followed by Christmas pudding with brandy custard. So today it was the day for Christmas Dinner with Turkey, stuffing, roast potatoes, pumpkin, sprouts and peas, this time followed by mince pies and brandy custard! I can't keep this up! Tomorrow we are having what we were supposed to be having today! I'll have to do an awful lot of exercise soon to work this off. I still have mince pies, Christmas pudding, chocolates, a full carton of whole cream and blueberries and apple to cook.

As there is no pool here (yet again) we decided we need to get out for some exercise and went back to Frenchman's Bay and we saw the most incredibly beautiful scenery. Fine very white sand, bright turquoise seas contrasting in colour where there were rocks beneath the water or seaweed, sheer cliffs, huge boulders, wild flowers, beautiful bays and not once did we see a shop or café and the only places we saw houses was in Frenchman Bay itself. It is a wild, wonderful and stunning area and it was a very hot day (we should have taken our swimming gear) with clear blue skies so the islands stood out in stark contrast to the colours of the ocean. So many photo opportunities, so many sights that took our breath away, so much beauty – you have to see this part of Western Australia.

We went first to **Newell Bay** and three young people who were going diving directed us towards the lookout and the views were absolutely breathtaking. Apparently it is not known if the area was named after a Jimmy Newell who was a convict or another man of the same name who was a deserter. The former served his time and settled, bringing his wife and children out from England to join him.

We drove down Stony Hill Road to the Lookout. We spent a long time there clambering over the rocks and looking at the beautiful views. I wanted to get to the Salmon Holes but this area surprises you because there are so many more places to see than those on the tourist brochures. We didn't get to the Salmon Holes until late in the afternoon because we bypassed it in the hope of finding something to eat in the settlement of Frenchman Bay itself. There isn't a shop in sight there so take food and drink with you! Point Possession Heritage Trail Whaling Cove was packed out with cars and the sand was so white. Many families were following a tradition here in Australia by gathering together for a barbecue or picnic on Boxing Day and this seemed to be a favourite destination.

We managed to find two beaches that the dogs were allowed on, the first being Vancouver Point. We went down to Frenchmans Bay towards Waterbay Point and then the second doggie beach, **Goode Beach**. The dogs were soaking wet which kept them cool whilst we looked at the places that they couldn't go.

Misery Beach was absolutely stunning with the added advantage of a huge, sheer rock face sliding down into the sand and the sea at one end of the bay. The Frenchman Bay Lookout provided spectacular views. I think it was at the Bald Head Walking Track that we didn't get any photos because it would have taken 6-8 hours to walk the track and there were warnings not to return via the beach as it can be dangerous.

As for **The Salmon Holes**, it was such a beautiful beach that I couldn't delete any photo even though I had too many! Having completed the **Vancouver Peninsular** we returned around the coast towards town and it had been a wonderful day, absolutely wonderful. As it is nearly all National Park it is pristine and natural and it would be a botanist's delight despite the fact that apparently the soil is poor. There are many different kinds of Banksia trees and there are some in bloom all year around. There is one species called the Bull Banksia which I find weird, another called Swamp Banksia which doesn't sound good but looks great and then there is the Cutleaf Banksia. Others with more normal names are the Coastal or Slender Banksia, Albany or Granite Banksia and the Oak-Leafed Banksia. I was taking photos of wild flowers but the foliage of many shrubs and plants delighted both John and I. It is unusual for John to point them out but the contrasting colours attracted the eye. Not that Captain George Vancouver liked it much when he visited the area in 1791 – if you read what he wrote you'd never bother visiting the area!

When we went to Eighty Mile Beach so many weeks ago I said that it was beautiful but that was one, albeit very long, beach and Coral Bay was beautiful too but here there are so many places with the same white sand and turquoise sea – so many beautiful bays within minutes of each other instead of several hundred kilometres!

For me it has only been from Bunbury onwards that W.A has met my expectations. By that I mean that I wouldn't bother to return to see the rest of W.A. Although I have realised my dream of the Horizontal Waterfalls and have seen Perth and have learnt so much and seen so much I don't feel the need to see them again. For the first time today I said to John that during these last few weeks we have seen so many places and things that I have loved, that I might even be tempted to return to W.A just to see this area again, just as I want to return to parts of the Queensland coast, the Southern Highlands of New South Wales and down to the coast there along as far as Narooma.

I have phoned my two brothers in England and they are talking about a family reunion in England next year and I told the first that he can't have it without me being there and the second that I'm not sure if I'm invited but I'm coming anyway! He cracked up laughing and told me he'd find a caravan park and a small van for us as we are obviously used to caravan parks. 'No, no, definitely not' I replied but then added that we had contemplated touring Spain and Portugal. Should we tour these countries – that would mean yet another diary? Oh, dear me. I told them we won't be home until May and then have to sort our finances out first!

Talking about finances, apparently in Queensland they are having the same problem with housing in the mining industry there as they are having in Western Australia. Unless you are on mining wages you cannot afford to rent the houses, so men are living for example at Mackay and driving 200 kilometre to work at the mine for four days, staying there in single men's units and then returning to the coast and their families for their four days off.

The rents and cost of housing here has shocked us all down the W.A coastline. At least the problem is more isolated in Queensland. The prices for food in this town do not seem quite so bad as we have previously experienced – or is it just that we are getting accustomed to paying more for our goods? I have no idea but should know when I first go shopping back in Queensland. I did refuse to buy a Rockmelon here at Christmas in Woolworths and a man who was shopping there was as stunned as I was that seedless grapes were priced at $19.98 per kilo and we both turned away. It will be interesting to find out when we get back home.

28th December 2006

Having spent yesterday running around until we eventually purchased a new printer as I'd had enough of the old one, we decided to do some more sight-seeing today before leaving tomorrow.

We were heading for Two Peoples Bay but our first stop was **Lower King** which had a 'one-stop-shop' store which had postal services and sold alcohol, groceries and fuel. It was along the

Esplanade there that we stopped to look at **Oyster Harbour** and Callie and Jack enjoyed their first swim. It was lovely there.

Then we stopped on the other side of the bridge at a park by the King River and took a couple of photos before moving on to **Nanarup**. We thought it was a village but it isn't and except for a house on the hill and a couple of beach houses there was nothing there but some toilets (don't go there!), an inlet and a beautiful surf beach. It was also a four wheel drive beach and it was busy and I spent most of my time fruitlessly (as he can't hear me) calling out to Jack to get out of the way of vehicles and it seemed almost as busy as Albany! It is a stunningly beautiful beach and Callie, in particular, had an absolute ball. Both of the dogs followed John over to the ocean but Callie galloped back from the sea at such a pace that I didn't know she was back until I heard a loud plop as she landed with glee in the waters of the inlet. She just lay down and grinned! Jack tried his best to limp back very quickly and barked his head off as he was annoyed that she beat him to it.

We then set off for **Peaceful Bay** not bothering to turn off to see Gull Rock and Ledge Point. It was mainly because it was such a blazingly hot day and I thought we would need to leave them in the car and would be walking over hot rocks without shade – I'll never know now! It was a pleasant drive by farmlands and wineries with hills and trees and wild plants to look at. We had been so looking forward to seeing Two Peoples Bay but the road was closed and a large sign explained that it was closed today because of 'Extreme High Fire Danger'. By this time we wanted our lunch so returned to the Bridge at Lower King again where we knew there was shade. We had just unpacked our picnic lunch when Callie leapt into the air and held one of her rear legs high off the ground. I couldn't see anything wrong with her leg or paw but she was limping. A wind had blown up that was so strong that we had to form a shield to get our coffee and sugar into our cups and were having to hold the flask to stop it from flying away. I took Callie into the water to try and ease her pain and she went back to where she had been lying before only to leap up into the air again. We found out that she had been resting on an ant's nest! They were huge and were a dull red colour with big black bums or balls at their rear end. They were really gross. We didn't stop long!

We did some last minute shopping on the way back as I don't think we are going to find a 'high street' at Bremer Bay and whilst unloading the car and packing the vegetables into the fridge I found that two more bottles of milk had been leaking and to cap it off the chocolate cake fell onto the carpet with the icing face down on the carpet! Although it was not one of our most wonderful days, the dogs wouldn't agree.

We've enjoyed our visit to Albany, mainly because of Frenchman Bay but we have not done a lot of the tourist attractions. For example we did not visit the **Wind Farm**, go to **Mount Romance** neither for their Emu oil nor for their Sandalwood products. At Mount Romance and at the **Tribal Dreaming relaxation centre** you can experience something called the 'Cone, Gong & Bowl'. You relax to the sounds of a gong, the aroma of sandalwood and relax in a softly lit conical structure so that the sounds move over and through the body for deep relaxation.

We did not go on a scenic cruise up the river nor visit the **Amity** (a replica of the Brig Amity) which brought the first settlers and convicts here in 1826. We had contemplated going out to sea with the **Eco Ocean Adventures** on a yacht and it was fairly reasonable at $55 per head including refreshments and didn't even get around to that. We didn't go to the Museum and we didn't go to the Convict Gaol Museum, nor take a ride on **Albany's Clydesdale Wagon Train**. To cap it off we did not go to **Mount Barker** and the **Stirling and Porongurup Ranges**. Perhaps it is because it was Christmas that we did not do all these things but there is plenty to return for isn't there! It will be Friday tomorrow and I still haven't finished last Saturday's paper (probably because a book about Catharine Hepburn took precedence). I also wasted time last night working out that when we leave Esperance and head inland to Norseman to cross the Nullarbor Desert to Ceduna in South Australia (S.A.), we will have to travel 1418 kilometres (880 miles – all but 2ks). I went into shock! I say that I wasted my time because we have to travel it anyway or we'll not get home so one step at a time or rather one hundred kilometres at a time!

Bremer Bay

Well we got here despite the fact that we do not have a GPS Navigation system – we use maps and they work really well! O.K. so we missed the caravan park and sailed right past but that was because we were quite understandably confused as they have changed the name of the park, earlier in the year and just forgot to tell us when we booked!

Within two minutes of arriving we had complete strangers greeting us and within an hour I was inside some strangers enclosed awning, being offered a second whisky and lemonade whilst chatting with two couples. 'Go and get John' it was suggested but he just wanted to relax with a cup of coffee and I was already under the influence of the alcohol and thought the van was rocking! Then we had some more visitors with their beautiful big white fluffy dog. Tonight we had some Skippies (kangaroos) come visiting which caused Jack such excitement that he was jumping around and barking straining on his leash. Apparently there is a queue of people drawing lots to be the first people to see inside our motor home!

We're cold again and have the van heater on so we are following a similar climate change every time we move further south We haven't had time to see anything yet because we've been socialising too much. Our new friends who hoped to spend Christmas with us now hope that they are booked into this park for New Years Eve, I had to dash back to the office to ask them to listen to their messages on their answering machine as I was receiving texts saying that the park had not returned their call. I was told that someone is leaving that day our friends can have that site, otherwise the park is fully booked.

I bought a Dusty Springfield C.D and John was surprised as he hadn't realised just how good she was. I spent the journey listening to that and listening to the Farmers program again on the ABC radio. I have learnt so much about farming since travelling and will miss this program on our return. I hadn't realised just how complicated modern farming is what with all the peculiarities of the various Boards, Egg Board, Wheat Board or the Milk Marketing Board. The problems of sugar cane growers, banana growers, distribution problems, government demands for information, water problems (likewise drought problems), genetically modified crops and so it goes on. Scientists are getting closer to having engineered genetically modified crops that are more drought tolerant. A drought affected crop may not be from lack of water but from drying winds apparently and one so different areas need different types of genetically modified crops and if they do grow them, will the public accept genetically modified grain foods. The next question that arose today was 'What if it rains too much?' and it seems that the farmers are supposed to guess what the weather is going to do before deciding on what seeds to plant. Try guessing the weather in Australia. The weather forecasters invariably get it wrong so how on earth are the farmers going to know. Today we here on the news that the El Nino affect is ending but that the rainfall will return slowly. Who would want to be a farmer?

I saw a cattle truck today parked on the side of the highway and could hear the cattle moaning in distress. To make matters worse, so could the cattle across the road in the field and they loped up to the fence line and called back to them and they were getting distressed. It was such an awful sight and sound it has really put me off beef and I am seriously considering changing my diet. I took a photo of the scene as a reminder.

I always buy organic chooks and at least I feel that they have had a normal life before one is killed for me to eat. Somehow that doesn't seem so bad, more like catching a fish for dinner. As for the veal, beef and pork though I am beginning to think more deeply about the cruelty the animals suffer before I buy my pre-packed cuts from the supermarket. I have been told before that if I visited an abattoir I probably would never eat meat again.

1ˢᵗ January 2007

Well we've driven everywhere that we can get to by car and some places by foot and the beaches are glorious and varied. The inland waterways around the town aren't as beautiful as there is so much green algae. It is believed that Bremer Bay was named by a man called John Septimus Roe. Now isn't that a wonderful name, Septimus? He was the Surveyor General who ambled around here in 1831. Apparently he served on the TAMAR and the between 1824 and 1827 and his Captain's name was John (popular name that isn't it) Gordon Bremer so it is assumed that he named the area after him. I wonder if J. Septimus Roe was here when the locusts were here or the whales, which sometimes are only 50 metres off shore. Good tucker in those days, the whale meat I mean, not the locusts.

We've covered both of our radiator grills, having first cleaned the radiators to get rid of the dead locusts. We had a great early evening New Years Eve because we had a couple who we really like in our van enjoying a few drinks and nibbles but they left at 10pm because he had been scuba diving yesterday and was due to go off diving again today at 6am despite the husband having had a quadruple heart bypass. His wife was telling us that he had one of the top surgeons who had told him not to dive again and over a period of time they got to know the surgeon really well who ended up in telling him 'You do a diving course and then call us and tell us whether or not you still think it is dangerous to dive'. Apparently he did the course and phoned and said 'Get back into the water.' The reason is that it is so relaxing and because his patient was so experienced he returns with half a tank of oxygen whereas those people not so experienced use most of theirs up. We were told that he is so relaxed that his blood pressure slows right down and apparently he was swimming with Leafy Sea Dragons, which are rare and are relatives of the sea horses. They look like frilly sea horses and are beautiful. It sounds wonderful and I wish I did not have an ear problem so that I could dive.

However, it is an experience just to see the turquoise sea, the white soft sand and the crashing waves breaking over rocky cliffs. One of our tourist information booklets states that 'People come to this part of the world to walk on the snow-white beaches, dip into the crystal clear water, fish, relax and get up close to the whales'.

We took too many photos of the sea breaking over the rocks at one beach and the surf rolling so fast that the sea was a mass of foam. We went down onto that beach with the dogs and they had a ball. In fact they have worn themselves out here as they have been allowed on so many of the beaches. Some of the bays are small and some are huge bays and all provide such picturesque scenery. We were quite awed by a couple of the bays as we stood on rocky headlands providing wide views of the stunning colours and islands

.We have now travelled countless kilometres from Queensland, across Northern Territory down to Uluru and back up via Alive Springs to Darwin. Then back down to Katherine, on to Kununurra and The Kimberley in Western Australia. Then from Dampier Land right down the coast to Perth and round to Margaret River and Bremer Bay.

The final diary 3 will continue the journey from Western Australia to South Australia, Victoria and New South Wales back to Queensland. After a break we visit Central Queensland as far as Bowen, returning to take the inland route via New South Wales and Victoria to Melbourne to spend three months exploring Tasmania. We hope you enjoy the journey with us.

Should I Go Walkabout in Australia Again

Diary 2 (Part 1 of The Big Lap)

The Route:
Page

Printed in the United States
By Bookmasters